INCOME INEQUALITY

Regional Analyses
within a Human Capital Framework

NATIONAL BUREAU OF ECONOMIC RESEARCH
Human Behavior and Social Institutions 4

Income Inequality
Regional Analyses within a Human Capital Framework

Barry R. Chiswick
National Bureau of Economic Research
and Queens College, C.U.N.Y.

National Bureau of Economic Research
New York
1974
Distributed by Columbia University Press
New York and London

64116

Relation of the Directors
to the Work and Publications
of the
National Bureau of Economic Research

1. The object of the National Bureau of Economic Research is to ascertain and to present to the public important economic facts and their interpretation in a scientific and impartial manner. The Board of Directors is charged with the responsibility of ensuring that the work of the National Bureau is carried on in strict conformity with this object.

2. The President of the National Bureau shall submit to the Board of Directors, or to its Executive Committee, for their formal adoption all specific proposals for research to be instituted.

3. No research report shall be published until the President shall have submitted to each member of the Board the manuscript proposed for publication, and such information as will, in his opinion and in the opinion of the author, serve to determine the suitability of the report for publication in accordance with the principles of the National Bureau. Each manuscript shall contain a summary drawing attention to the nature and treatment of the problem studied, the character of the data and their utilization in the report, and the main conclusions reached.

4. For each manuscript so submitted, a special committee of the Directors (including Directors Emeriti) shall be appointed by majority agreement of the President and Vice Presidents (or by the Executive Committee in case of inability to decide on the part of the President and Vice Presidents), consisting of three Directors selected as nearly as may be one from each general division of the Board. The names of the special manuscript committee shall be stated to each Director when the manuscript is submitted to him. It shall be the duty of each member of the special manuscript committee to read the manuscript. If each member of the manuscript committee signifies his approval within thirty days of the transmittal of the manuscript, the report may be published. If at the end of that period any member of the manuscript committee withholds his approval, the President shall then notify each member of the Board, requesting approval or disapproval of publication, and thirty days additional shall be granted for this purpose. The manuscript shall then not be published unless at least a majority of the entire Board who shall have voted on the proposal within the time fixed for the receipt of votes shall have approved.

5. No manuscript may be published, though approved by each member of the special manuscript committee, until forty-five days have elapsed from the transmittal of the report in manuscript form. The interval is allowed for the receipt of any memorandum of dissent or reservation, together with a brief statement of his reasons, that any member may wish to express; and such memorandum of dissent or reservation shall be published with the manuscript if he so desires. Publication does not, however, imply that each member of the Board has read the manuscript, or that either members of the Board in general or the special committee have passed on its validity in every detail.

6. Publications of the National Bureau issued for informational purposes concerning the work of the Bureau and its staff, or issued to inform the public of activities of Bureau staff, and volumes issued as a result of various conferences involving the National Bureau shall contain a specific disclaimer noting that such publication has not passed through the normal review procedures required in this resolution. The Executive Committee of the Board is charged with review of all such publications from time to time to ensure that they do not take on the character of formal research reports of the National Bureau, requiring formal Board approval.

7. Unless otherwise determined by the Board or exempted by the terms of paragraph 6, a copy of this resolution shall be printed in each National Bureau publication.

(Resolution adopted October 25, 1926, and revised February 6, 1933, February 24, 1941, April 20, 1968, and September 17, 1973)

To my mother,
and the memory of my father

The Committee on the Distribution of Income is in process of organization to meet a growing demand for a scientific determination of the distribution of national income among individuals . . . A knowledge of this distribution is of vital consequence in the consideration of almost every important political and social problem . . .

June 4, 1917 memorandum of the Committee on the Distribution of Income, which evolved into the National Bureau of Economic Research in 1920.

Contents

Tables

Figures

Acknowledgments

I am greatly indebted to Gary Becker and Jacob Mincer for their encouragement and constructive criticism during the gestation period of this book. Comments received from the staff reading committee—V. K. Chetty, Sherwin Rosen, and Finis Welch—and from the Board of Directors' reading committee—Robert Lampman, Lloyd Reynolds, Alice Rivlin, and Robert Will—were also most helpful. In addition, comments by Victor Fuchs, John Meyer, Robert Michael, and Carmel Ullman, as well as those received at seminars at the National Bureau, Columbia University, the University of Chicago, the University of California, Los Angeles, and Queens College C.U.N.Y., aided in sharpening my analysis and exposition.

Financial support was provided primarily by the National Bureau of Economic Research through grants from the Carnegie Corporation of New York for studies on education, and the Economic Development Administration, Department of Commerce for regional studies. Additional aid was provided by a Ford Foundation fellowship, a visiting research appointment at Princeton University's Industrial Relations section, and by the research facilities of Columbia University, the University of California, Los Angeles, the University of Chicago, Queens College, and the Graduate Center of the City University of New York.

I wish to thank Martin Carnoy for lending me his sample data on Mexican wage earners, and Jennie Podoluk and Statistics Canada (formerly the Dominion Bureau of Statistics), for access to unpublished census data.

Martha Jones Lichtenstein's initial help in the processing of the data, and research assistance from Irene Abramson, Neville Beharie, and Hope Wong were invaluable. Hedy D. Jellinek's skillful editing is also appreciated.

Part B is primarily a revision of the income inequality chapters in my doctoral dissertation, "Human Capital and the Personal Distribution of Income," Columbia University, 1967. The section on earnings inequality and economic growth in Chapter 5 is based on my "Earnings Inequality and Economic Development," *Quarterly Journal of Economics*, February 1971.

Barry R. Chiswick

PART A

Introduction

1

Introduction and Summary

For a long time there has been substantial interest in the determinants of the distribution of personal income. This interest may arise from a concern with either the effects of that distribution (on such factors as incentives for greater efficiency and income allocation between consumption and investment) or its equity. The purpose of this study is to construct a theoretical framework for analyzing regional differences in the distribution of labor market income, and to apply this framework empirically to several countries.[1] Two dimensions of regional differences are studied—the central tendency (level) and dispersion (inequality) in the distribution of income.[2]

Expressing an interest in the determinants of the distribution of income in 1776, Adam Smith wrote: "The five following are the principal circumstances which, so far as I have been able to observe, make up for a small pecuniary gain in some employments,

---

1. For surveys of the literature on regional differences in the distribution of earnings, see Jacob Mincer, "The Distribution of Labor Incomes: A Survey," *Journal of Economic Literature*, March 1970, pp. 1–26; and Harold Lydall, *The Structure of Earnings*, Oxford, Clarendon Press, 1968, Chapter 2. A nontechnical survey of several dimensions of income distribution in the United States is presented in Council of Economic Advisers, *Economic Report of the President*, 1974, Chapter 5.

2. For an analysis of regional differences in the asymmetry of the distribution of income, see Barry R. Chiswick, "An Interregional Analysis of Schooling and the Skewness of Income," W. Lee Hansen, ed., *Education, Income, and Human Capital*, New York, NBER, 1970.

and counter-balance a great one in others: first, the agreeableness
or disagreeableness of the employments themselves; secondly, the
easiness and cheapness, or the difficulty and expense of learning
them; thirdly, the constancy or inconstancy of employment in
them; fourthly, the small or great trust which must be reposed in
those who exercise them; and fifthly, the probability or improba-
bility of success in them."[3]

Smith's second point is the basis of "human capital" analysis—
and the major focus of this book, which uses differences in years
of training and in the rate of return from training to explain differences in the level and inequality of labor market income.
Smith's third point, "the constancy or inconstancy of employment," is explicitly included in my analysis in Part C.

As in most other empirical research in the social sciences,
availability of data influenced the method of analysis adopted and
the number and diversity of data sets analyzed in this study. For
example, investments in schooling can be measured in either dollars (direct plus opportunity costs) or "time equivalents" (years
of schooling completed). Since data on dollar investments in
schooling are nearly nonexistent while data on years of schooling
completed are available for many regions, my theoretical model
and empirical analysis relate income to years of schooling. For
similar reasons, investments in postschool training are measured
in years of experience (i.e., years since leaving school).

The human capital model I use in my analysis relates the natural logarithm of an individual's income to his years of training.
The level and inequality of income in a region can be related to
the distribution of years of training by computing the mean and
variance of both sides of the micro-level human capital equation.
The measure of "level" is the mean log of income (or the log of
the geometric mean), while the measure of "inequality" is the
variance of the log of income, a commonly used measure of income inequality.

Although the purpose of this study is to analyze the distribution of labor market income (earnings), some of my analysis deals
with money income (i.e., earnings plus nonlabor income) because
of data limitations. The terms income and earnings are used inter-
changeably for labor market income, unless it is clear from the
context that total money income rather than labor market income (earnings) is under discussion. Also, because of the measurement problems surrounding years of labor market experience, the

3. Adam Smith, *The Wealth of Nations*, Book I, Chapter 10, New York,
Modern Library, 1937, p. 100.

analysis is restricted to males, who are assumed to have a continuous work history since leaving school.[4] (This assumption would be far less tenable for women.)

OUTLINE OF THE BOOK

Research reports, whether by economists or others, are written far too often for that small group of colleagues who speak the author's specialized jargon and understand the basic principles underlying his study. The nonspecialist is occasionally awed and more often "turned off." Chapter 2, "A Nontechnical Analysis of the Distribution of Income," is an attempt to bridge this communication gap. It presents an elementary analysis of the distribution of labor market income, much of it quite standard,[5] and the incorporation into this framework of the findings in Parts B and C (the technical parts) of this study. Thus, the "uninitiated" reader is provided with a nontechnical explanation of my analysis, thereby gaining an understanding of its approach and contribution.

In recent years there has been considerable interest in whether or not schooling affects the distribution of income among individuals. Much of the criticism of schooling as a means of improving economic well-being has focused on the allegedly weak link between the distribution of schooling and the distribution of income. The purpose of Part B—Chapters 3 to 5—is to examine explicitly the relation between these two distributions for adult males. In this connection, the analysis is performed on two levels. The first is *within* regions, and is concerned with the extent to which an individual's years of schooling can statistically explain his income. The second is *between* regions, and deals with the extent to which the inequality of schooling and the rate of return from schooling can statistically explain the inequality of income.

---

4. The data are for white and nonwhite males. In 1960, 11 per cent of the U.S. male population was nonwhite, 92 per cent of which was black. The proportion of nonblacks among nonwhites varies considerably among the states. For the four major regions, the percentage of nonwhites who are nonblack varies from 1.7 per cent in the South to 52.4 per cent in the West (*U.S. Census of Population: 1960, General Population Characteristics*, Vol. 1, B., Summary, Table 56). Therefore, the census term "nonwhite" is used in this study.

5. What I refer to as the "standard" theory has been developed largely over the last two decades. Gary Becker, Jacob Mincer, and Theodore W. Schultz have been most prominent in its development and dissemination.

The relevant theoretical model is developed in Chapter 3. It predicts that income inequality is larger, the larger the inequality of schooling and the higher the rate of return from schooling. The model is applied empirically in Chapter 4 to the political subdivisions of the United States, Canada, and the Netherlands, and in Chapter 5, to the United States, Canada, Puerto Rico, Mexico, Great Britain, and Israel.

Part C focuses on this question: To what extent and in what manner are state differences in the level and inequality of labor market income of males due to state differences in human capital and employment variables? In searching for answers, it goes beyond Part B's relatively restricted use of the human capital framework, which analyzes earnings merely as a function of schooling. In Part C a broader notion of human capital is employed, incorporating on-the-job experience acquired over time and weeks worked in the survey year as additional determinants of earnings.

The relationships between the distribution of labor market income and that of years of schooling, years of investment in postschool training, rates of return from these investments, and employment during the year are examined.[6] In so doing, this analysis represents a departure from previous regional studies of income distribution, which have tended to rely on ad hoc models. It also departs from previous research by broadening the scope of coverage.

While there has been considerable empirical research on the income distribution of all males and of white males, and on white-nonwhite income differences, a search of the literature reveals little explicit study of regional differences in the level and inequality of labor market income among nonwhites in the United States.[7] Part C of this book, on the other hand, presents an analysis of state differences in the level and inequality of income for all males, white males, and nonwhite males in the United States (including a comparison of the white and nonwhite distributions), and of provincial differences in the level and inequality of income in Canada.

---

6. The expanded human capital earnings equation was initially developed by Jacob Mincer in his *Schooling, Experience, and Earnings*, NBER, 1974. Two recent nonregional studies have applied the expanded human capital model to an interoccupation analysis of the level of income and a time series analysis of the inequality of income. See C. M. Rahm, "Investment in Training and the Occupational Structure of Earnings," Ph.D. dissertation, Columbia University, 1971; and B. R. Chiswick and J. Mincer, "Time-Series Changes in Personal Income Inequality in the United States from 1939, with Projections to 1985," *Journal of Political Economy, Supplement*, May-June 1972, pp. S34–S66.

7. One such study is Sharon M. Oster's "Are Black Incomes More Unequally Distributed?," in *American Economist*, Fall 1970, pp. 6-20.

TABLE 1-1

Means and Standard Deviations Across States of the Level
and Inequality of Income and Earnings for Males

	Income (Y) or Earnings (E)	Av(lnE) or Av(lnY)		Var(lnE) or Var(lnY)	
		Mean	Standard Deviation	Mean	Standard Deviation
United States	Y	1.3094	0.2397	0.7867	0.1184
(51 states)	E	1.2644	0.2132	0.7743	0.1076
Non-South	Y	1.3748	0.1356	0.7241	0.0795
(34 states)	E	1.3530	0.1459	0.7283	0.0902
South	Y	1.1786	0.1144	0.9119	0.0758
(17 states)	E	1.0872	0.2193	0.8662	0.0770

Note: Income and earnings are in thousand dollar units. Earnings are for males 14 years of age and older, while income (earnings plus nonlabor income) is for males 25 years of age and older. The District of Columbia is treated as a state.

Source: See Appendix A.

The expanded human capital earnings function, which relates an individual's income to his years of schooling, years of labor market experience, and employment during the year, is presented in Chapter 6. This is converted into a relationship to explain regional differences in the level of income in Chapter 7, and in inequality of income, in Chapter 8.

Table 1-1 presents interstate data on the level and inequality of income and earnings of males in the United States.[8] The average log of income (Av(lnY)) and the variance in the log of income (Var(lnY)) are the measures of level and inequality used in this study.[9] The data indicate that there is considerable interstate variability in the level and inequality of income and that, although this variability is reduced, it is not eliminated when separate computations are made for the Southern and non-Southern states.

SUMMARY OF FINDINGS

This study demonstrates that the distribution of income can be related to investment in human capital. Its theoretical and statistical analyses of personal income distribution among males in

---

8. See Appendix A for definitions of the income and earnings data.

9. This choice is based on the structure of the human capital model and data availability. Further, the variance of logs is a commonly used measure of inequality.

the United States and several other countries indicate quite strongly that schooling is an important determinant of individual differences in income and of regional differences in its distribution. In addition, postschool training is also found to be an important determinant of income distribution.

Individual differences in years of schooling is an important variable for understanding individual differences in income. The intrastate explanatory power varies considerably, from 17 per cent for Nevada to 51 per cent for Mississippi, with the average value for the states at 29 per cent. This explanatory power is high, considering that individual differences in other variables which influence annual income (e.g., quality of schooling, investment in postschool training, ability, weeks employed, health, pleasantness of the job) are not held constant.[10]

When we look at a model relating income to schooling, income inequality is found to be greater, the higher the rate of return from investment in schooling and the wider the variation in years of schooling in a region. Interstate differences in the rate of return and in schooling inequality by themselves explain 60 per cent of interstate differences in the inequality of income. Income inequality is greater in the Southern states than in the non-South, due partly to (a) greater inequality of schooling, but mainly to (b) a higher rate of return from schooling stemming from the existence of a national labor market for highly educated workers in contrast to the preponderance of local labor markets for those with little schooling.[11]

The schooling model predicts that the strong negative simple correlation between the level of schooling and the inequality of income disappears when the rate of return and inequality of schooling are held constant.

---

10. For a fuller analysis of the relation between individual differences in income and schooling, postschool training, and employment, see Jacob Mincer, *Schooling, Experience, and Earnings*, NBER, 1974. For a survey of the literature on this general topic, see Mincer, "The Distribution of Labor Incomes," 1970.

11. Because interstate migration tends to be quite easy for those with high levels of training, there is virtually only one single national (and, in some professions, one international) labor market for their services. Highly trained workers in poorer states receive incomes similar to what they would receive in a wealthier state. This is not true, however, for those with less skill, for whom migration is more difficult. Therefore, less skilled workers are paid wages determined by the local labor market, and these wages are lower in the poorer (lower average income) states. Thus, the per cent increase in income for an extra year of schooling, or the rate of return from schooling, is higher in the poorer (Southern) states.

Our analysis is expanded by adding the distribution of years of postschool experience and weeks of employment during the year to our model. This increases from 60 per cent to 85 per cent the proportion of interstate differences in income inequality which we can explain via our model of income distribution. (The additional variables explain over 60 per cent of the variation in income inequality *not* explained by the rate of return from schooling and by schooling inequality.) If the data are restricted to white males, our analysis explains 92 per cent of interstate differences in income inequality; the comparable analysis for nonwhite males explains 85 per cent. The important variables are the rate of return from schooling, the inequality of schooling, the inequality of weeks worked, and the inequality of age (or experience) except for inequality of age for nonwhite males.

The reason why inequality of age is an unimportant factor in the analysis for nonwhite males lies in the small change in income of older nonwhites as we look at older age groups at a particular moment in time. This change in income is referred to as a cross-sectional "experience-earnings profile." In principle, the observed fairly flat nonwhite profile may stem from several, not mutually exclusive, forces: low investments in postschool training, low rates of return from postschool training, and a more rapid rise over time in the quality of schooling and the quantity of job opportunities for nonwhites compared to whites. Evidence developed in this volume and elsewhere suggests that each of these forces may be operative.

The inequality of annual income within states is smaller among nonwhite males than among white males. Nonwhites, however, show a larger inequality in weeks worked during the year. These two observations imply a smaller inequality in weekly wages within states for nonwhite males than for white males. This is not due to differences in the distribution of years of schooling or of years of experience in the labor market; rather, it is a consequence of the lower rate of return from schooling and the flatter cross-sectional experience-earnings profile.

The schooling model of income inequality is also applied within Canada, within the Netherlands, and across various countries. As was found in the United States, income inequality is larger where the rate of return from schooling and the inequality of schooling are larger. Among the Canadian provinces, the rate of return and schooling inequality by themselves explain 65 per cent of provincial differences in income inequality. This rises to 75 per cent when the distribution of years of experience is added to the analysis. Thus, the distribution of experience explains 30 per cent

of the variation left unexplained by the rate of return and schooling inequality. It is also demonstrated that the model provides a
useful framework for interpreting the income distribution effects
of historical events (mass migration into Israel), institutional differences (Great Britain versus the United States), and economic
growth.

Regional differences in the level of income of male workers are
related to differences in the distribution of schooling, age (experience), and employment. Interstate differences in the distribution
of schooling and age explain 65 to 70 per cent of interstate differences in the level of earnings of all males and all white males in
the United States, but these variables perform less well where income data are used. For nonwhite males, however, schooling and
weeks worked account for a high proportion (80 per cent) of interstate differences in the level of income and earnings.[12] Over 80
per cent of white-nonwhite differences in the level of income are
due to the smaller number of years of schooling and the smaller
number of weeks worked by nonwhites. The model performs very
well (95 per cent explanatory power) when we analyze Canadian
provincial differences in the level of income.

---

12. Weeks worked is not a significant variable for white males because it
varies too little across the states, and age is not significant for nonwhite
males because of the low slope of the nonwhite experience-earnings profile.

2

A Nontechnical Analysis
of the Distribution of Income

Designed to make the fruits of my research effort intelligible
to the nonspecialist, this chapter presents an elementary analysis
of the determinants of the distribution of labor market income.
Within this framework it also discusses some of the more important aspects of the theory and findings comprising the technical
chapters in Parts B and C.

EQUALIZING WAGE DIFFERENTIALS AND NONMONEY
ASPECTS OF JOBS

No discussion of the theory of labor market income can ignore
Adam Smith's contribution. In his 1776 volume, *The Wealth of
Nations*, Smith introduced the idea of compensating wage differentials in competitive labor markets.[1] He wrote: "The whole of the
advantages and disadvantages of the different employments of
labor and stock must, in the same neighborhood, be either perfectly equal or constantly tending to equality. If in the same neighborhood there was any employment evidently either more or less
advantageous than the rest, so many people would crowd into it
in the one case, and so many would desert it in the other, that its

---

1. Modern Library edition, Book I, Chapter 10, p. 99. I am willing to
wager that Smith's Chapter 10 is the most frequently cited work written
prior to 1960 on reading lists in labor economics.

advantages would soon return to the level of other employments."
That is, if in a single geographical area workers of equal ability can
freely sell their labor services to any one of many employers, competition among workers for the jobs with more desirable nonmoney characteristics will make, on balance, all jobs equally attractive—the sum of the money and nonmoney benefits are equal.

Let us define a "job" as an employment at particular tasks, in
a particular firm, in a particular location, under given working
conditions. A change in a job can be thought of as a change in any
of these characteristics. For example, acting as short-order cook
for Nathans, located in Times Square in New York City, during
the day shift, represents a job. An employment with a different
task (manager), or firm (Chock Full O'Nuts), or location (Nathan's
in Coney Island), or working condition (the night shift) would
represent a different job.

Suppose there are two jobs, A and B, employing large numbers
of workers, alike in all respects except for one characteristic. Job
A is dirty, or physically strenuous, or dangerous, et cetera. Suppose
for the moment that all workers are identical in all respects.
Everyone views the different characteristic to be unfavorable to
job A. For an equal wage in jobs A and B no one would select job
A; everyone would want to enter job B. Suppose we wish to bribe
people to enter job A by paying a sufficiently higher wage in job A
(W_A) than in job B (W_B). Since we assume workers to be identical,
they would all be willing to leave job B and enter job A for the
same positive wage differential, which we call d_0 ($d = W_A - W_B$).
For example, suppose job A represents employment as a short-order cook in the summer without air conditioning or a fan, and job
B represents employment as a short-order cook in the summer with
an electric fan. For the same wage, no one would want to work in
job A, but, for a sufficiently larger wage in job A, job A would be
preferable to job B.

Curve S_0 in Figure 2-1 shows the number of workers who supply their labor to job A at each wage differential.[2] If the difference
in wages between jobs A and B were less than d_0, everyone would
prefer to enter job B and no worker would choose job A. At a differential above d_0, all workers would want to enter job A and none
job B. At the differential d_0, the workers are indifferent between
jobs A and B.

Curve D_A in Figure 2-1 is a downward-sloping market demand
curve for workers in job A relative to job B. The negative slope of

---

2. We assume a fixed population that will work in either job A or job B.

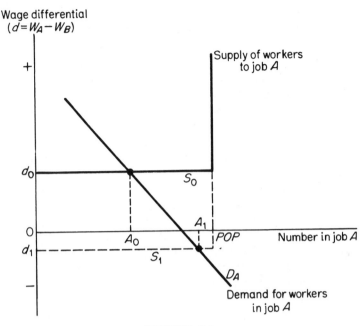

FIGURE 2-1
Supply and Demand for Labor—Homogeneous Tastes

the demand curve is based on the assumption that there is imperfect substitution of workers for one job compared to the other. The point where the demand curve and the supply curve intersect indicates the equilibrium number of workers in job A and the equilibrium wage differential between jobs A and B.

Shifts would occur in the supply curve if working conditions, or the perception of the working conditions, were to change. Job A initially has supply curve S_0 and a positive wage differential. Now, however, let us assume that demand conditions are unchanged, but that an air conditioner is added to job A, so that now job A is preferred to job B. The new supply curve is S_1, and a negative wage differential emerges; job A now pays less than job B.

Up to this point we have assumed that all workers have the same tastes for the characteristics of a job. People differ, however, in their evaluation of the same working conditions. Some have strong preferences for an air-conditioned office, while others prefer an office with a fan. In the context of our simple example, those who have a preference for the working conditions in job A compared to job B offer their services to job A even when the wage is lower than in job B. Those who are indifferent will enter job A if the wage in A is at least as large as in job B. Finally, those who prefer the characteristics in job B to those in job A require the inducement of a higher wage in A than in B to enter job A. The supply of labor at a given wage equals the sum of all workers who would enter at that wage or at a lower wage. Thus, differences in tastes for the nonmoney characteristics of jobs result in a rising labor supply curve. (See curve S in Figure 2-2.)

Thus far we have considered the distribution of tastes for the two jobs and the resulting shape of the supply curve. The market wage differential (d) and the number employed in jobs A and B depend on both supply and demand conditions. The supply curve in Figure 2-2 depicts a situation where the majority of people dislike job A compared to job B. There are some, however, who prefer A to B. On the demand side, Figure 2-2 features three demand curves. With demand curve D_1, the quantities demanded and supplied are equal at a negative wage differential.[3] Suppose the relative demand curve for labor in job A shifts outward to D_2 and then to D_3. For the same supply relation, the outward shift of demand increases the wage differential $(d = W_A - W_B)$, and more workers enter job A.

Note the difference between average tastes $(\bar{d})$ and marginal tastes (i.e., tastes at the intersection of the supply and demand curves). Market wages are determined by tastes at the equilibrium, and wage differentials depend on both supply and demand. Those who have a stronger-than-market taste for an activity (i.e., those who would enter at a wage differential below d_1) will be in that activity—in this case, job A. Those who have weaker-than-market tastes will be in the alternative activity.[4]

---

3. Although most people dislike job A, there are enough who like it, given the demand D_1 for labor in job A, for the number of workers offering themselves at a zero differential to exceed the number demanded. For example, suppose 5 per cent of a 1,000-man workforce enjoys climbing poles so much that they are willing to be telephone pole climbers for lower wages than for otherwise "similar" work on *terra firma* (supply curve S). Suppose that for equal wages the phone companies wish to employ only thirty workers as pole climbers (demand curve D_1). Clearly, at equal wages in the two jobs, the supply of labor is greater than the demand for labor (fifty men compared to thirty jobs), so that pole climbers' wages will fall relative to wages in the other job. The fall in wages has two effects which help bring about market equilibrium. Because of the rising supply curve, fewer workers want to be pole climbers, and because of the downward-sloping demand curve more such workers are demanded.

4. The difference between the wage differential a worker requires to induce him to enter an activity (d_i) and the market wage differential (d_1) is called economic rent. Only the "man at the margin" does not receive economic rent.

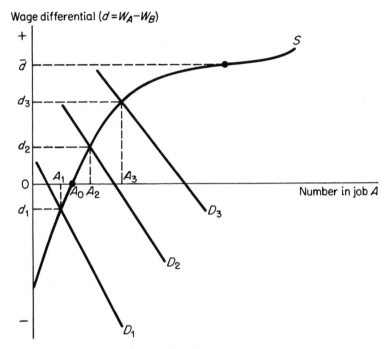

FIGURE 2-2
Supply and Demand for Labor—Heterogeneous Tastes

SEASONALITY AND ANNUAL INCOME

The analysis of compensating wage differentials is used in Part C's theoretical discussion of the effect of seasonality of employment on weekly wages and on annual earnings.

Let us assume that two jobs, A and B, have similar working conditions. At the start of each year (or each working life), a worker freely chooses between entering job A or job B, but he cannot reverse his decision within the year (or worklife). Job B involves a full year of employment, but job A is seasonal, providing work for only forty weeks per year. During the twelve weeks of unemployment in job A, the worker receives no wage from A. For simplicity let us assume he is unemployed during these twelve weeks. Although workers place a positive value on the weekly "income" received while unemployed (i.e., unemployment insurance and leisure), let us assume that they all evaluate this to be less than the weekly wage in job B.

Under equilibrium conditions, the real annual compensation in the two activities, job A and job B, would be equal. Since lower real weekly income is received in the "off season" in job A, workers enter job A only if the weekly wage while working in job A exceeds that of job B. Suppose the weekly wage in job B is $100, providing a $5,200 annual income. A worker receives $45 per week as unemployment insurance for each week unemployed and values the leisure gained at $30 per week. His annual income in job A at a weekly wage W_A would then be $40(W_A) + 12(45 + 30)$. The worker prefers job A if this sum exceeds $5,200. At the weekly wage $W_A = \$107.50$, the worker earns the same annual income in the two activities; he enters job A only if the weekly wage in job A is equal to or greater than $107.50. This simple model of wages in seasonal industries implies that jobs offering relatively less employment during the year offer higher weekly or hourly wages for the time actually worked. The higher wage compensates for less income during the period of unemployment.

If the wage rate were the same regardless of the number of weeks worked, annual income could be written as the product of annual income from a full year's employment and the fraction of the fifty-two weeks in the year the individual worked. A 1 per cent increase in the fraction of the year employed would then increase annual income by 1 per cent. The seasonality of employment model, however, postulates that those who work more weeks per year have a higher annual income but a smaller weekly income; a 1 per cent increase in the fraction of weeks worked would increase annual income, but by less than 1 per cent. The relationship between the per cent change in annual income and the per cent change in the fraction of weeks worked is called "the elasticity of income with respect to weeks worked" and is designated by γ. The seasonality of employment model implies that γ is positive but less than unity. (The parameter γ plays an important role in our analysis of income distribution in Part C.)

HUMAN CAPITAL

The basic framework employed in this study of income distribution is one in which the returns to an individual from labor market activity are a function of his stock of training—or "human capital." The concept of human capital will become clearer, and sound less cold-blooded, if each of the two component words are examined separately.

Capital may be defined as anything produced at a cost and providing useful services over time in either production or consumption. Thus, a drill press or a clothes washing machine are capital goods. Rainfall is not capital unless it is influenced by man.

There are some human characteristics which satisfy this definition of capital. For example, my knowledge of economics was created at a cost and has produced a stream of services over time. The cost of producing my stock of knowledge involved my foregoing both what I would have otherwise done with my time (opportunity cost of time) and what I would have otherwise purchased (goods and services). The services yielded over time by this capital include teaching and research, as well as my own consumption benefits from my knowledge of the subject.

There is, however, a fundamental difference between my "knowledge of economics" as capital and my "washing machine" as capital—my knowledge of economics is embodied in me. I can sell my "washing machine" and become unaffected by its use thereafter. I cannot sell my "knowledge," but can only rent its services to others. In addition, I must endure the conditions under which the renting of my labor services takes place: thus, I care whether I teach in an overheated classroom or one in which airplanes pass overhead every few minutes. Capital (productive power) embodied in a person is referred to as *human* capital.

Since human capital is created at a cost, no one would willingly invest in human capital unless it generated sufficient monetary or nonmonetary benefits to compensate for the cost. The analysis of investment in human capital is part of the broader analysis of compensating wage differentials.

Human capital can be acquired in several different ways. Schooling, vocational training, formal on-the-job training, learning by doing, medical care, acquiring information, and migration are means by which individuals can increase their productivity. Hence they create human capital. Unfortunately, we cannot directly measure units of human capital (i.e., productive power). This study focuses on the *money income*-producing effects of years of formal *schooling* and years of labor market *experience* after schooling, all of which are quantifiable.[5]

---

5. This does not imply that training is not productive outside of the market place. Several recent studies do, in fact, suggest that schooling is productive in household activities. For example, holding income constant, those with more schooling appear to be more efficient consumers, to have better health, and to provide a higher quality of child care. See, for example, Robert Michael, *The Effect of Education on Efficiency in Consumption*,

ONE PERIOD OF TRAINING

Training is not without costs. A year of schooling, for example, involves direct and opportunity costs. Direct costs are out-of-pocket expenditures that otherwise would not have been incurred, such as tuition charges and the cost of books. Opportunity costs, sometimes called indirect costs, are the monetary equivalent of the time devoted to the investment in schooling.

Suppose jobs A and B are alike in all respects except one: job A requires a year of training beyond high school, whereas job B requires only a high school education. If the two jobs offer the same annual income, all high school graduates will choose job B over job A and none will acquire the extra training required for job A. If the benefits from the two jobs are equal but job A requires expenditures before a worker can enter it, job A is inferior to job B. If, however, the annual income from job A exceeds the annual income from job B by an amount sufficiently large to compensate for the training cost, workers will be induced to acquire the extra training and enter job A. If there are individual differences in the ability to learn the task required for job A or individual differences in the evaluation of income received in the future, workers will differ as to the wage differential that will make them view the two jobs as equally attractive. That is, the supply of labor to job A relative to job B will be upward rising. With a demand curve for labor and a supply curve of labor, a market income differential (d) between jobs A and B emerges.

Under a few simplifying assumptions,[6] the rate of return from an investment (r) can be written approximately as the ratio of the

New York, NBER, 1972; Michael Grossman, *The Demand for Health: A Theoretical and Empirical Investigation*, New York, NBER, 1972; Arleen Leibowitz, "Women's Allocation of Time to Market and Nonmarket Activities: Differences by Education," Ph.D. dissertation, Columbia University, 1972; and Zvi Griliches and William Mason, "Education, Income and Ability," *Journal of Political Economy*, Supplement, May-June 1972.

6. The assumptions are that the costs (c) occur in one period, the annual increment in wages (d) is constant over time, and that the differential is received for a very long period of time. The internal rate of return (r) is the rate of discount which sets the cost of an investment equal to the present value of the benefits from the investment. That is,

$$c = \sum_{t=1}^{N} \frac{d}{(1 + r)^t}$$

where N is the number of periods in which benefits are received. However, if

annual differential (d) to the cost (c) of the investment, $r = d/c$. Therefore, the annual income of a worker in job A can be written as

$$Y_A = Y_B + d = Y_B + rc.$$

This is shown in Figure 2-3. The income line Y_A is higher than the income line Y_B by d dollars. The shaded area represents the cost of the training needed for job A.

Let us assume everyone in job A has the same income, and everyone in job B has the same income. Average income is higher, the larger the proportion of the population in job A, or the higher the average level of training in the population. There is no inequality in income if everyone is in job A or everyone is in job B. There is inequality if some workers are in job A and the others are in job B. In Figure 2-3 income inequality is largest when half of the workers are in job A and half in job B, that is, when the inequality of training is at a maximum.

We are also interested in the effect of the rate of return from training (r) and the amount of dollars invested in the year of training (c) on the average level and the inequality of income. Recall that the wage differential (d) was $d = rc$. For a particular distribution of investment in years of training (i.e., some workers in A and the others in B), the level and inequality of income is larger, the greater the differential (d). (See Figure 2-4.) Thus, the level and inequality of income is larger, the larger the rate of return from training or the larger the dollar investments.

$$S = \sum_{t=1}^{N} \frac{d}{(1 + r)^t}$$

$$(1 + r) S = \sum_{t=1}^{N} \frac{(d)(1 + r)}{(1 + r)^t}$$

and

$$(1 + r) S - S = \sum_{t=0}^{N-1} \frac{d}{(1 + r)^t} - \sum_{t=1}^{N} \frac{d}{(1 + r)^t}$$

$$r S = d - \frac{d}{(1 + r)^N}$$

$$S = \frac{d}{r} \left(1 - \frac{1}{(1 + r)^N} \right).$$

As N becomes large, S approaches d/r, and $c = d/r$. Hence, $r = d/c$.

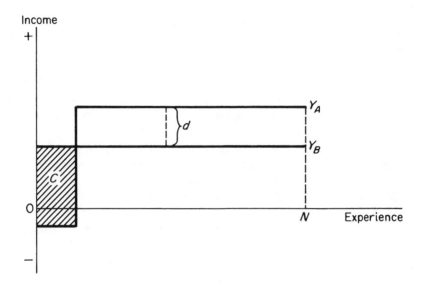

C = opportunity costs (c_0) plus direct costs (c_d)

$Y_A = Y_B + r(c_0 + c_d) = Y_B + d$

FIGURE 2-3
One Period of Training

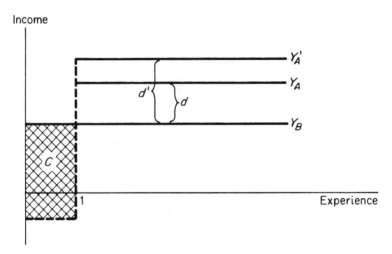

FIGURE 2-4
One Period of Training—An Increase in the Differential

SCHOOLING MODEL OF INCOME INEQUALITY

Part B develops and tests empirically a model that relates income to schooling. Data for the United States, Canada, and several other countries are employed and the effects of schooling computed for both differences in individual incomes within a region and differences in relative income inequality across regions.

Individual differences in years of schooling are found to be an important variable for explaining individual differences in income within regions. For the United States, differences in years of schooling explain from 17 to 51 per cent of individual differences in the income of adult males within each state, and 29 per cent is the average intrastate explanatory power of schooling. State differences in the rate of return from schooling and the inequality of schooling explain 60 per cent of state differences in the inequality of income. The greater income inequality in the Southern states can be explained by the greater inequality of schooling and the higher rate of return from schooling in the South.

The interregional analyses of income inequality for Canada and the Netherlands, as well as the various international analyses, provide additional support for the hypothesis that income inequality is larger, the higher the rate of return from schooling and the greater the inequality of schooling. Although less developed countries tend to have a larger inequality of income, this is not true when we adjust for intercountry differences in the inequality of years of schooling and the rate of return from schooling. That is, with the latter two variables held fixed, there is no relation, empirically, between income inequality and the level of income.

The model also provides a framework for understanding the income distribution effects of historical events and institutional arrangements which alter either the distribution of schooling or the rate of return from schooling. This is done through analyses of the income distribution effects of mass immigration into Israel, the effects of minimum schooling legislation on the distribution of schooling and hence also income in Great Britain and the United States, and the effects of economic change per se on income inequality.

MIGRATION AND THE RATE OF RETURN
FROM SCHOOLING

If workers with high levels of schooling were perfect substitutes for those with low levels of schooling, relative wages would
depend solely on technical production considerations (i.e., the substitution coefficient). For example, if one college graduate were
always as productive as two high school graduates, the wage of the
former would always be twice that of the latter, regardless of the
relative supply of college graduates. There is evidence, however, to
show that high-level manpower (college graduates) is qualitatively
different from less-skilled manpower, and that the two factors are
not perfect substitutes.[7] Hence, there is a downward-sloping demand curve for skilled manpower relative to less-skilled manpower.
In terms of the analysis of income distribution, this negatively
sloped relative demand curve plays an important role.

Let us view each state of the United States as a labor market.
Wages of college graduates vary little across the states because of
their high mobility. There is, in effect, a national labor market for
college graduates. For those with less schooling, the tendency to
migrate is weaker and there are significant state differences in wage
rates.[8] The result: higher rates of return from schooling in the
poorer states.[9]

Those with more schooling have a higher propensity to migrate
for several reasons. First, schooling may increase a person's awareness of other areas and thereby reduce the cost of moving to a new
environment. Second, college schooling itself often entails moving
to a new area and thus loosens ties to the place of origin. Third,
since those who acquire more schooling tend to be wealthier—and
since greater wealth facilitates investment in all forms of human

---

7. See Carmel J. Ullman, "The Rise of Professional Occupations in the
American Labor Force," Ph.D dissertation, Columbia University, 1972; and
Finis Welch, "Education in Production," *Journal of Political Economy*,
January-February 1970, pp. 35-59.

8. See Rashi Fein, "Educational Patterns in Southern Migration,"
Southern Economic Journal, Supplement, (Part 2), July 1965, pp. 106-124;
June O'Neill, "The Effect of Income and Education on Inter-Regional Mi-
gration," Ph.D. dissertation, Columbia University, 1970; and Thomas J.
Courchene, "Interprovincial Migration and Economic Adjustment," *Cana-
dian Journal of Economics*, November 1970, pp. 550-577.

9. See Chapter 5 below; see also W. Lee Hansen, "Total and Private Rates
of Return to Investment in Schooling," *Journal of Political Economy*, April
1963, pp. 128-140; and Giora Hanoch, "An Economic Analysis of Earnings
and Schooling," *Journal of Human Resources*, Summer 1967, pp. 310-329.

capital (including migration)—those with more schooling also tend to be those who invest more in migration. Fourth, because of direct costs of migration that are unrelated to skill level, the rate of return from migration tends to be higher for those with more skill.[10]

A higher rate of migration from the poorer states by skilled workers relative to unskilled workers increases the ratio of skilled to unskilled workers in the wealthier states and decreases it in the poorer states. Given the same negatively sloped demand curve for labor, the wage ratio of skilled to unskilled workers is depressed in the wealthier states and boosted in the poorer states. The result is a decline in the rate of return from schooling in the wealthier region and a rise in the poorer region.

The higher rate of return from schooling in the poorer regions within a country proves to be a major explanation for the larger inequality of income in the southern states of the United States (see Chapter 5). In addition, although the Atlantic provinces of Canada (the poorer provinces) have small inequalities of schooling, they have higher rates of return, and this tends to reduce interprovincial differences in income inequality.

An additional illustration is furnished by a time series study of income inequality in the Jewish population of Israel (see Chapter 6). Relative to the size of its population, Israel has experienced large exogenous immigration. During the two decades before independence (1948), the immigrants contained a high proportion of skilled workers. If we assume that the relative demand curve remained stable, the outward shift of labor supply should have depressed the relative wage of skilled workers—as, in fact, it did. In the decade after independence, the immigration primarily brought unskilled workers, and the relative wage of skilled to unskilled workers increased. These changes in the relative wage can be translated into movements in the rate of return from schooling. As predicted by the schooling model of income distribution, income inequality was small and showed a contracting tendency in the pre-independence period and an uptrend after independence.

POSTSCHOOL TRAINING AND INCOME DISTRIBUTION

In the section entitled "One Period of Training" (p. 18) above, a simple training model was used to demonstrate that the level and inequality of income are a function of the level and in-

10. For a proof of this, see Chapter 5 below.

equality of training, the rate of return from the training, and the dollar intensity of the relevant investment among individuals. Postschool training, however, is not an all-or-nothing investment made in the first year after the completion of formal schooling. In Part C, postschool training is viewed as a continuous variable in which the ratio of dollar investments to potential income is assumed to decline over time.[11] This permits dollar investments in training to be translated into years of experience (postschool training). The scarcity of data on dollar investments in training versus the availability of data on years of schooling and age virtually dictate that the empirical analysis be specified in terms of years of experience, where experience is measured by the number of years since leaving school.

The conclusions of the one-period-of-training model are generalized into years of experience (or age, if schooling is held constant), measured as a continuous variable. Within the levels of schooling, the average level of earnings of adults is expected to be higher the greater the average age (or the average level of experience) of the population. Similarly, the inequality of earnings is expected to be greater the more unequal the distribution of age (experience). The effect of a year of experience on income is referred to as the slope of the "experience-earnings profile." This slope steepens with larger dollar investments in postschool training and a higher rate of return from this training. Finally, the more the slope of the profile steepens, the stronger the effect of the age distribution on income distribution becomes. These are the basic hypotheses examined in Part C of this volume.

POSTSCHOOL TRAINING AND EMPLOYMENT

The relationship between the distribution of employment during the year and the distribution of annual income is explicitly examined in Part C below (p. 107). In this chapter we have already examined the concept of compensating wage differentials and the relationship between seasonality of employment and annual and weekly income. Here we turn to the theory behind another factor that influences individual differences in employment during the year: investment in postschool training.

---

11. The relative decline in investments occurs because life is finite (and, thus, there are a smaller number of periods in which to receive benefits from investments made later in life) and because the most profitable postschool training investments are made during the first few years in the labor market.

Investment in postschool training may be of two types: general and specific.[12] General training is training that is useful (productive) both in the firm in which it is acquired and in many other firms. Specific training, on the other hand, is productive only in the firm in which it is acquired. It includes learning the layout of the work-place, the procedures peculiar to the company, and the characteristics of fellow employees (supervisors and subordinates).

Since a worker with only general training is equally productive in many firms, he would stay in the firm in which he acquired the training only if it paid a wage at least equal to what he could obtain elsewhere. Thus, the firm would not be able to benefit from investing in the worker's general training, and therefore would not make such investments. Consequently, the worker finances the investments in his general training himself.

A worker with specific training is more productive in the firm in which he acquired the training than elsewhere. He would tend to stay with the firm in which he acquired his training if he is paid a wage greater than his best alternative. The firm is willing to finance some of the specific training if the worker, once trained, receives a wage less than his value to the firm.[13] Because of specific training, a worker's wage in a firm can be greater than his next best alternative and still less than his value to the firm.

Stability of employment increases with greater amounts of specific training because of the wedges between the cost to the firm of the worker (his wage), the worker's value to the firm, and his value to other firms. For example, assuming that wages do not decline during recessions, the value to the firm of workers with only general training decreases when a recession occurs, making it costly to the firm to retain the worker, since his wage exceeds his value. As a result, disemployment of workers begins. However, the case is different for workers with some specific training. Since their value to the firm is higher than their wage in a nonrecession year, when a recession does occur it may still be profitable for the firm to retain the workers, although their value to the firm may decline. Also, workers with more specific training have lower quit rates than those with less. This is so because the worker is more productive in the firm in which the specific training is acquired than elsewhere.

---

12. The distinction between general and specific training and the analysis of the employment effects were developed by Gary S. Becker. See his *Human Capital: A Theoretical and Empirical Analysis, with Special Reference to Education*, New York, NBER, 1974.
13. The value of a worker to the firm is the value of the extra output produced by him.

Workers who have more than average human capital of one type usually have more of other types, too. For example, those with higher levels of schooling also have higher rates of migration and make larger dollar investments in their postschool training.[14] It seems reasonable to conclude that those with more general training also have more specific training and consequently lower quit and layoff rates. Thus, because of specific training, ceteris paribus, the higher the weekly wages, the greater the fraction of weeks worked during a year.

Recall that we previously used the symbol γ to designate the elasticity of annual earnings with respect to the fraction of weeks worked during the year. If a 1 per cent increase in weeks worked does not change the weekly wage, annual earnings go up 1 per cent and $\gamma = 1$. In the case of specific training, however, those with 1 per cent more weeks worked have *higher* weekly wages and thus annual incomes which are larger by more than 1 per cent. Hence, γ exceeds unity. The seasonality of employment model discussed above suggests that, holding specific training constant, those who work 1 per cent more weeks per year have *lower* weekly wages and annual incomes that are larger, but by less than 1 per cent—hence γ is positive but less than unity.

In the empirical analysis of Part C, the elasticity γ is computed for white and nonwhite males and is compared to the value of unity. For white males the estimated value of γ does not differ from unity. For nonwhite males, however, the estimated γ is less than unity. This racial difference may be explained by smaller investments in postschool training and a greater seasonality of employment for nonwhite males.[15]

ANALYSIS OF LEVEL OF INCOME

If we pull together the analyses of the schooling, postschool training, and employment models discussed in this chapter, we can develop a framework for explaining regional differences in the

---

14. For migration, see references in footnote 8, p. 22. For postschool training, see Jacob Mincer, "On-the-Job Training: Costs, Returns and Some Implications," *Journal of Political Economy, Supplement*, October 1962, pp. 50–79, and *Schooling, Experience, and Earnings*, NBER, 1974, Part 2; also Thomas Johnson, "Returns from Investment in Human Capital," *American Economic Review*, September 1970, pp. 546–560.

15. For a study of racial differences in postschool training, see Mincer, "On-the-Job Training" and Johnson, "Returns from Investment in Human Capital." For racial differences in the seasonality of employment, see Chapter 7, p. 126, footnote 18.

level of earnings (or income) of adult males.[16] The level of earnings is positively related to the levels of schooling, age, and employment (weeks worked) during the year.[17]

Let us recall that the rate of return from training and dollar investments in training translate the distribution of years of training into a distribution of earnings. Thus, the greater the rate of return and dollar investments, the stronger the effect of the level of schooling and age on the level of earnings. Independent empirical evidence shows lower rates of return from training and smaller investments in postschool training for nonwhites than whites for the period under study.[18] Therefore, the schooling and age distributions can be expected to have a weaker effect on the earnings level of nonwhite males than on that of white males.

In the analyses for all males and all white males, the schooling and age variables explain approximately 70 per cent of interstate differences in the level of earnings. The variables have the expected effects and tend to be statistically significant.[19] The model is less successful in explaining interstate differences in the level of income.

In the case of nonwhite males, the schooling and employment (weeks worked) variables affect earnings in the expected direction and explain nearly 80 per cent of interstate differences in the levels of earnings and income.[20] The distribution of age appears to have no effect, and the distribution of schooling a weaker effect for nonwhites than for whites, on interstate differences in the level of earnings or income. White-nonwhite differences in the level of earnings across states are found to be due largely (80 to 90 per cent) to racial differences in the explanatory variables (particularly the lower levels for nonwhites in schooling and weeks of employment during the year).

---

16. Chapter 7 is devoted to the development and testing of this model for the United States and Canada.

17. For technical reasons developed in Chapter 7, the level of income is also related to the inequalities of schooling and age.

18. Becker, *Human Capital*, Chapter IV; Finis Welch, "Black-White Differences in Returns to Schooling," *American Economic Review*, December 1973, pp. 893–907; Mincer, "On-the-Job Training"; Johnson, "Returns from Investment in Human Capital." An alternative explanation for the flatter nonwhite experience-earnings profile is a more rapid rise in school quality and job opportunities for young nonwhites compared to young whites.

19. The variable for the level of employment is not significant, but this may be because of its very small variation across the states for all males and all white males.

20. The employment variable, the mean log of weeks worked, has twice the variation across states for nonwhite males than it has for all males or white males.

In Canada, the schooling and age variables explain 95 per cent of provincial differences in the level of income of nonfarm males. Although the level of age does not have an independent effect, the level of schooling (and the inequality of schooling and age) have strong effects in the expected direction. The results are quite similar, therefore, to those obtained for the United States.

ANALYSIS OF INEQUALITY OF INCOME

Regional differences in the inequality of earnings or income can be analyzed by combining the implications of the schooling, postschool training, and employment models. These suggest that income inequality is greater the larger the inequalities of schooling, age, and weeks worked during the year. Each of these variables is included in the empirical analysis.[21] Higher rates of return from schooling and postschool training and larger dollar investments per year of training also increase income inequality. Rates of return from schooling are computed by race in each unit of observation (state or province). If, as appears to be the case, nonwhites have flatter experience-earnings profiles in the cross-section than whites, the effect of the inequality of age will be weaker for nonwhites than for whites.

The elasticity of earnings with respect to the fraction of weeks worked (γ) can be estimated from the analysis of income inequality. Since it appears that nonwhite male workers may invest in less postschool training and have greater seasonality in their employment than white males, the parameter γ is expected to be lower for the former than for the latter.

In the empirical analyses (Chapter 8) for all males and all white males in the United States, the model explains a large proportion of interstate differences in income inequality (85 to 92 per cent) and earnings inequality (approximately 80 per cent). The inequalities of schooling, age, and employment and the rate of return from schooling have strong positive effects on income inequality. In the parallel analysis for nonwhite males, the model performs equally well—approximately 85 per cent of the differences in inequality are attributable to the model. The inequalities of school-

---

21. The income inequality model for the United States and Canada is developed and tested in Chapter 8. Under the set of simplifying, yet technical, assumptions developed there, three additional variables enter the analysis—the covariance of schooling and age, the years of schooling, and the years of postschool experience.

ing and weeks of employment and the rate of return from school-ing have significant positive effects on interstate differences in nonwhite income inequality. The elasticity of earnings with respect to the fraction of weeks worked (γ) is less than unity for nonwhite males, but not for white males.

Within states, the observed inequality of annual income is smaller for nonwhites than for whites. Since nonwhites experience a larger inequality in weeks worked during the year than whites, it follows that their inequality of weekly income is even smaller than the inequality based on annual income. This small intrastate non-white inequality of weekly income is not due to differences in the distribution of schooling or age, but to the rate of return from schooling and the effect on income of differences in age (ex-perience). Thus, the smaller within-state inequality in income of nonwhites may be due, in part, to less investment in postschool training. A more important role can possibly be assigned to the greate. rise in the quality of schooling and the quantity of job op-portunities for young nonwhites than for young whites in the decade or two prior to 1960. This would tend to flatten the experience-earnings profile in the cross-section for nonwhites compared to whites.

Regional differences in income inequality are also studied with the Canadian provinces as the unit of observation. The school-ing and age variables, including the rate of return from schooling, explain 75 per cent of provincial differences in the income in-equality of adult nonfarm males.[22] The Canadian pattern is similar to that for nonwhite males in the United States: on the one hand, an insignificant effect of the inequality of age, and, on the other, significant positive effects of the rate of return and schooling inequality.

Thus, the human capital and employment model of income distribution outlined in this chapter (developed and tested in greater detail in Part C of this volume) appears to be a very power-ful tool for studying regional differences in the level and inequality of labor market income.

---

22. Appropriate data are not available for analyzing the effects of differences in the distribution of weeks worked.

PART B

Income as a
Function of Schooling

3

The Schooling Model

The theoretical model on which Part B rests, relating labor market income (earnings) to years of schooling, is presented in the following pages. We note its statistical characteristics and see how it can be used to analyze interregional differences in income inequality.

An individual's earnings are assumed to depend upon the earnings he would receive without any training, on his dollar investment in training, and on the rate of return received from his investment. Training is defined in terms of both years of formal schooling completed and years of labor market experience.

Further, the chapter is devoted to methods of computing the explanatory power of schooling for the two levels of aggregation in the income-schooling relationships that form the basis of our discussion. The first is intraregional, and relates the natural logarithm of earnings to an individual's level of schooling and to his average rate of return from investments in schooling. The second is interregional, and relates a measure of the relative variance of earnings in a region to the variance of schooling and the level of the rate of return from schooling in that region. Thus, the schooling model is used to explain (a) *individual* differences in earnings within regions via years of schooling; and (b) *regional* differences in the relative inequality in earnings via the rate of return from, and the inequality in the years of, schooling.

The schooling model shows, under simplifying assumptions, how the natural log of labor market income can be expressed as a

TABLE 3-1
Annual Earnings during and after Training

Years of Training	1	2	3	...	$N-1$	N	$N+1$	∞
0	E_0	E_0	E_0	...	E_0	E_0	E_0	E_0
1	0	$E_0(1+r)$	$E_0(1+r)$	...	$E_0(1-r)$	$E_0(1+r)$	$E_0(1+r)$	$E_0(1+r)$
2	0	0	$E_0(1+r)^2$	...	$E_0(1+r)^2$	$E_0(1+r)^2$	$E_0(1+r)^2$	$E_0(1+r)^2$
$\cdots$				...				
N	0	0	0	...	0	0	$E_0(1+r)^N$	$E_0(1+r)^N$

Note: E_0 = earnings in the absence of investment in training;
 0 = zero earnings in years in which investment is undertaken;
 r = rate of return on investment in training;
 N = number of years of training.

linear function of the product of two terms: the individual's level of schooling, measured in years, and the (adjusted) average rate of return on the investment in his schooling. If the rate of return is assumed constant across individuals, the variance of the natural log of income across individuals in a region (for example, a state) becomes a function of the square of the rate of return from schooling and the variance in years of schooling in that region. Since average rates of return from schooling are not readily available on a regional basis, they are computed from a linear regression of the natural log of income on schooling with individual or microdata within each region.

THE THEORETICAL MODEL

Individual Earnings Function

Let us designate the perpetual annual earnings after N years of training as E_N, and the perpetual earnings if there were no training as E_0.[1] It is assumed initially that all persons are of equal ability, that the only private costs of training are forgone earnings, and that during the training period there are no earnings. With these assumptions, Table 3-1 will help clarify the derivation of the relation between training and earnings.

A person without training would earn E_0 every year, as shown in row 1 of Table 3-1. A person who invests in training for one year is assumed to have forgone the amount E_0; that is, no earnings were received during that year. This is shown by the zero in the second row of the first column. If a rate of return of r were received on his investment, he would earn $E_1 = E_0 + rE_0 = E_0(1 + r)$ in year two and all subsequent years, where rE_0 is the perpetual return on the investment E_0. This is shown in the second row of Table 3-1. If the rate of return were the same for all years of training, a person with two years of training would have received no earnings during years one and two, and after that an amount equal to

$$E_2 = E_0 + r(E_0) + r(E_0 + rE_0) = E_0(1 + r)(1 + r) = E_0(1 + r)^2,$$

where $r(E_0 + rE_0) = rE_1$ is the perpetual annual return to the investment in the second year of $E_0 + rE_0 = E_1$. A person with N

---

1. The assumption that earnings do not rise with age greatly simplifies the model. The effects of a rise in earnings with age on the analysis of schooling data are discussed below.

years of training would receive nothing during the first N years
and

$$E_N = E_0 + r(E_0) + rE_0(1 + r) + \cdots + rE_0(1 + r)^{N-1},$$

or

$$E_N = E_0(1 + r)^N \qquad\qquad (3\text{-}1)$$

after the investment period.

If the rate of return were not the same for all years of training,
the product terms in the equations above could not be combined,
and the postinvestment income stream would be represented by

$$E_N = E_0 \prod_{j=1}^{N} (1 + r_j), \qquad\qquad (3\text{-}2)$$

where $\prod$ is the mathematical symbol for multiplication.

The assumptions that there are no direct costs of training and
no earnings during the period of investment are not realistic. A
year of schooling ordinarily leaves the summer free for working,
and, for some levels of schooling, direct costs (tuition, school
supplies, and other expenses necessitated by schooling) are far
from negligible. Those engaged in on-the-job training usually receive positive incomes in excess of direct costs, in contrast to the
past, when payments for the privilege of being in an apprentice-
ship program were quite common.

Let C_j equal the direct plus forgone-earnings costs of the investment in the jth year of training. E_{j-1} is the income which
would be received after $j - 1$ years of training if no further investments were undertaken. Furthermore, let us designate by K_j the
ratio C_j/E_{j-1}. That is, K_j equals the proportion of potential income
during year j that is invested. We previously assumed that the only
cost of education was a full year of forgone earnings, so that
$C_j = E_{j-1}$ and $K_j = 1$. Now K_j may differ from unity. If the total
costs of the investment were greater than potential earnings during
the year of training, K_j would be greater than one. If the potential
earnings exceeded the total costs, K_j would be less than one.

The introduction of the investment-income ratio, K, modifies
the earnings equation. If there were no investment, E_0 would still
be earned. If, in year one, the amount $C_1 = K_1 E_0$ were invested at
a rate of return of r_1, the postinvestment income would be

$$E_1 = E_0 + r_1(K_1 E_0) = E_0(1 + r_1 K_1). \qquad\qquad (3\text{-}3)$$

If N years of investments were undertaken,

$$E_N = E_0 \prod_{j=1}^{N} (1 + r_j^*),$$ (3-4)

where $r_j^* = r_j K_j$ is the "adjusted" rate of return to the jth year of education.

Individual differences may be introduced into equation (3-4) by the inclusion of a residual U_i^* and an allowance for differences in rates of return to a given level of training. The earnings equation then becomes

$$E_{N,i} = E_0 \prod_{j=1}^{N} (1 + r_{ij}^*) U_i^*,$$ (3-5)

where r_{ij}^* is the adjusted rate of return to the ith individual for the jth year of training. Taking logarithms of both sides of equation (3-5) and using the relation $\ln (1 + a) \approx a$ when a is small results in

$$\ln E_{N,i} = \ln E_0 + \sum_{j=1}^{N} r_{ij}^* + U_i,$$ (3-6)

where $U_i = \ln U_i^*$ and the "approximately equal to" sign has been replaced by the symbol for "equal to."[2]

Earnings Inequality

Since the purpose of this study is to analyze the effects of regional differences in schooling on regional differences in inequality of income, we must first select a measure of income inequality. Let it be stated at the outset that no one measure is ideal.[3] In referring to several measures of inequality, Lydall writes: "As has frequently been pointed out, they are not unambiguous

2. Rates of return (r) tend to range from 5 per cent to 20 per cent, and K generally does not greatly exceed unity. Hence, rK is sufficiently small to keep the approximation appropriate. Individual differences in the zero investment level of earnings may be considered to be in the residual.

3. This problem is not unique to the dispersion of a distribution—there are several measures of a central tendency, i.e., the mode, the median, the arithmetic mean, and the geometric mean. The ranking of a series of distributions by a measure of central tendency will be sensitive to the measure selected if the distributions have different shapes. There are also several different ways of measuring skewness, the asymmetry of a distribution.

indicators of the degree of inequality, since distributions of various shapes may have the same concentration coefficient. If the distribution is exactly log normal, of course, this problem does not exist; and we can measure the degree of relative dispersion either by the coefficient of concentration, or by the standard deviation of the logarithm of income, or by several other coefficients. . . .The use of a single index of inequality is, therefore, not an ideal arrangement, except where one can be fairly confident that the essential shape of the distribution, i.e., its functional form, is constant."[4] Although the distribution of labor market incomes within regions is not precisely log normal, it does have a universal positive skewness.[5]

The measure of dispersion I use in this study is the variance of the logarithm of income—the square of the standard deviation of the log of income. It has several advantages. First, it is a measure of *relative* inequality and is therefore devoid of units. This permits a comparison of income inequality across regions even if the measuring units (U.S. dollars, Canadian dollars, et cetera) differ. Second, there is probably more social concern about relative income inequality than about absolute income inequality. For example, if all incomes and all prices doubled, there would be no real change in relative wealth or in the equity of the income distribution. The variance in logs would, in fact, remain unchanged. Yet the absolute variance of income would quadruple.[6] These two reasons argue for a measure of relative inequality, but not necessarily for the variance in logs.

There is, however, a third advantage, which dictates the use of the variance in the log of income as the measure of dispersion. The human capital model I use here relates income to investments. When investments are measured in dollars, the appropriate measure of income is also in dollars.[7] However, when investments are measured in *time equivalents* (such as years of schooling, years of

4. See Harold Lydall, *The Structure of Earnings*, Oxford, Clarendon Press, 1968, pp. 137-138. For a discussion of various measures of income inequality, see also Mary Jean Bowman, "A Graphical Analysis of Personal Income Distribution in the United States," *American Economic Review*, September 1945, pp. 607-628.

5. See, for example, H. P. Miller, *Income of the American People*, New York, John Wiley, 1955, p. 3; and Barry Chiswick, "An Interregional Analysis of Schooling and the Skewness of Income," in W. L. Hansen, ed., *Education, Income, and Human Capital*, New York, NBER, 1970.

6. If the variance of X is $\text{Var}(X)$, the variance of $2X$ is $\text{Var}(2X) = 4 \text{Var}(X)$. The variance of the log of $2X$ is $\text{Var}(\ln 2X) = \text{Var}(\ln X)$.

7. See Gary Becker, *Human Capital*, New York, 1964, Chapter III.

labor market experience), the appropriate measure of income is the natural log of income. This latter measure is a linear function of years of investment. Taking the variance of both sides of the relation, it is the variance of the natural log of income that is related to the variance in years of schooling. While data on dollar investments in human capital are very scarce, data on time-equivalent investments in one form of human capital, namely schooling, abound. Since the availability of data, as mentioned before, determines much of the form of this analysis, the measure of dispersion—the variance of the natural logarithm of income—is related to investments in schooling measured as years of schooling completed.

Effect of Training on Earnings Inequality

To find the effect of training on the inequality of earnings, the variance of both sides of equation (3-6) is computed. This results in

$$\text{Var } (\ln E) = \text{Var} \left(\sum_j r_j^* \right) + \text{Var } (U) + 2 \text{ Cov} \left(U, \sum_j r_j^* \right), \quad (3\text{-}7)$$

where Var means variance and Cov means covariance.

The sum of the adjusted rates of return $\Sigma_j\, r_{ij}^*$ can be rewritten as

$$\sum_j r_{ij}^* = \bar{r}_i^* N_i = \bar{r}^* N_i + (\bar{r}_i^* N_i - \bar{r}^* N_i),$$

where $\bar{r}_i^*$ is the ith person's average adjusted rate of return and $\bar{r}^*$ is the average $\bar{r}_i^*$ for the population.[8] If it were assumed that

---

8. In mathematical terms,

$$\bar{r}_i^* = \sum_{j=1}^{N_i} \frac{r_{ij}^*}{N_i} = \sum_{j=1}^{N_i} \frac{r_{ij} K_{ij}}{N_i},$$

where N_i is the number of years of training and

$$\bar{r}^* = \sum_{i=1}^{p} \frac{\bar{r}_i^*}{p},$$

where p is the size of the population.

deviations from the population's average adjusted rate of return appear in the residual U', $[U_i' = U_i + (\bar{r}_i^* - \bar{r}^*)N_i]$, equation (3-6) could be rewritten as

$$\ln E_{N,i} = \ln E_0 + \bar{r}^* N_i + U_i' \tag{3-8}$$

and

$$\text{Var } (\ln E) = (\bar{r}^*)^2 \text{ Var } (N) + \text{Var } (U') + 2\bar{r}^* \text{ Cov } (U', N). \tag{3-9}$$

The model generates as a parameter a commonly used measure of relative inequality, the variance of the log of earnings. This measure of income inequality is related to the rate of return from, and the inequality of investments in, years of training (see equation 3-9). The statistical analysis developed below rests on this equation.

STATISTICAL IMPLEMENTATION OF THE MODEL

Data on money investments in schooling are scarce. There is, however, considerable information on the number of years of schooling. For this reason it is the measure chosen for the empirical analysis in Part B, despite the fact that it masks the effect of differences in the money cost and quality of a given level of schooling. There is also considerable public interest in the role of years in school in determining the distribution of income. A model which explicitly includes postschool training is presented and analyzed in Part C of this volume.

Years of Schooling

Years of training can be separated into two components, schooling and postschool (on-the-job) training. Thus, the earnings function (equation 3-6) becomes

$$\ln E_{N,i} = \ln E_0 + \sum_{j=1}^{S_i} r_{S_{ij}}^* + \sum_{j=1}^{J_i} r_{J_{ij}}^* + U_i, \tag{3-10}$$

where S_i and J_i are the number of years of schooling and postschool training, respectively, and N_i equals $S_i + J_i$.

If schooling were the only explanatory variable, the relevant earnings equation would be

$$\ln E_{S,i} = \ln E_0 + \sum_{j=1}^{S_i} r_{S_{ij}}^* + U_{S,i}. \tag{3-11}$$

Since $\bar{r}_i^*$ was previously defined as the ith person's average adjusted rate of return, equation (3-11) could be rewritten as

$$\ln E_{S,i} = \ln E_0 + (\bar{r}_i^*) S_i + U'_{S,i}. \qquad (3\text{-}12)$$

For simplicity's sake, let us temporarily neglect individual differences in the residual $U'_{S,i}$. Then, if we calculate the variances of both sides of equation (3-12) we obtain

$$\text{Var }(\ln E) = \text{Var }(\bar{r}_i^* S_i). \qquad (3\text{-}13)$$

Thus, the relative variance of income depends on the absolute variance of the product of the adjusted rate of return and the number of years of schooling.

Schooling and the Rate of Return

The variance of the product of two independent random variables, $\bar{r}_i^*$ and S_i, can be expressed as[9]

$$\text{Var}(\bar{r}_i^* S_i) = \bar{r}^{*2} \text{ Var }(S_i) + \bar{S}^2 \text{ Var }(\bar{r}_i^*) + \text{Var }(S_i) \text{ Var }(\bar{r}_i^*). \quad (3\text{-}14)$$

Thus, if $\bar{r}_i^*$ and S_i were independent, the relative variance of income would be positively related to both the average level and the variance of each of the two variables.[10] There are theoretical reasons which make this assumption plausible.

With wealth held constant, those with higher marginal rates of return for a given level of schooling have a greater incentive to invest. This implies a positive correlation between schooling level and rate of return. For a given level of ability, those with greater wealth have a lower discount rate and therefore a greater incentive to invest. As a consequence, they receive a lower rate of return. This implies a negative correlation between schooling level and rate of return. Thus, using a priori analysis, the sign of the correlation between the average rate of return to an individual and his level of schooling is ambiguous.[11] Empirically, Mincer has shown that the rate of return from schooling is uncorrelated with the person's level of schooling (holding experience and weeks worked in the year constant).[12]

---

9. Leo Goodman, "On the Exact Variance of Products," *Journal of the American Statistical Association*, December 1960, pp. 708-713.

10. This differs from Lydall's view that, to explain income dispersion, "what matters is the *inequality* (*sic*) of environment and education, not its average level." (See Lydall, *The Structure of Earnings*, 1968, p. 10).

11. See Gary Becker, *Human Capital and the Personal Distribution of Income*, Ann Arbor, 1967.

12. Mincer, *Schooling, Experience, and Earnings*, Part 2.

The variance of a product of two variables that are not independent can be evaluated,[13] but this is not necessary for the present purpose. The foregoing implies that the intraregional relative variance of income is positively related to the average levels and variances in both years of schooling and rates of return from schooling, even if, for individuals, the level of schooling and the rate of return are not perfectly independent. Data on regional differences in the average rate of return are scarce, but a procedure used in this study permits the computation of estimates for many regions. Data on regional differences in the variance in rates of return are nonexistent. Thus, equation (3-14) is of restricted applicability in an empirical analysis.

Returning to equation (3-12), substituting the population's average adjusted rate of return from schooling into the equation and placing deviations from this population average into the residual, $U'' = U' + (r_i^* - \bar{r}^*)S$,

$$\ln E_{S,i} = \ln E_0 + \bar{r}^* S_i + U''_{S,i}. \tag{3-15}$$

Then,

$$\text{Var } (\ln E_{s,i}) = (\bar{r}^*)^2 \text{ Var } (S) + \text{Var } (U'') + 2\bar{r}^* \text{ Cov } (S,U''). \tag{3-16}$$

Although some average rates of return from schooling have been calculated in recent years, their number is still very small, and relying on the income inequality formulation presented in equations (3-14) and (3-16) would severely limit an empirical analysis. Therefore, rates of return from schooling are computed specifically for this study for many regions. Two methods of estimation, named for their method of computation, are employed: the "regression estimate" of the rate of return, computed for the United States, Canada, Mexico, and Puerto Rico; and the "overtaking age" estimate of the rate of return, computed indirectly only for the states of the United States.[14]

Biases in Computing Regression Rates of Return

The regression estimate of the rate of return is obtained via equation (3-15) by regressing the natural logarithm of earnings on

---

13. Goodman, "On the Exact Variance of Products," 1960.

14. The procedure used to compute the "overtaking age" estimate is discussed in Appendix A-2. Because it is computed indirectly it is subject to considerable measurement error. Mincer developed a shortcut for estimating the overtaking age rate of return; see his *Schooling, Experience, and Earnings*.

years of schooling completed:

$$\ln E_{S,i} = (\widehat{\ln E_0}) + \hat{r} S_i + \hat{U}_i, \qquad (3\text{-}17)$$

where $\hat{r}$ and $(\widehat{\ln E_0})$ are the least-squares linear regression estimates of the average adjusted rate of return from schooling and the zero schooling level of earnings, respectively, and $\hat{U}$ is the residual. Unbiased estimates of the adjusted rate of return are obtained when S_i and U_i'' from equation (3-15) are uncorrelated, that is, when schooling and the omitted variables are uncorrelated and when there are no errors of measurement. The residual contains the effects of differences in luck, tastes, ability, investments in human capital other than schooling, and wealth. By definition, luck is uncorrelated with schooling. There is reason to believe, however, that the other variables may be correlated with schooling. For example, we would expect a positive, although not perfect, correlation between schooling and family wealth.

Due to the secular increase in schooling, those with low levels of schooling tend to be older and are receiving their return on earlier investments in postschool training. Thus, a regression of the log of earnings on years of schooling in which all age groups are pooled results in a downward-biased estimate of the slope coefficient of schooling, and hence of the regression estimate of the rate of return. The downward bias would not be fully eliminated by restricting the regressions to specified age groups. For a given age, an additional year of schooling implies one year less of experience (investment in postschool training). Since years of schooling and of experience are negatively correlated in the cross section, the omission of experience from the regression equation results in a downward bias in the slope coefficient of schooling.

An individual's dollar investments in health and migration are positively correlated with his level of schooling.[15] This generates a positive correlation between years of schooling and the component of the residual reflecting the money return from those forms of capital, since it is unlikely that their rates of return are sufficiently (if at all) negatively correlated with the level of schooling.

Another component in the residual is differential ability, as

---

15. See Michael Grossman, *The Demand for Health: A Theoretical and Empirical Investigation*, NBER, 1972; Selma Mushkin, "Health as an Investment," *Journal of Political Economy*, October 1962, pp. 129–157; Rashi Fein, "Educational Patterns in Southern Migration," *Southern Economic Journal*, July 1965, pp. 106–124; and June O'Neill, "The Effect of Income and Education on Inter-Regional Migration," Ph.D. dissertation, Columbia University, 1970.

reflected in differences in the rate of return from investments in schooling. For simplicity of presentation, let us assume that $K_i = 1$ for all i in equation (3-12). Then, for each individual,

$$\ln E_{S,i} = \ln E_0 + \bar{r} S_i + (d_s S_i + U'_{S,i}), \qquad (3\text{-}18)$$

where $(d_s S_i + U'_{S,i})$ is the residual and $d_s = (\bar{r}_i - \bar{r})$ is the difference between the rate of return received by the ith person and the average rate of return. Since the expected value of d_s is zero, S and $d_s S$ would be uncorrelated and there would be no bias from this source if S and d_s were independent of each other.[16] It is not clear a priori or empirically whether d_s and S are positively or negatively correlated.[17]

Errors in measurement of the variables may also bias the regression coefficient. If there were random errors in both S and $\ln Y$, and these errors were uncorrelated, the effect would be a downward bias. If these errors were positively correlated (for example, if in sample data there were a tendency for those who overreport their level of schooling to overreport their earnings), the effect would be unclear a priori.[18]

To summarize, it appears that wealth, migration, and health are positively correlated with earnings—with schooling held constant—and positively correlated with schooling. Thus, omitting these variables biases the slope coefficient of schooling upward. The effect of ability and errors of measurement is unclear. Omit-

---

16. It is not sufficient for S and d_s to be uncorrelated. If $\bar{r}_i$ is uncorrelated with S_i, Cov $(d_s, S) = 0$. We know that $E(d_s) = 0$. Then Cov $(d_s, S) = E[d_s (S - \bar{S})] = E(d_s S) = 0$. Thus, Cov $(S, d_s S) = E[(S - \bar{S}) (d_s S)] = E(d_s S^2) - \bar{S} E(d_s S) = E(d_s S^2)$.

Hence, Cov $(S, d_s S) = 0$, if Cov $(d_s, S^2) = 0$, which necessarily holds when d_s and S are independent.

17. If ability were measured by the average rate of return from schooling for a given level of schooling, and if average and marginal rates of return were positively correlated, then (since those with higher marginal rates of return have a greater incentive to invest in schooling) there would be a positive relation between ability (d_s) and schooling (S) if all individuals had the same supply curve of funds. If, however, differences were greater in supply conditions than in demand conditions, and if those with greater ability had lower investment costs, d_s and S would be negatively related.

18. Let $y = a + b x + U$ be the true relation and let $X = x + w$ and $Y = y + v$ be the observed values, where w and v are normally distributed with zero expectation and constant variance, and are independent of x, y, and U. Then $Y = a + bX + (U - bw + v) = a + bX + z$, where $z = U - bw + v$ and $E(z) = 0$. Since $E(X) = x$, $w = X - E(X)$, and Cov $(X, z) = E[(X - E(X))(z)] = E[(w) (U - bw + v)] = -b$ Var $(w) + $ Cov (w, v). If x and y were positively correlated, a sufficiently strong positive correlation between w and v could produce an upward bias of the slope coefficient.

ting years of experience biases the slope coefficient downward because the variable is negatively correlated with schooling in cross-sectional data.[19] Indeed, in empirical work, regression-estimated rates of return (when schooling is the only explanatory variable) are lower than directly estimated internal rates of return and lower than regression-estimated rates of return, with investments in experience held constant.[20]

The downward bias notwithstanding, these estimates are employed in the empirical analysis that follows because experience cannot be held constant for the data sets studied.

Schooling as an Explanatory Vehicle

Taking the variance of both sides of regression equation (3-17) results in

$$\text{Var } (\ln E_{s,i}) = (\hat{r})^2 \text{ Var } (S_i) + \text{Var } (\hat{U}_i) \qquad (3\text{-}19)$$

for each region.[21] The ratio of the explained variance ($\hat{r}^2$ Var S) to the total variance (Var(ln E)), called the "coefficient of determination," indicates the proportion of the variability in the dependent variable in that region "explained" by the variation in the explanatory variables. If the regression slope coefficient were an unbiased estimate of the average adjusted rate of return and if the two variances were unbiased, the coefficient of determination would be an unbiased estimate of the explanatory power of schooling. A bias in the slope coefficient, however, produces a bias in the same direction in the coefficient of determination.

If an unbiased estimate of the adjusted rate of return ($\bar{r}^*$) were known, then equation (3-16) could be used to calculate

$$1 = \frac{(\bar{r}^*)^2 \text{ Var } (S)}{\text{Var } (\ln E)} + \frac{\text{Var } (U'')}{\text{Var } (\ln E)} + \frac{2\bar{r}^* \text{ Cov } (S, U'')}{\text{Var } (\ln E)} . \qquad (3\text{-}20)$$

The first ratio indicates the direct explanatory power of schooling, the second measures the direct explanatory power of other variables, while the third shows the explanatory power of the covariation of schooling and these other variables. The latter would be

---

19. The negative correlation is due to both secular trends in schooling and the negative correlation between schooling and experience for a given age, as discussed above.

20. For a comparison of internal and regression rates of return, see Table 4-2. For an analysis of the effect on the regression estimate of including experience, see Table 5-3, and Mincer, *Schooling, Experience, and Earnings.*

21. The regression forces Cov(S, U) = 0 for each region.

positive (or negative) if, on balance, S and U'' were positively (or negatively) correlated. If the covariance term were zero [Cov $(S, U'') = 0$], the direct contribution of schooling would be the same as the total contribution and the regression estimate of the contribution.

For each region the coefficient of determination shows the proportion of differences in earnings within that region that can be explained by differences in schooling, given the regression estimate of the adjusted rate of return. We are also concerned, however, with the proportion of the variation across regions in the inequality of earnings [Var(ln$E$)] that can be explained by differences in the educational component of income inequality [$\hat{r}^2$ Var(S)] and the variation in "all other variables" [Var($\hat{U}$)]. There is no unique estimate of these values because of the covariation of the education component and the residual variance. We can, of course, estimate the separate explanatory powers of schooling, the residual, and the covariation of schooling with the residual. If for the ith region

$$v_i = \text{Var} (\ln E)_i,$$

$$s_i = \hat{r}_i^2 \ \text{Var} (S)_i,$$

and

$$t_i = \text{Var} (\hat{U})_i,$$

then from equation (3-19), $v_i = s_i + t_i$. Taking variances across regions,

$$\text{Var}(v) = \text{Var}(s) + \text{Var}(t) + 2 \ \text{Cov}(s,t), \qquad (3\text{-}21)$$

and the interregional explanatory power of

(a) the education component is $\dfrac{\text{Var} (s)}{\text{Var} (v)}$,

(b) the residual variance is $\dfrac{\text{Var} (t)}{\text{Var} (v)}$,   (3-22)

and

(c) the covariation is $\dfrac{2 \ \text{Cov} (s,t)}{\text{Var} (v)}$.

An alternative procedure for estimating the interregional explanatory power of schooling is to regress the variance of the log of income on the education component. Then the regression's adjusted coefficient of determination is schooling's interregional explanatory power of income inequality. This procedure forces the covariance term ín equation (3-22) to equal zero, and biases upward the education component's direct explanatory power of schooling.

Schooling is measured in years and is used in the same units for all regions.[22] The variances of the log of earnings [$\text{Var}(\ln E)$] and the residual [$\text{Var}(\hat{U})$] in equation (3-19) are both pure numbers and can be compared across countries without converting to a common currency. In subsequent chapters these parameters are analyzed within and among regions in order to ascertain what patterns of relationships exist.

---

22. Note, however, that, while the unit is "years," the length and quality of a school year vary within and across regions. No attempt is made here to adjust for these differences.

4

Interregional Applications

The relationships between income inequality and the rate of return from schooling, the variance of schooling, and the residual variance—the focal points of the model developed in the preceding chapter—are analyzed here empirically on an interregional basis for the United States, Canada, and the Netherlands. A summary of the findings and a discussion of the relationships among the relevant parameters conclude Chapter 4.

The empirical analyses—here as well as in Chapter 5—rest on the theoretical model of Chapter 3. A linear regression (equation 3-17) of the log of income on years of schooling is run for each region of the United States and Canada and for Puerto Rico and Mexico. This regression provides data on the regression estimate of the rate of return $(\hat{r})$, the residual variance $(\text{Var } (\hat{U}))$, and the intra-regional explanatory power $(\bar{R}^2)$ for each region. These data, together with the inequalities of income and schooling, are then used as the inputs in the second level of the analysis. Here interregional differences in income inequality are related to interregional differences in the rate of return from schooling, the inequality of schooling, the education component $(\hat{r}^2 \text{ Var } (S))$, and the residual variance $(\text{Var } (\hat{U}))$.

Two estimates of the explanatory power of schooling are calculated: (1) the proportion of individual differences in the log of income $(\ln E)$ within a region that can be explained by years of schooling (S) and (2) the proportion of the variations in income inequality $(\text{Var } (\ln E))$ across regions that can be explained by the

48

education component ($\hat{r}^2$ Var (S)). As will be shown below, there is a systematic downward bias in the fraction of the differences in the log of income explained by schooling within each region. If these biases are similar in each region, the fraction of interregional differences in income inequality explained by schooling may be unaffected by the intraregion bias.

As to coverage, it is a truism that, as a prerequisite for an empirical analysis, the data must first be delimited, the relevant population and income concepts defined. All inhabitants of a region cannot be included in the data for the purposes of this study. Students, for example, must be removed because the model is designed to cover those who have already completed their investment in schooling. Wives, whose labor force behavior is strongly influenced by their husband's income and the number and age distribution of their children, should also be excluded from the data base. Finally, the aged should be excluded, since many of them have low labor force participation rates due to ill health, discrimination, and pension income. Thus, we approximate the desired group by restricting the data to males between the ages of twenty-five and sixty-four.[1] Where possible and practicable, separate calculations are made to remove the effects of racial differences.

On the income side, the dependent variable used is market earnings. This is dictated by the fact that the model is developed for labor income and data on nonmarket and psychic earnings are unavailable. The total annual money earnings of those with some earnings reflect unemployment, but persons unemployed for the entire year are omitted from the study.[2]

THE UNITED STATES

In examining the effects of schooling on the intraregional and interregional differences in labor market income inequality, we first look at the two major regions of the United States—the South and the non-South. Next comes an extensive interstate analysis,

---

1. The model was developed under the assumption of an infinite working life. However, for positive rates of return and long labor force participation, the difference in the rate of return between assuming an infinite and a finite working life is trivial.

2. Unemployment compensation and home production during the period of unemployment are omitted from the earnings data. The proportion of adult males unemployed for an entire year, however, is very small.

TABLE 4-1

Regression of Natural Log of Earnings on Schooling:
Males, Twenty-five to Sixty-four, South versus Non-South, 1959

	Summary Statistics				Regression: $\ln E$ on S_2			
	SD($\ln E$)	SD(S)	AV($\ln E$)	AV(S)	$\ln E_{0,1}$	$\hat{r}_1$	$\dfrac{\overline{R}^2_1}{R^2_1}$	Var(U)
	(1)	(2)	(3)	(4)	(5)	(6)	(7)	(8)
1. Non-South, white	.65	3.36	1.66	10.78	.96 (.26)	.06 (.02)	.10 .11	.38
2. South, white	.74	3.90	1.43	9.96	.60 (.23)	.08 (.02)	.18 .20	.44
3. Non-South, total	.65	3.41	1.63	10.67	.94 (.23)	.06 (.02)	.10 .11	.38
4. South, total	.76	4.03	1.32	9.42	.47 (.20)	.09 (.02)	.22 .23	.45

Note: The following definitions hold for Table 4-1 and all subsequent tables:

E = annual earnings in thousands of dollars.
Y = annual income in thousands of dollars.
S = years of schooling attended.
U = residual income or earnings.
$\hat{r}$ = regression estimate of adjusted rate of return, slope computed from regression equation (3-17).
$\ln E$ = natural log of E, similar for $\ln Y$.
$\ln E_0$ = zero education level of earning, intercept computed from regression equation (4-17), similar for $\ln Y_0$.
$\overline{R}^2$ = adjusted coefficient of determination; R^2 = unadjusted, computed from regression equation (3-17).
SD = standard deviation.

based, for the most part, on money income rather than earnings data (since for the individual states the latter are available only for males of fourteen years and over). Attention is focused on the rate of return, and a procedure is developed to improve the model's explanatory power by correcting for the downward bias inherent in the regression estimate of the rate of return.

To test the general validity of the relationships found, the interstate analysis is repeated for the income inequality of white males alone, for the earnings inequality of all males, and for another measure of the rate of return from schooling called the "overtaking age rate of return."[3] Finally, the relationship between the level of schooling and income inequality is also examined.

---

3. See Chapter 3, footnote 14.

TABLE 4-1 (Concluded)

		Regression: $\ln E$ on $\not\pounds$, $\$$, and H			
$\ln E_{0,3}$	$\hat{r}_{\not\pounds}$	$\hat{r}_{\$}$	$\hat{r}_H$	$\dfrac{\bar{R}_3^2}{R_3^2}$	Var(U)$_3$
(9)	(10)	(11)	(12)	(13)	(14)
1.09	.05	.06	.08	.07	.39
(.67)	(.09)	(.06)	(.06)	.11	
.66	.07	.09	.09	.16	.46
(.50)	(.08)	(.07)	(.06)	.2C	
1.06	.05	.06	.08	.08	.39
(.58)	(.08)	(.05)	(.05)	.12	
.50	.08	.09	.09	.20	.46
(.40)	(.07)	(.07)	(.06)	.23	

AV = average.
Var = variance.
Subscripts 1, 3, $\not\pounds$, $\$$, H: 1 is used when schooling is treated as a single variable; 3 and $\not\pounds$, $\$$ and H are used when it is treated as three variables; $\not\pounds$ or "low" education is defined as 0–8 years of school, $\$$ or "medium" as 8–12 years, and H or "high" as more than 12 years.
In calculating the adjusted coefficients of determination for the regression of the natural log of earning on schooling, the number of degrees of freedom was assumed equal to the number of cells minus the number of parameters estimated. For the regions there were 7 schooling intervals and 11 income intervals for a total of 77 cells.
Standard errors are in parentheses.
Source: U.S. Census of Population: 1960, Subject Reports, Occupation by Earnings and Education, Tables 2 and 3.

SOUTH VERSUS NON-SOUTH

The relationships between schooling and income inequality in the South and the non-South are compared by regressing the natural log of earnings on years of schooling for males between the ages of twenty-five and sixty-five in the Census Bureau's "South" and "non-South."[4] The results appear in Table 4-1, with rows 1

---

4. The "South" consists of sixteen Southern states plus the District of Columbia. The remainder of the country, the "non-South," is also referred to as the "North."

The data are from a 5 per cent sample of the population grouped into seventy-seven cells. The midpoint of each closed earnings interval represents the earnings of all persons in the interval. The shape of the lower end of the earnings distribution is not definitely known, and with census definitions

and 2 reporting the results for white males only, and rows 3 and 4, for all males—white and nonwhite.

Reading down columns (1) through (14), we see that the inequalities of earnings, "residual" earnings and schooling, and adjusted rates of return from education are higher in the South than in the non-South.[5] The education component ($\hat{r}^2$ Var (S)) and the coefficient of determination are also larger in the South, while levels of earnings and education are lower there. A comparison of rows 1 and 2 with rows 3 and 4 indicates that the same patterns exist when both whites and nonwhites are covered in the data, but that the inclusion of nonwhites widens the regional differences.[6]

Regression estimates of the rate of return for college and secondary education are presented in Table 4-2. These can be isolated by assuming that the appropriate investment-income ratios are $\overline{K}_H = 1.0$ and $\overline{K}_{\cancel{S}} = 0.75$.[7] Clearly, the regression technique

---

there can never be negative earnings. Therefore, the class mean of the lower open-end interval is considered to be the midpoint between zero earnings and the upper limit of the interval. The effect of any error introduced in this estimate would be small since the lowest earnings group contains only a small part of the samples analyzed. The Pareto equation, which provides a fairly good fit for the income distribution in the higher income ranges, is used to estimate the mean income in the upper open-end interval. See M. J. Bowman, "A Graphical Analysis of Personal Income Distribution in the United States," *American Economic Review*, September 1945; and N. O. Johnson, "The Pareto Law," *Review of Economics and Statistics*, February 1937, pp. 20–26.

5. Since direct estimates of rates of return from schooling by state are not available for the states, equation (3-17) is used here to generate estimates from census data. The data for the South and non-South are from the 1960 *Census of Population* and cover 1959 earnings of all males in the experienced labor force between the ages of twenty-five and sixty-four.

The pair-wise product moment correlations among the explanatory variables when schooling is divided into three components are not large, but due to the definitions of the variables, the multicollinearity is substantial. Note that the standard error of the slope coefficient increases from 0.02 to a low of 0.05 and a high of 0.09.

Hanoch's estimates also show higher internal rates of return from schooling in the white South. See G. Hanoch, "Personal Earnings and Investment in Schooling," Ph.D. dissertation, University of Chicago, 1965, pp. 71 and 84.

6. The effects of the inclusion of nonwhites are discussed in Appendix B-1 with special reference to the interstate analysis.

7. For college education in the United States, Becker estimates that direct costs are approximately equal to potential summer earnings, or $\overline{K}_H = 1.0$. (See his *Human Capital*, Chapter 4.) A low estimate for $\overline{K}_{\cancel{S}}$, the high-school investment income ratio, is 0.75. This is based on the assumption of a nine-month academic year and no direct costs of schooling. Positive direct costs would raise the ratio. No estimate has been made of $\overline{K}_{\cancel{S}}$, and therefore $\hat{r}_{\cancel{S}}$ cannot be separated into its components $\overline{r}$ and $\overline{K}_{\cancel{S}}$.

TABLE 4-2

Calculated Rates of Return for Adult Males in the United States and Canada
(per cent)

	Elementary School (0-8 Years)	High School (9-12 Years)	College (13+ Years)
United States			
Becker (white)	—	20.0	13.0
Hansen (all)			
I	15.0	11.4	10.2
II	∞	14.5	10.1
Hanoch (white, North)			
I	>100.0	16.1	9.6
II	33.6	18.0	10.0
Regression estimate			
(all)	—	9.2	8.0
(white)	—	8.9	7.8
(North)	—	8.2	7.6
(white, North)	—	8.4	7.6
Canada			
Podoluk	—	16.3	19.7
Regression estimate	—	10.0	7.6

Sources:
United States

G. S. Becker, *Human Capital*, New York, NBER, 1974, Chapters 4 and 6. Marginal internal private rates of return based on earnings for graduates. No rate of return was calculated for elementary education. College is for 13 to 16 years of education. Data from *U.S. Census of Population: 1950.*

W. L. Hansen, "Total and Private Rates of Return to Investment in Schooling," *Journal of Political Economy*, April 1963, pp. 128–140, for income of adult males as reported in the *U.S. Census of Population: 1950.* College refers to 13 to 16 years of schooling. I: p. 134, Table 3. Internal rate of return on total resources. II: p. 137, Table 5. Internal rate of return to private resources after taxes. Infinite rate of return to elementary education, given assumption of costless education to the individual through the eighth grade.

G. Hanoch, "Personal Earnings and Investment in Schooling," Ph.D. dissertation, University of Chicago, 1965. Private internal rates of return from two methods of calculation, based on earnings from *U.S. Census of Population: 1960.* Hanoch assumes that potential earnings equal the cost of the investment. I: p. 71, Table 6. II: p. 84, Table 7.

Regression estimate: Adjusted rates of return divided by $\overline{K}_H$ = 1.0 for college and $E_{\mathcal{g}}$ = 0.75 for high school. Estimated rates of return are not presented for elementary school because the appropriate value for $K_{\mathcal{g}}$ is unclear. Calculated from regressing log earnings on three education variables for males aged 25 to 64. *(U.S. Census of Population: 1960, Subject Reports, Occupation by Earnings and Education*, Washington, Bureau of the Census, Tables 1, 2, and 3.) See Table 6-1.

Canada

J. R. Podoluk, *Education and Earnings*, Ottawa, Dominion Bureau of Statistics, Central Research and Development Staff, 1965, pp. 60–65. Rates of return to private investments in schooling for completing secondary school
(Continued)

TABLE 4-2 *(Concluded)*

and receiving a university degree. Based on earnings before taxes for nonfarm males as reported in the *Census of Canada: 1961.*

Regression estimate: Adjusted rates of return from regressing the natural log of earnings on three education variables for nonfarm males, age 25 to 64, divided by K_H = 1.0 for college and K_S = 0.75 for high school. (*Census of Canada: 1961, Population Sample. Income of Individuals,* Bulletin 4.1-2, Ottawa, Dominion Bureau of Statistics, Table B6). See Table 6-1.

results in lower estimates of rates of return to secondary and higher education than the internal rate of return method.[8] The differences are quite large in the case of secondary schooling in the United States and Canada and of university education in Canada.

The regression slope coefficient and therefore the intraregional explanatory power of schooling appear to be downward-biased. A negative covariation term (i.e., a negative correlation between schooling and the residual) would result if the unbiased rates of return were used. The downward bias notwithstanding, column 7 of Table 4-1 indicates that the explanatory power of schooling is substantial, especially in the South.

The percentage of the variance of the log of earnings which is attributable to the education component and the percentage attributable to the residual variance can be calculated on the basis of the following equation. According to equation (3-21), where v = Var (ln$E$), $s = \hat{r}^2$ Var (S), and t = Var ($\hat{U}$), with two regions and with s and t positively related, then necessarily $R_{s,t}$ = 1.0 and

$$\text{Var} (v) = \text{Var} (s) + \text{Var} (t) + 2 R_{s,t} \text{SD} (s) \text{ SD} (t)$$

$$\text{Var} (v) = [\text{SD} (s) + \text{SD} (t)]^2$$

$$\text{SD} (v) = \text{SD} (s) + \text{SD} (t).$$

---

8. This is not due to the pooling of age groups. The adjusted rate of return and explanatory power are low for all age groups, as seen in the table below, but rise when experience rather than age is held constant (see Mincer, *Schooling, Experience, and Earnings*).

Regression of Natural Log of Earnings in 1959 on Schooling

Age Group	Non-South Males		Non-South White Males	
	$\hat{r}$	R^2	$\hat{r}$	R^2
25–34	.051	.063	.049	.061
35–44	.077	.135	.077	.134
45–54	.078	.126	.078	.121
55–64	.070	.096	.070	.094

Note: Based on 77 cells.
Source: United States Census of Population: 1960, Subject Reports, Occupation by Earnings and Education, Tables 2 and 3.

The proportion of the variation in income inequality explained by the education component is SD (s)/SD (v), and the proportion explained by the residual is SD (t)/SD (v).

Applying this method to the data on Table 4-1, we find that the interregional explanatory power of the education component is approximately 48 per cent for white males and 54 per cent for all males. (See Table 4-5.) Thus, the interregional explanatory power of schooling is very large, both in absolute terms and relative to the intraregional explanatory power. This may result from a number of important factors. For example, differences in ability and luck vary considerably within regions but presumably have fairly similar distributions across regions. It seems plausible that the smaller the variation of these traits, the larger the explanatory power of schooling. Note that the inclusion of nonwhites in the data tends to increase this explanatory power.

INTERSTATE ANALYSIS

In contrast to the preceding two-region, South–non-South comparison, we turn to variations in the effects of schooling on income distribution among fifty states and the District of Columbia (fifty-one states).

Income Inequality

Regression equation (3-17) is computed for each state, with the natural log of personal income (ln Y) for 1959 as the dependent variable.[9] The data cover males of twenty-five years and over with some income.[10]

Table 4-3 shows the correlation matrix for the parameters under study. Here each of the fifty-one states represents an observation. Column 1 of Table 4-3 indicates a significant positive correlation of the log variance of income with the rate of return

---

9. While it would be preferable to restrict the state data to earnings of adult males under sixty-five, such statistics are unobtainable. However, including males over sixty-five and income other than earnings does not disturb the qualitative regional results, although the values of the parameters are altered (see Appendix B-2).

10. The income data come from the *U.S. Census of Population: 1960*, *Vol. 1, Characteristics of the Population*, Parts 2-52, Table 138; they are based on a 25 per cent sample cross-classified by schooling and income in seventy-two cells—eight intervals for schooling and nine intervals for income.

TABLE 4-3

Matrix of Correlation Coefficients for Fifty-one States

	Var(lnY) (1)	$\hat{r}_1$ (2)	lnY$_{0,1}$ (3)	$\bar{R}^2$ (4)	Var(S) (5)	Var(U) (6)	$\hat{r}_1^2$ (7)	$\hat{r}_1$ Var(S) (8)	AV(lnY) (9)
$\hat{r}_1$	.77								
lnY$_{0,1}$	-.86	-.94							
$\bar{R}^2$	.79	.77	-.68						
Var(S)	.48	.24	-.19	.76					
Var(U)$_1$	.90	.78	-.77	.46	.18				
$\hat{r}_1^2$	.77	1.00	-.94	.79	.27	.76			
$\hat{r}_1^2$ Var(S)	.88	.86	-.79	.98	.69	.62	.87		
AV(lnY)	-.79	-.79	.94	-.67	-.32	-.66	-.81	-.76	
AV(S)	-.73	-.66	.70	-.78	-.62	-.51	-.68	-.81	.84

Note: The null hypothesis is that the correlation coefficient in the population is zero. The probabilities represent the chance that sample estimates of R will be further from zero than the values given (one-tailed test). The probabilities are based on the number of degrees of freedom equal to, or nearest to, the number of observations minus two. See R. A. Fisher and F. Yates, *Statistical Tables*, London, Oliver and Boyd, 1938, Table VI, pp. 36–37. The critical values for the correlation coefficient (R), under alternative type I errors (α), are $R(\alpha = .05) = .23$, $R(.025) = .27$, $R(.01) = .32$. The critical values are based on 50 degrees of freedom.

Source: See Table A-1.

($\hat{r}$), the inequality of schooling (Var (S)), and the education component ($\hat{r}^2$ Var (S)), but a negative correlation with the level of income and schooling.

The relationship between the rate of return ($\hat{r}$) and the variance of schooling (Var (S)) (Table 4-3, row 4, column 2) is quite weak (0.24), and the hypothesis that no statistically significant correlation exists cannot be rejected. There is a strong positive correlation between the variance of residual income and the variance of log income. However, the intrastate explanatory power of schooling [$R^2 = 1 - $ Var (U)/Var (ln$Y$)] is significantly positively correlated with income inequality. This implies that interstate differences in the residual variance (Var (U)) are smaller than interstate differences in the variance of income. In other words, education increases interstate differences in the variance of income.

The explanatory powers of the education component, the residual, and their covariation are shown in Table 4-5, row 3. It appears that each of the components explains approximately one-third of the interstate variances in income inequality. Again, while education explains an important part of *interstate* differences in the variance of income, it has less *intrastate* explanatory power. The adjusted coefficient of determination ranges from 32 per cent for Mississippi to 11 per cent for Nevada, with a mean value of 18.4 per cent.[11]

Regression Estimate of Rate of Return Corrected

The results of the regression of Var (ln$Y$) on $\hat{r}^2$ Var (S) across fifty-one states appear in row 1 of Table 4-4. The slope $b = 1.58$ suggests that the estimate of the average rate of return across the states is $\bar{r}_c = \bar{\hat{r}}\sqrt{b} = (0.102)\sqrt{1.58} = 0.126$.[12]

---

11. The relatively low coefficients of determination reflect the large variation of individual income and rates of return within a given level of schooling, possibly due to individual differences in rates of return, experience, and employment. The variance and coefficient of variation in rates of return from schooling have received little attention in the literature. Two exceptions are Mincer's *Schooling, Experience, and Earnings* (Part 2) and my "Racial Differences in the Variation in Rates of Return from Schooling" in G. von Furstenberg et al., eds., *Patterns of Racial Discrimination*, Vol. 2, D. C. Heath, 1974.

12. Recall equation (3-16): Var (ln$E_{S,i}$) = ($\bar{r}^*$)^2 Var(S) + Var(U'') + 2($\bar{r}^*$) Cov (S, U''). The regression across states may be run:

$$\text{Var } (\ln E_{S,i}) = a + b[(\hat{r})^2 \text{ Var } (S)] + V_i,$$

where a is the average Var (U'') + 2($\hat{r}$) Cov (S, U'') and V_i is a random residual. The value b ($\hat{r}$)^2 is our estimate of ($\bar{r}^*$)^2.

TABLE 4-4

Regression Analysis of U.S. Data for Fifty-one States

Regression	Slope Coefficient[a]	Coefficient of Determination
Var(ln Y) on $\hat{r}^2$ Var(S)	1.58 (0.11)	0.77
Var(ln Y) on r_M^2 Var(S)	0.52 (0.05)	0.68
Var(ln$E$) on $\hat{r}^2$ Var(S)	1.30 (0.14)	0.63
Var(ln$E$) on r_M^2 Var(S)	0.45 (0.05)	0.61

Source: Data from Tables A-1 and A-4.
[a]Standard errors are in parentheses.

An adjustment for the corrected rate of return $\hat{r}_{ci} = \hat{r}_i$ ($\sqrt{1.58}$) alters the interregional and intraregional explanatory power of schooling. This correction raises the education component's direct explanatory power of interstate differences in income inequality to (1.58) × (30.5) = 48.2, or approximately 50 per cent.[13] The proportion of differences in income within states explained by schooling is also increased if each state's rate of return were corrected by the factor $\sqrt{1.58}$. Rankings would not change, but the adjusted coefficient of determination would range from (1.58) × (32) = 51 per cent for Mississippi to (1.58) × (11) = 17 per cent for Nevada, with a mean value of (1.58) × (18.4) = 29 per cent.

Interstate Analysis of White Males

In an attempt to determine whether the interstate results are the consequence of different proportions of nonwhites in the data, the regression analysis was performed for the fifty-one states, but with nonwhites deleted from the data of seventeen states. These states include all those in which nonwhites constitute eight per cent or more of the relevant population.[14]

The regression analysis for white males substantiates the findings for all males, but shows generally weaker results. The average

---

13. Under the assumption that the covariance between $(r_c)^2$ Var (S) and the residual variance is nonnegative.

14. The results are discussed in Appendix B-1.

TABLE 4-5

The Explanatory Power of Schooling in the United States and Canada
(per cent)

Region	Education Component (1)	Residual (2)	Covariation of Education Component and Residual (3)	Average Intra-Area Explanatory Power (4)
North-South				
(whites) (2 areas)	47.6	52.4	—	14.1
North-South (2 areas)	54.0	46.0	—	16.1
States (51 states)	30.5	32.0	37.5	18.4
Corrected $\hat{r}$	48.2	51.8		29.1
States (17 states adjusted for nonwhites)	22.3	43.2	34.5	17.4
Non-South (34 states)	13.3	57.9	28.8	15.4
South (17 states)	48.2	40.0	11.8	24.4
Non-South (34 states adjusted for nonwhites)	16.5	57.0	26.5	15.0
South (17 states adjusted for nonwhites)	18.8	66.5	14.7	21.9

Note: If $s = \hat{r}^2 \text{Var}(S)$, $t = \text{Var}(\hat{U})$, and $v = \text{Var}(\ln Y)$, then $v = s + t$ and
$$1 = \frac{\text{Var}(s)}{\text{Var}(v)} + \frac{\text{Var}(t)}{\text{Var}(v)} + \frac{2 \text{Cov}(s,t)}{\text{Var}(v)}.$$
The three ratios are the interregional explanatory powers of schooling, the residual, and their covariation, respectively. If there were only two regions and the education component and the residual variance were positively correlated, $1 = \frac{\text{SD}(s)}{\text{SD}(v)} + \frac{\text{SD}(t)}{\text{SD}(v)}$ where the two ratios would be the explanatory powers of schooling and the residual.
Source: Tables 4-1, A-1, A-2, A-3.

explanatory power of schooling within the states decreases slightly from 18.4 per cent to 17.4 per cent, while a comparison of rows 3 and 5 of Table 4-5 indicates that the interstate explanatory power of schooling decreases by a larger proportion. Schooling is still a very important variable, and more so interstate than intrastate, even though both explanatory powers are reduced.

Intra-South and Intra–non-South

In the South–non-South analysis (p. 51) we saw a clear regional difference. To ascertain whether the interstate conclusions are due solely to North-South differences, correlation matrices are cal-

TABLE 4-6
Matrix of Correlation Coefficients, All Males, Seventeen Southern States
(17 observations)

	$Var(\ln Y)$ (1)	$\hat{r}_1$ (2)	$\ln Y_{0,1}$ (3)	$\bar{R}^2$ (4)	$Var(S)$ (5)	$Var(U)$ (6)	$\hat{r}_1^2$ (7)	$\hat{r}_1^2 Var(S)$ (8)	$AV(\ln Y)$ (9)
r_1	.79								
$\ln Y_{0,1}$	-.85	-.91							
$\bar{R}^2$	.58	.82	-.70						
$Var(S)$	.15	-.08	.04	.43					
$Var(U)$	.73	.28	-.44	-.14	-.19				
$\hat{r}_1^2$	.79	1.00	-.93	.81	-.08	.28			
$\hat{r}_1^2 Var(S)$	.79	.89	-.83	.96	.39	.15	.89		
$AV(\ln Y)$	-.84	-.78	.95	-.61	-.08	-.50	-.79	-.77	
$AV(S)$	-.80	-.74	.81	-.68	-.23	-.40	-.73	-.79	.89

Note: The critical values for the correlation coefficient (R), under alternative type I errors (α), are $R(\alpha = .10) = .33$, $R(.05) = .41$, $R(.025) = .48$, $R(.01) = .56$. The critical values are based on 15 degrees of freedom. See notes to Table 4-3.
Source: Table A-1.

culated for the seventeen Southern and thirty-four non-Southern states; they appear in Tables 5-6 and 5-7.

Within the South and non-South, the variables in equation (3-19), the adjusted rate of return ($\hat{r}$), and the education component ($\hat{r}^2$ Var (S)) show a significant positive correlation with the variance of log of income (Var (ln Y)). The variance of the residual (Var ($\hat{U}$)) and the adjusted coefficient of determination also exhibit a significant positive correlation with the inequality of income. The variance of schooling does not fit the previously observed patterns, is not significantly related to income inequality, and has a significant negative correlation with the rate of return in the non-South. The levels of schooling and income appear to be negatively related to income inequality, especially in the South.

The average intrastate explanatory power of schooling in the South is 24.4 per cent, compared with 15.4 per cent in the non-South. An adjustment for the corrected rate of return, $\hat{r}_{ci} = (1.26)\,\hat{r}_i$, raises the average explanatory power to 38.6 per cent in the South and to 24.3 per cent in the non-South. In the non-South (row 6 of Table 4-5) schooling explains 13.3 per cent and the residual, 57.9 per cent of the variation in income inequality, compared with 48.2 per cent and 40.0 per cent, respectively, in the South (row 7). The correlation between the education component and the residual variance is insignificant in the South but significant in the remainder of the country (row 7, column 6 in Tables 4-6 and 4-7). This results in a much smaller interstate explanatory power of their covariation in the South than in the non-South.

In the white South (Table 4-8), income inequality is significantly positively correlated with the adjusted rate of return, the education component, and the residual variance.[15] It is not significantly positively correlated with the inequality of schooling and the adjusted coefficient of determination. Schooling inequality is almost significantly negatively related to the adjusted rate of return.

The average coefficient of determination adjusted for degrees of freedom for the white South is 21.9 per cent. It is clear from column 4 of Table 4-5 that this is below the figure for the total

---

15. In only three of the seventeen Southern states was the proportion of nonwhites among adult males very small. These were Kentucky (7.0 per cent), Oklahoma (7.7 per cent), and West Virginia (4.5 per cent). The data for all males in these three states were combined with the data computed for whites in the other fourteen states in order to ascertain the parameters for the "white" South.

TABLE 4-7

Matrix of Correlation Coefficients, All Males, Thirty-four Non-Southern States

(34 observations)

	$\text{Var}(\ln Y)$ (1)	$\hat{f}_1$ (2)	$\ln Y_{0,1}$ (3)	$\bar{R}^2$ (4)	$\text{Var}(S)$ (5)	$\text{Var}(U)$ (6)	$\hat{f}_1^2$ (7)	$\hat{f}_1^2\,\text{Var}(S)$ (8)	$AV(\ln Y)$ (9)
$\hat{f}_1$	.89								
$\ln Y_{0,1}$	-.75	-.89							
$\bar{R}^2$	.45	.38	-.14						
$\text{Var}(S)$	-.12	-.40	.51	.61					
$\text{Var}(U)$	.95	.86	-.78	.16	-.34				
$\hat{f}_1^2$	.90	1.00	-.89	.40	-.36	.86			
$\hat{f}_1^2\,\text{Var}(S)$	.78	.68	-.45	.90	.36	.56	.70		
$AV(\ln Y)$	-.48	-.57	.86	.02	.36	-.54	-.58	-.20	
$AV(S)$	-.18	-.06	.14	-.30	-.38	-.11	-.09	-.26	.46

Note: The critical values for the correlation coefficient (R), under alternative type I errors (α), are $R(\alpha = .05) = .30$, $R(.025) = .35$, $R(.01) = .41$. The critical values are based on 30 degrees of freedom. See notes to Table 4-3.

Source: Table A-1.

TABLE 4-8
Matrix of Correlation Coefficients, Whites, Seventeen Southern States
(17 observations)

	Var(ln Y) (1)	$\hat{r}_1$ (2)	ln$Y_{0,1}$ (3)	$\bar{R}^2$ (4)	Var(S) (5)	Var(U_1) (6)	$\hat{r}_1^2$ (7)	$\hat{r}_1^2$Var(S) (8)	AV(ln Y) (9)
$\hat{r}_1$	.60								
ln$Y_{0,1}$	-.62	-.92							
$\bar{R}^2$	.17	.77	-.61						
Var(S)	.00	-.31	.35	.15					
Var(U_1)	.91	.24	-.33	-.26	-.04				
$\hat{r}_1^2$	.60	1.00	-.92	.76	-.32	.25			
$\hat{r}_1^2$Var(S)	.62	.92	-.81	.87	.08	.23	.91		
AV(ln Y)	-.11	-.36	.51	-.42	-.04	.09	-.37	-.41	
AV(S)	.18	-.20	.29	-.48	-.22	.39	-.19	-.32	.88

Note: The critical values for the correlation coefficient (R), under alternative type I errors (α), are $R(\alpha = .10) = .33$, $R(.05) = .41$, $R(.025) = .48$, $R(.01) = .56$. The critical values are based on 15 degrees of freedom. See notes to Table 4-3.
Source: See Tables A-1 and A-2.

TABLE 4-9

Matrix of Correlation Coefficients, Whites, Thirty-four Non-Southern States
(34 observations)

	Var(lnY) (1)	$\hat{r}_1$ (2)	lnY$_{0,1}$ (3)	$\bar{R}^2$ (4)	Var(S) (5)	Var(U$_1$) (6)	$\hat{r}_1^2$ (7)	$\hat{r}^2$Var(S) (8)	AV(lnY) (9)
$\hat{r}_1$	.87								
lnY$_{0,1}$	-.76	-.92							
$\bar{R}^2$	.45	.58	-.38						
Var(S)	.06	-.01	.19	.77					
Var(U$_1$)	.93	.75	-.71	.10	-.26				
$\hat{r}_1^2$	.88	1.00	-.91	.56	-.03	.77			
$\hat{r}^2$Var(S)	.75	.77	-.58	.92	.60	.47	.77		
AV(lnY)	-.59	-.73	.90	-.19	.32	-.59	-.72	-.37	
AV(S)	-.40	-.54	.54	-.45	-.13	-.29	-.52	-.48	.69

Note: The critical values for the correlation coefficient (R), under alternative type I errors (α), are $R(\alpha = .05) = .30$, $R(.025) = .35$, $R(.01) = .41$. The critical values are based on 30 degrees of freedom. See notes to Table 4-3.
Source: Tables A-1 and A-2.

South but above that for the North. In the white South, schooling explains 18.8 per cent, the residual, 66.5 per cent, and their covariation, 14.7 per cent of the differences in income inequality. Although the removal of nonwhites from the data substantially reduces their interstate explanatory power, schooling is still important in explaining differences in income inequality. However, contrary to the findings for all males, for all white males, and for all males in the South, schooling for white males in the South is a less important factor in variations between states than in variations within states.

Calculations were also made for the thirty-four non-Southern states, with nonwhites excluded from the data for Alaska, Hawaii, and New York.[16] The data of Tables 4-7 and 4-9 indicate that the algebraic value of the correlation coefficients between the variance of schooling and the inequality of income, the adjusted rate of return, the residual variance, and the adjusted coefficient of determination are increased by the exclusion of nonwhites. On the other hand, the average intrastate explanatory power is decreased from 15.4 to 15.0 per cent. Rows 5 and 7 of Table 4-5 indicate that the "adjustment" for nonwhites slightly increases the interstate explanatory power of schooling in the non-South.

Additional Analyses

An alternative definition of income inequality and an alternative measure of the rate of return from schooling are used in this section to test the robustness of the model for explaining income inequality. Virtually identical results emerge from calculations based on the income inequality of adult males and the earnings inequality for all males. Similarly, when the overtaking age rate of return is used rather than the regression estimate, there is no fundamental change in the patterns that emerge. A conservative estimate of the interstate explanatory power of schooling for alternative definitions of income and the rate of return appears to be 60 per cent. Thus, the model is found to be robust.

Analysis of Earnings Inequality

Thus far the empirical analysis has been restricted to income rather than earnings. The 1960 census does contain data by state

---

16. In 1960 the proportions of nonwhites were: Alaska, 17.6 per cent; Hawaii, 68.9 per cent; and New York, 8.0 per cent. All other non-Southern states had very small proportions of nonwhites.

on the distribution of earnings in 1959 of males fourteen years of age and older who were in the experienced labor force in 1960.[17] This made it possible to calculate the variance of the natural log of earnings of males fourteen years of age and older for each state. Unfortunately, neither are the data cross-classified by schooling, nor can youths of fourteen to twenty-four be eliminated. The inclusion of young males tends to raise, and the exclusion of property income tends to lower, the variance of the log of earnings compared to the variance of the log of income of males aged twenty-five and over, the data used in the other interstate analyses. However, the variance of the log of income and the variance of the log of earnings for the states are very similar. Their product-moment correlation coefficient is $R = +.91$, and neither their means nor their variances differ significantly from each other.

As shown in Table 4-10, the regression estimate of the rate of return ($\hat{r}$), schooling inequality, and the education component show a significant positive correlation with the inequality of earnings. The correlations are lower for earnings inequality than for income inequality, but the differences are not statistically significant at a 10 per cent level. The lower correlations may be due to the large investment in schooling and postschool training on the part of nonadult males. It may also be due to the omission, because of data limitations, of young labor force males in the calculation of the variance in schooling and the rate of return.

TABLE 4-10

Correlation Matrix for Males in Fifty-one States,
Income and Earnings Inequality,
Regression and Overtaking Age Rates of Return

	Var(ln$E$)	Var(ln$Y$)	$\hat{r}$	r_M	Var(S)	$\hat{r}^2$ Var(S)
Var(ln Y)	.91					
$\hat{r}$	.71	.77				
r_m	.81	.80	.73			
Var(S)	.36	.48	.24	.19		
$\hat{r}^2$ Var(S)	.79	.88	.86	.73	.69	
r_m^2 Var(S)	.78	.82	.70	.91	.54	.88

Note: The critical values for the correlation coefficient (R), under alternative type I errors (α), are $R(\alpha = .05) = .23$, $R(.025) = .27$, $R(.01) = .32$. The critical values are based on 50 degrees of freedom. See notes to Tables 4-3 and A-4.

Source: Tables A-1 and A-4.

---

17. *U.S. Census of Population: 1960, Vol. 1, Characteristics of the Population,* Parts 2–52, Washington, D.C., Table 124.

The direct interstate explanatory power of the education component can be calculated by the procedure shown on p. 55. The ratio of the variance of the education component ($\hat{r}^2$ Var (S)) to the variance of the natural log of earnings is .320.[18] Thus, the direct explanatory power on the basis of earnings is approximately equal to that on the basis of income (.305, see Table 4-5).

"Overtaking Age" Estimate of Rate of Return

Up to this point the "regression estimate" has been the only measure of the rate of return discussed in this study. Yet, it has been shown that these rates of return are systematically biased downward. It would be useful to see whether our findings are specific to this measure; that is, would similar conclusions emerge if an alternative method for computing the rate of return were employed? Such an alternative is available. In his study *Schooling, Experience, and Earnings*, Jacob Mincer presents an alternative shortcut technique for calculating an unbiased rate of return from a given level of schooling, which he calls the "overtaking age" rate of return. The overtaking age rate of return from high school employed had to be computed indirectly due to the lack of appropriate data and is therefore subject to measurement error.[19] The findings shown in Table 4-10 are based on this technique.

The overtaking age estimate (r_M) is highly and significantly correlated with the regression estimate of the rate of return ($\hat{r}$) from schooling (R ($\hat{r}$, r_M) = 0.73). The estimates of the overtaking age rate of return, however, are consistently larger; and average r_M equals 0.151, while the average $\hat{r}$ is equal to 0.102.

The overtaking age rate of return can be used to analyze the effect of schooling on the variance of the log of earnings of all males and on the variance of the log of income of adult males. The statistic r_M is significantly and highly positively correlated with both the earnings and income inequalities, and is not significantly correlated with the inequality of schooling. (See Table 4-10.)

We can calculate a measure of schooling's intrastate explanatory power of earnings and income inequality with r_M as the measure of the rate of return. Table A-4 contains the ratio of the ex-

---

18.

Variable	Variance
$\hat{r}^2$ Var(S)	.0047
Var(ln$E$)	.0116

Source: Tables A-1 and A-4.

19. Estimating procedure and data sources are presented in Appendix A-2.

plained (r^2 Var (S)) to total variation for income and earnings in the case of r_M, and for earnings in the case of $\hat{r}$. The ratio for income and $\hat{r}$ (with the trivial adjustment for degrees of freedom) is in column 6 of Table A-1. For a given measure of the rate of return but different income concepts there are no significant differences. For a given income concept but different rates of return, the explanatory powers differ, being consistently high when r_M is employed. Note, however, that there is a negative correlation between schooling and the residual when r_M is the regression slope coefficient.

The statistic developed to measure the education component's direct interstate explanatory power of schooling breaks down when r_M is used as the rate of return. The education component r_M^2 Var (S) has a larger variance than Var $(\ln E)$ or Var $(\ln Y)$, thereby implying that the education component and the residual are negatively correlated.[20]

An alternative procedure for estimating schooling's interstate explanatory power with respect to income inequality is to look at the coefficient of determination when income inequality is regressed on the education component. The results of regressing Var $(\ln Y)$ and Var $(\ln E)$ on $\hat{r}^2$ Var (S) and also on r_m^2 Var (S) are shown in Table 4-4.

If the education component were uncorrelated with the residual in the regression, with the model properly specified, the slope coefficients in Table 4-4 would equal unity. The slope coefficient in row 1 of Table 4-4 is significantly greater than 1. This means that the coefficient of determination of 0.77 is an upward-biased estimate of the true explanatory power of the education component. When earnings inequality is used (row 3), the slope coefficient is also significantly greater than unity. This suggests that the explanatory power of 0.63 is upward-biased.

The slope coefficients obtained using the estimated overtaking age rate of return are significantly less than 1. This suggests the existence of a downward bias in the slope coefficient. The procedure for estimating the overtaking age rate of return for the

---

20.

Variable	Variance
r^2 Var(S)	.0047
r_m^2 Var(S)	.0353
Var$(\ln Y)$	.0140
Var$(\ln E)$	.0116

Source: Calculated from data in Tables A-1 and A-4.

states assumed that the shape of the experience log of income profile is the same for each state as it is for the nation as a whole. This introduces errors of measurement in r_M. If these errors are random, there is a downward bias in the estimate of the slope coefficient and the coefficient of determination. The coefficient of determination for the variance of the log of income is 0.68 and for the variance of the log of earnings, 0.61. Thus, the schooling model's interstate explanatory power re inequality may be conservatively estimated at 60 per cent for earnings and somewhat higher for income.

State Differences in the Rate of Return from Schooling

Our analysis of income inequality highlights the importance of the rate of return from schooling as an explanatory variable. The correlation matrices indicate that the rate of return is higher in the poorer states. This negative correlation is not due to chance, but is a consequence of differences in regional mobility across schooling levels.

If workers with high levels of schooling were perfect substitutes for those with low levels of schooling, relative wages would depend solely on the substitution coefficient. There is evidence, however, that high-level manpower (professional) is qualitatively different from nonprofessional manpower and that the two factors are not perfect substitutes.[21] Hence, a downward-sloping demand curve results for high-level relative to lower-level manpower. This negatively sloped relative demand curve plays an important role in the analysis of income distribution.

Let us view each state of the United States as a labor market with a negatively sloped demand curve for college graduates versus high school graduates. The relative wage in each state for the two schooling levels depends on relative factor supplies. Relative factor supplies, in turn, are a function of wage rates and mobility.

Wages of college graduates vary very little across the states because of their high mobility. For college graduates there is, in effect, a national labor market, in contrast to those with less schooling, where the tendency to migrate is weaker and there are

---

21. Using the states as units of observation and a three-factor constant elasticity of substitution production function for professionals, nonprofessionals, and physical capital, the elasticity of substitution is computed to be 2.5. See Carmel J. Ullman, "The Rise of Professional Occupations in the American Labor Force," Ph.D. dissertation, Columbia University, 1972.

significant state differences in wage rates.[22] Those with more schooling have a higher propensity to migrate for several reasons. First, schooling may increase a person's awareness of other areas and thereby reduce the psychic cost of moving to a new environment. Second, college schooling itself often entails moving to a new area, thus loosening ties to the place of origin. Third, those who acquire more schooling tend to be wealthier: since migration is an investment in human capital and discount rates vary inversely with wealth, those with more schooling also tend to be those who invest more in migration. Fourth, due to the presence of direct costs of migration which are unrelated to skill level, the rate of return from migration tends to be higher for those with more skill,[23] encouraging greater migration on their part.

A higher rate of migration out of the poorer region by skilled workers relative to unskilled workers tends to increase the ratio of skilled to unskilled workers in the wealthier region and to decrease

---

22. Rates of migration across the states of the United States, across the provinces of Canada, and from Canada to the United States are higher for those with higher levels of schooling. See Rashi Fein, "Educational Patterns in Southern Migration," *Southern Economic Journal*, July 1965, pp. 106–124; June O'Neill, "The Effects of Income and Education on Inter-Regional Migration," Ph.D. dissertation, Columbia University, 1970; Bruce Wilkinson, "Some Economic Aspects of Education in Canada," Ph.D. dissertation, Massachusetts Institute of Technology, 1964, pp. 84–85, 87, and 106; Thomas J. Courchene, "Interprovincial Migration and Economic Adjustment," *Canadian Journal of Economics*, November 1970, pp. 550–577.

23. Suppose the wages of a worker of skill i in region j are written as W_{ij}. The worker can either be skilled (s) or unskilled (u), and reside in the North (n) or South (s), where the South is the poorer region. Suppose there is no migration between the North and the South and wages are uniformly higher by 100 (h) per cent in the North:

$$W_{s,n} = (1 + h) W_{s,s}; W_{u,n} = (1 + h) W_{u,s}.$$

Let us designate the fraction of the year devoted to the migration investment by k' and the direct costs of migration by C_d. Then, using the simplified formula for the rate of return, r = annual differential/cost, the rate of return to northward migration for the skilled worker is

$$r_{m,s} = \frac{W_{s,n} - W_{s,s}}{k'W_{s,s} + C_d} = \frac{W_{s,s}(h)}{k'W_{s,s} + C_d} = \frac{h}{k' + \dfrac{C_d}{W_{s,s}}}.$$

The rate of return to northward migration for the unskilled worker is

$$r_{m,u} = \frac{W_{u,n} - W_{u,s}}{k'W_{u,s} + C_d} = \frac{W_{s,s}(h)}{k'W_{u,s} + C_d} = \frac{h}{k' + \dfrac{C_d}{W_{u,s}}}.$$

it in the poorer region. Given the same negatively sloped demand curve for labor,[24] the ratio of the wages of skilled workers to those of unskilled workers is depressed in the wealthier region and raised in the poorer region. The result is a decline in the rate of return from schooling in the wealthier region and a rise in the poorer region.

Higher rates of return from schooling in the poorer states have already been noted. In the analysis of income distribution in Canada (pp. 73–77), higher rates of return are similarly found in the poorer provinces. This model suggests that among regions with little mobility there is no clear prediction as to the relation between the level of income and the rate of return from schooling. This is supported by studies of international differences in rates of return from schooling, which find no consistent pattern.[25]

The Average Level of Schooling

Thus far, the empirical analysis has been concerned primarily with the rate of return, schooling inequality, and what has been called the education component of income inequality, r^2 Var (S). In some of our analyses the level of schooling has a significant negative simple correlation with income inequality. Equations (3-13) and (3-14), however, suggest a positive partial relative between schooling level and income inequality.

Across the states, the level of schooling tends to be negatively correlated with the rate of return. In addition, schooling inequality is larger in the South. What would be the relation between the

---

If the fraction of the year devoted to migration (k') and direct costs (C_d) do not vary with the skill level, since the wages of unskilled workers in the South are lower than those of skilled workers in the South $(W_{u,s} < W_{s,s})$, $r_{m,s} > r_{m,u}$, or the rate of return from migration is higher for skilled workers. This higher average rate of return to migration induces greater migration out of the poorer region by skilled than unskilled workers.

24. The assumption of the same negatively sloped demand curve is not unrealistic. Information about productive techniques spreads rapidly in developed countries such as the United States. This implies similar coefficients for the aggregate production function in each state. Using the states as units of observation, Ullman (op. cit.) found the data to be consistent with a three-factor constant elasticity of substitution production function. Then, interstate variations in the amount of physical capital play no role in determining the relative wage of highly skilled to lower-skilled manpower.

25. See Martin Carnoy, "Rates of Return From Schooling in Latin America," *Journal of Human Resources*, Vol. 2, Summer 1967, pp. 354–374; and T. Paul Schultz, "Returns to Education in Bogota, Colombia," RAND Memorandum, Santa Monica, Rand Corporation, 1968, Table 9.

TABLE 4-11

Income Inequality and Average Level of Schooling for the United States and Canada

Region (1)	Partial Regression Coefficients			AV(S) Significance (5)	Simple Correlations		Change in Significance (8)
	AV(S) (2)	r̂ (3)	VAR(S) (4)		Coefficient (6)	Significance (7)	
U.S., total (51 observations)	−0.005 (−0.360)	6.864 (12.491)	0.010 (4.158)	NS	−0.733	0.1	+
U.S., white (51 observations)	+0.033 (+2.734)	6.945 (10.961)	0.012 (3.822)	1.0	−0.161	NS	+
North, total (34 observations)	−0.002 (−0.156)	7.476 (12.947)	0.009 (3.297)	NS	−0.177	NS	0
North, white (34 observations)	+0.017 (+1.053)	6.698 (8.743)	0.003 (0.896)	NS	−0.396	5.0	+
South, total (17 observations)	−0.041 (−1.766)	2.935 (2.078)	0.004 (0.566)	10.0	−0.799	0.1	+
South, white (17 observations)	+0.042 (+2.008)	5.910 (3.757)	0.020 (1.605)	10.0	+0.175	NS	+
Canada (11 observations)	−0.005 (−0.148)	7.205 (2.647)	0.041 (1.557)	NS	−0.543	10.0	+

Note: NS = not significant at a 10.0 per cent level two-tailed test. *t* ratios are in parentheses. Degrees of freedom equal the number of regions minus two (for the simple correlations) or four (for the partial regression coefficients). Change in significance from simple (column 7) to partial (column 5) relation: less negative (+), more negative (−), or no clear change (0). For additional notation, see notes to Table 4-1. Significance levels from H. M. Walker and J. Lev, *Statistical Inference*, New York, Holt, Rinehart and Winston, 1953, pp. 465 and 470.

Source: See Tables A-1, A-2, and A-3.

average level of schooling and income inequality if the rate of return and schooling inequality were held constant?[26] To answer this question, a multiple linear regression of the variance of the log of income was run on the average level of schooling, the adjusted rate of return from schooling, and schooling inequality. The results appear on Table 4-11.

The sign of the slope coefficient of average schooling shows whether income inequality and average schooling are positively or negatively correlated when the rate of return and schooling inequality are held constant. For five of the six divisions of the United States (as well as for the provinces of Canada) the partial relation is either less negative or more positive than the simple relation. The only exception is the total North, where there is no perceptible change.

Thus, the negative simple correlation between income inequality and the level of schooling tends to become a nonsignificant relation when schooling inequality and the rate of return are held constant.

CANADA

Unpublished tables from the *1961 Census of Canada* permit an analysis of the effect of schooling on income for the ten provinces and the Yukon territory (referred to as the eleven provinces).[27] Within each province income is cross-classified by years of schooling for nonfarm males between the ages of twenty-five and sixty-four. A comparison of the means and standard deviations of the variables under study for the states vis-à-vis the provinces (see Table A-4) reveals only two substantial differences: both the standard deviation of years of schooling within the provinces and

---

26. Samarrie and Miller, as well as Aigner and Heins, analyzed interstate differences in family income inequality through multiple regression analysis. They found a negative partial relation between level of schooling and income inequality. They did not hold constant (either explicitly or through a proxy) the rate of return or schooling inequality. See A. Al Samarrie and H. P. Miller, "State Differentials in Income Concentration," *American Economic Review*, March 1967, pp. 59-72; and D. J. Aigner and A. J. Heins, "On the Determinants of Income Equality," *American Economic Review*, March 1967, pp. 175-184.

27. The census data are from a 20 per cent sample of private nonfarm households. They have been processed in the same manner as for the United States. The intraprovince regression results appear in Table A-3.

the range of the standard deviation of schooling are smaller in Canada than in the United States.[28]

Part of the apparently low education inequality within the provinces may be traced to the grouping of the data. The Canadian data contain fewer intervals than the U.S. data for schooling, particularly primary education.[29] In addition, a higher proportion of Canadian males are in the lower-level schooling category.[30] This

---

28. The standard deviation of schooling in Canada ranges from 3.0 years for Prince Edward Island to 3.5 years for Quebec. For the United States the range is from 3.2 years in Iowa to 4.8 years in Hawaii. (See Tables A-1 and A-3.)

29. Note the comparison below:

Number of Groups in the Education Data for
the United States and Canada

| | United States | | Canada | |
	Total and Regions (1)	States (2)	Total (3)	Provinces (4)
Zero schooling	} 2	1	} 1	1
Primary schooling		3		1
Secondary schooling	2	2	2	2
College or university	3	2	2	2
Total	7	8	5	6

Sources:

(1) *U.S. Census of Population: 1960, Subject Reports, Occupation by Earnings and Education,* Washington, D.C., Tables 1, 2, and 3.

(2) *U.S. Census of Population: 1960, Vol. 1, Characteristics of the Population,* Parts 2–52, Washington, D.C., Table 138.

(3) *Census of Canada: 1961, Population Sample. Incomes of Individuals,* Bulletin 4.1-2, Ottawa, Dominion Bureau of Statistics, Table B6.

(4) *Census of Canada: 1961,* Ottawa, Dominion Bureau of Statistics, Table A.11, unpublished.

30.   Proportion of Adult Males with No More than
Elementary School Education
(per cent)

	Proportion of Males
Canada	
(nonfarm, excludes those with zero schooling)	
Total	44.1
Newfoundland	49.4
Prince Edward Island	50.0
Nova Scotia	51.2
New Brunswick	55.3
Quebec	51.5
Ontario	42.2
Manitoba	35.4

is particularly true of the Atlantic provinces, which are the poorer provinces. Thus, there is a greater loss of variability for schooling in Canada than in the United States, and a greater loss in the Atlantic provinces than in Canada's other provinces. Note also that the population under examination in the Canadian case—nonfarm males—is more homogeneous with respect to occupation than the population studied for the United States.

Table 4-12 presents the correlation matrix for the Canadian provinces. Income inequality, the residual variance, the rate of return from schooling, and the education component (r^2 Var (S)) are positively correlated with each other. They are negatively correlated with the levels of income and schooling. However, as in the case of the United States, the significant negative correlation of schooling level with income inequality disappears when the rate of return and schooling inequality are held constant (see Table 4-11). Schooling inequality is not correlated with income inequality, whether the rate of return is held constant or not.

The observed higher rate of return in the poorer provinces (lower levels of income and schooling) may be a consequence of the greater propensity to migrate on the part of those with higher levels of schooling.[31] Schooling inequality, however, is smaller in the poorer provinces. The rate of return appears to be more important than the inequality of schooling for explaining income inequality.

A regression of income inequality on the education component (r^2 Var (S)), with the provinces as the unit of observation, has a coefficient of determination (adjusted for degrees of freedom) equal to 68 per cent.

Saskatchewan	42.3
Alberta	34.5
British Columbia	33.1
Yukon	34.2
United States	
(males with earnings, includes those with zero education)	
Total	34.4
U.S., white	32.0
Non-South	30.8
Non-South, white	29.6
South	43.6
South, white	36.9

Sources: Census of Canada: 1961, Population Sample. Schooling by Age Groups, Bulletin 1.3-6, Ottawa, Dominion Bureau of Statistics, Tables 102 and 103; and *U.S. Census of Population: 1960, Subject Reports. Occupation by Earnings and Education,* Washington, D.C., Tables 1, 2, and 3.

31. See the citations for Canada on p. 70.

TABLE 4-12

Matrix of Correlation Coefficients, Eleven Provinces of Canada
(11 observations)

	Var(lnY) (1)	$\hat{r}$ (2)	lnY$_{0,1}$ (3)	$\bar{R}^2$ (4)	Var(S) (5)	Var(U) (6)	$\hat{r}^2$ (7)	$\hat{r}^2$ Var(S) (8)	AV(lnY) (9)
$\hat{r}$	.71								
lnY$_{0,1}$	-.67	-.95							
$\bar{R}^2$	.29	.79	-.67						
Var(S)	-.15	-.63	.73	-.35					
Var(U)	.99	-.62	-.59	.18	-.10				
$\hat{r}^2$	.70	1.00	-.96	.76	-.67	.61			
$\hat{r}^2$ Var(S)	.84	.94	-.85	.76	-.33	.76	.92		
AV(lnY)	-.62	-.83	.94	-.56	.62	-.56	-.84	-.75	
AV(S)	-.54	-.58	.64	-.49	.15	-.49	-.57	-.65	.82

Note: The critical values for the correlation coefficient (R), under alternative type I errors (α), are $R(\alpha = .05) = .52$, $R(.025) = .60$, $R(.01) = .69$. The critical values are based on 9 degrees of freedom. See notes to Table 4-3.
Source: Table A-3.

The intraprovince explanatory power of schooling is low, but this may be due to the small number of schooling intervals.[32]

THE NETHERLANDS

This section of the interregional analysis focuses on the level and inequality of income among the seventy-five "geographic-economic" regions of the Netherlands. It is based on data from Schultz's study of income distribution in the Netherlands.[33]

Across regions, the level and inequality of schooling appear to be positively related to the proportion of males with higher education.[34] For the years 1950, 1955, and 1958, Schultz regressed his measure of income inequality, the Gini concentration ratio,[35] on the proportion of males with higher education between the ages of forty and sixty-four, and on several other variables. The other variables included the number and average wealth of taxpayers paying wealth taxes, measures of relative unemployment, the average number of persons on public relief, and the number of in-

---

32. The explanatory power ranges from 8.7 per cent for British Columbia to 15.9 per cent for New Brunswick (averaging 13.4 per cent). However, this is not corrected for the downward bias in the regression estimate of the rate of return.

33. T. Paul Schultz, "The Distribution of Income: Case Study of The Netherlands," Ph.D. dissertation, Massachusetts Institute of Technology, 1965, Chapter 8.

34. Ibid., pp. 339-340. The nationwide minimum school leaving age truncates the distribution of schooling, particularly in the poorer areas. This may be responsible for the positive interregional correlation between the level and inequality of schooling. See Barry R. Chiswick, "Minimum Schooling Legislation and the Cross-Sectional Distribution of Income," *Economic Journal*, September 1969, pp. 494-507.

35. Ibid., pp. 175-176. The Gini concentration ratio, a measure of relative inequality, is

$$C = \frac{1}{2mN^2} \sum_{i=1}^{n} \sum_{j=1}^{n} |Y_i - Y_j| f(Y_i) f(Y_j)$$

where m is the arithmetic mean, Y_i $(i = 1, \ldots, n)$ is the average income of the ith income class, $f(Y_i)$ is the class weight, and

$$\sum_{i=1}^{n} f(Y_i) = N.$$

A higher concentration ratio means a larger inequality of income.

TABLE 4-13

Netherlands: Cross-Sectional Regressions on Concentration
Ratio (C), by Region
(75 observations)

Dependent Variable (1)	Constant (2)	ΔA (3)	Ed_{47} (4)	W_t (5)	W (6)	Unp (7)	Rel (8)	$\bar{R}^2$ (9)	N (10)
C_{1958}	.3828	.096	.013	.062	a	a	-.660	.446	75
		(.073)	(.003)	(.015)			(.325)		
C_{1955}	.3691	.541	.012	.073	-.0011	a	-.783	.544	75
		(.237)	(.003)	(.014)	(.0007)		(.320)		
C_{1950}	.3866	a	.012	.068	-.0009a	b	b	.419	75
			(.003)	(.015)	(.0008)				

Note: Standard errors are in parentheses.
Source: T. P. Schultz, "The Distribution of Income: Case Study of The Netherlands," Ph.D. dissertation, Massachusetts Institute of Technology, 1965, Table 8-12, p. 352, and Table 8-10, pp. 346–348.
[a]Regression coefficient not statistically significant at .05 level of significance. Where no numbers are reported they were absent in the source.
[b]Data not available.

come taxpayers in the region. Table 4-13, column 4, shows that the partial regression coefficients between income inequality and the proportion with higher education are all positive and significantly different from zero. A measure of wealth, W_t, is the most significant variable. Its significance, however, is only slightly greater than that of education. The variables used are defined below.

Definitions of Variables

$\bar{Y}_t$ Mean income of taxpayers by region in year t (in thousands of current guilders).

C_t Concentration ratio of incomes of income tax units by region, in year t.

$\bar{W}$ Mean wealth of wealth-taxpayer in 1951 (in tens of thousands of current guilders).

w The number of wealth-taxpayers in 1951 as a proportion of income-taxpayers in region in current year.

W_t Total wealth taxed in 1951, divided by the number of income-taxpayers in current year (in tens of thousands of guilders).

Ed_{47} The percentage of males with a higher education between the ages of forty and sixty-four in May 1947, by region. Higher education is defined to include doctorates and candidates for the doctorate. The doctorate usually requires six years of higher education.

Unp The quarterly average number of totally unemployed persons as a proportion of the income-taxpayers by region, in current year.

Rel The quarterly average number of persons on public relief works as a proportion of the income-taxpayers by region in current year.

Urb The proportion of the population in a region living in a municipal center as of 1950.

A The annual average rate of change in the number of income-taxpayers in region since previous regional income distribution sample (1946, 1950, 1955, and 1958), rounded to thousands of persons.

Note that the concentration coefficient is significantly positively correlated with W_t, a measure of average wealth, as well as the level of schooling, and significantly negatively correlated with *Rel*, the average number on public relief. Thus, it seems that inequality of income is positively correlated with average level of income, since the independent variables are presumably positively correlated with level of income, except for the inverse relation for the relative number on relief.

Schultz regressed average income on the proportion with higher education and several other variables. As can be seen from Table 4-14, column (4), the coefficient of schooling is positive and very significant. A positive relation between the level of income and the inequality of schooling was found among the Canadian provinces, but not across the states of the United States.

In conclusion, it appears that in the Netherlands there are very significant positive interregional correlations among the levels and inequalities of income and schooling. No correlations can be established between these variables and the rate of return since there are not enough data available to estimate relative rates of return by region.

SUMMARY

Comparisons between the two major regions and among the various states of the United States (for all males and for white

TABLE 4-14

Netherlands: Cross-Sectional Regressions on Regional Mean Income per Taxpayer ($\overline{T}$)

(75 observations)

Dependent Variable (1)	Constant (2)	$\overline{W}$ (3)	Ed_{47} (4)	Urb (5)	Rel (6)	Unp (7)	w (8)	$\overline{R}^2$ (9)	n (10)
$\overline{Y}_{1958}$	3.989	0.234 (0.057)	0.358 (0.057)	-0.0043 (0.0013)	0.577[a] (6.88)	-18.70 (6.29)	0.035 (0.014)	0.712	75
$\overline{Y}_{1955}$	3.027	0.229 (0.056)	0.256 (0.056)	-0.0040 (0.0013)	-15.28 (5.09)	-0.403[a] (1.733)	0.024 (0.013)	0.609	75
$\overline{Y}_{1950}$	2.190	0.151 (0.043)	0.163 (0.043)	-0.0028 (0.0010)	[b]	[b]	0.019 (0.009)	0.465	75

Note: Standard errors are in parentheses.

Source: Schultz, "The Distribution of Income," 1965, Table 8-11, p. 349.

[a]Regression coefficient not statistically significant at .05 level of significance.

[b]Data not available.

males) reveal that the inequalities of income, of residual income, and of schooling, the rate of return, the education component (r^2 Var (S)), and the explanatory power of schooling tend to be (1) positively correlated with each other and (2) negatively correlated with the levels of income and schooling. When the rate of return and schooling inequality are held constant, the level of schooling ceases to be correlated with income inequality. The higher rate of return in the poorer states can be attributed to higher rates of migration on the part of those with more schooling. A virtually national labor market appears to exist for highly skilled workers, side by side with a tendency toward more local labor markets for those with less skill.

The relationships found among the states are only partly attributable to North-South differences. Similar, although somewhat weaker, relationships are generally found within the non-South and within the South.

When corrected for the downward bias in the regression estimate of the rate of return, schooling explains from 17 to 51 per cent of the variation in income, with a mean value of 29 per cent. The explanatory power is higher in the South than in the non-South, and higher for all males than for white males alone. It appears that the education component ($\hat{r}^2$ Var (S)) can explain half of the North-South differences in income inequality. Among all the states (on the basis of the regression estimate of the rate of return) the education component itself can explain approximately one-third of interstate differences, the intrastate residual variance (Var (U)) can explain another one-third, and their correlation explains the remaining third. When income or earnings inequality is correlated with the education component (r^2 Var (S) or $\hat{r}^2_M$ Var (S)), schooling's interstate explanatory power is at least 60 per cent. The rate of return appears to be more important than the inequality of schooling in explaining interstate differences in income inequality.

In the case of Canada, the analysis for the provinces indicates positive correlations among the inequality of income, the inequality of residual income, the rate of return, and the education component. Provincial variations in the education component explain ($\overline{R}^2$) 68 per cent of provincial variations in income inequality. The rate of return is more important than the inequality of schooling for explaining income inequality. And, the significant negative effect of the level of schooling on income inequality disappears when the rate of return and schooling inequality are held constant. These results are similar to those obtained for the United

States. The brief analysis for the regions of the Netherlands indicates that income inequality is greater the larger the inequality of schooling.

Thus, the schooling model appears to be a powerful tool for explaining differences in the inequality of personal income among the regions of a country.

5

International Applications

Thus far, the empirical analysis of Part B has been concerned only with comparisons among regions within a country. The goal of this chapter is to discover whether the relationships found in the interregional data exist on an international level, too. To this end, the first section presents a comparative regression analysis for the United States, Canada, Puerto Rico, and Mexico, applying the procedures of the schooling model as in the preceding chapter. Next a different international data set is used to test the effect of schooling inequality and the level and growth rate of income per capita on the inequality of earnings of nonfarm males. In addition, the influences of some institutional arrangements and historical events on the parameters under review and on the mechanism through which income inequality is generated are examined, via the effects of mass immigration and distribution of capital (physical and human) in Israel and a comparison of Great Britain with the United States.

A FOUR-COUNTRY ANALYSIS

United States and Canada

Table 5-1 shows the results from regressing the log of earnings on schooling for males between the ages of twenty-five and sixty-

TABLE 5-1

Results from Regressing the Natural Log of Earnings on Schooling
for Males, Twenty-five to Sixty-four, in the United States and Canada

	Summary Statistics				Regression: ln$E$ on S			
	SD(ln$Y$) (1)	SD(S) (2)	AV(ln$E$) (3)	AV(S) (4)	ln$E_{0,1}$ (5)	$\hat{r}_1$ (6)	Var(U)$_1$ (7)	R^2 (8)
United States	.70	3.66	1.54	10.31	.75 (.22)	.08 (.02)	.41	.15
White	.68	3.53	1.60	10.57	.83 (.25)	.07 (.02)	.40	.13
Non-South	.65	3.41	1.63	10.67	.94 (.23)	.06 (.02)	.38	.10
Non-South, white	.65	3.36	1.66	10.78	.96 (.26)	.06 (.02)	.38	.10
South	.76	4.03	1.32	10.42	.47 (.20)	.09 (.02)	.45	.22
South, white	.74	3.90	1.43	9.96	.60 (.23)	.08 (.02)	.44	.18
Canada, nonfarm	.68	3.38	1.36	8.70	.68 (.14)	.08 (.01)	.39	.15

Note: The U.S. data are based on a 5 per cent sample and contain 77 cells—7 schooling intervals and 11 earnings intervals. The Canadian data are for a 20 per cent sample of private nonfarm households and contain 78 cells—6 schooling intervals and 13 income intervals. Standard errors are in parentheses. See Chapter 4, pp. 50–51 for definitions of symbols.

four in the United States and nonfarm Canada.[1] Compared with the total South and the white South, Canada has lower inequalities of income, schooling, and residual income, as well as a lower rate of return and adjusted coefficient of determination. Compared with the total non-South and the white non-South, Canada has higher values for these parameters, except for the standard deviation of schooling. However, as indicated in Chapter 4, grouping causes a greater downward bias of this parameter in Canada than in the non-South. The total U.S. results are a weighted average of the North and South figures. The values of the parameters for the United States and Canada differ only very slightly (with one exception: the standard deviation of schooling), and no pattern emerges.

To summarize, these comparisons show that the inequalities of income, residual income, and schooling—as well as the rate of return—seem to be (1) higher in the South than in Canada, (2) approximately equal in Canada and the United States, and (3) higher in Canada than in the non-South.

---

1. The data are for individuals classified into schooling and income cells.

TABLE 5-1 (Concluded)

Regression: ln$E$ on $£$, $\$$, and H					
ln$E_{0,3}$ (9)	$\hat{r}_£$ (10)	$\hat{r}_\$$ (11)	$\hat{r}_H$ (12)	Var$(U)_3$ (13)	$\bar{R}^2_3$ (14)
.70	.09	.07	.08	.43	.13
(.48)	(.07)	(.06)	(.05)		
.84	.07	.07	.08	.42	.10
(.59)	(.09)	(.06)	(.06)		
1.06	.05	.06	.08	.39	.08
(.58)	(.08)	(.05)	(.05)		
1.09	.05	.06	.08	.39	.07
(.67)	(.09)	(.06)	(.06)		
.50	.08	.09	.09	.46	.20
(.40)	(.07)	(.07)	(.06)		
.66)	.07	.09	.09	.46	.16
(.50)	(.08)	(.07)	(.06)		
.63	.09	.07	.08	.40	.14
(.40)	(.06)	(.06)	(.05)		

Sources: (1) *U.S. Census of Population: 1960, Subject Reports. Occupation by Earnings and Education*, Washington, D.C., Tables 1, 2, and 3. (2) *Census of Canada: 1961, Population Sample. Incomes of Individuals*, Bulletin 4.1–2, Ottawa, Table B6.

Puerto Rico

Since Puerto Rico is a self-governing Commonwealth of the United States, the 1960 U.S. Census of Population includes an enumeration for the island. It contains a cross-classification of 1959 income data by schooling for all males, as well as urban males separately, twenty-five and over, with income.[2] Table 5-2 shows regression results based on these data for total and urban Puerto Rico, the United States, and nonfarm Canada, with the log of income as the dependent variable.

It is clear that Puerto Rico shows higher values than the United States for the three measures of inequality (income, residual income, and schooling), as well as for the rate of return, the explanatory power, and the education component. Presumably the same qualitative results would hold true if property income and aged males were excluded from all of the data. Note that, except for

2. *U.S. Census of Population: 1960, Vol. 1, Characteristics of the Population*, Washington, D.C., Part 53, p. LII and Table 117. The data are processed in the same manner as the U.S. data.

TABLE 5-2

Results from Regressing the Natural Log of Income on Schooling for Males,
Twenty-five and Over, in Puerto Rico, the United States, and Canada

	Summary Statistics			Regression: ln Y on S		
	SD(ln Y)	SD(S)	$\frac{AV(\ln Y)}{AV(S)}$	$\ln Y_{0,1}$	$\hat{r}_1$	$\frac{Var(U_1)}{\bar{R}^2}$
	(1)	(2)	(3)	(4)	(5)	(6)
Puerto Rico	1.19	4.75	-0.05	-0.93	0.14	0.97
			6.17	(0.15)	(0.02)	0.32
Urban	1.14	5.01	+0.40	-0.62	0.13	0.89
			7.95	(0.16)	(0.02)	0.31
Canada	0.83	3.41	1.21	+0.40	0.10	0.58
			8.38	(0.09)	(0.01)	0.16
United States	0.91	3.95	1.34	+0.30	0.11	0.66
			9.80	(0.23)	(0.02)	0.20

Note: See notes to Tables 4-1 and 5-1. The Puerto Rico data are based on
a 25 per cent sample of the population cross-classified in 117 cells, 9 schooling intervals, and 13 income intervals. Income is in thousand dollar units. A
negative AV(ln Y) results from mean income being less than $1,000. Standard
errors are in parentheses.

Sources: (1) *U.S. Census of Population: 1960*, Vol. 1, *Characteristics of
the Population*, Part 53, Puerto Rico, Washington, D.C., Table 117. (2) *U.S.
Census of Population: 1960, Subject Reports. Educational Attainment*, Wash-
ington, D.C., Table 6. (3) *Census of Canada: 1961*, Vol. 4, *Population Sample,
Income of Individuals*, Bulletin 4.1-1, Ottawa, Dominion Bureau of Statistics,
Table A.11.

schooling inequality, urban Puerto Rico seems to be less divergent
from the United States than total Puerto Rico.

The data for Puerto Rico are defined in the same manner, and
were obtained from the same sampling procedure, as those for the
United States. Therefore, we can test the null hypothesis that the
relationship between the education component and income inequality is the same in Puerto Rico as among the states.

This test is done in a three-stage procedure. First, income inequality is regressed on the education component for the states.
Second, the observed value of the education component for Puerto
Rico is inserted into the regression equation to obtain the predicted value of income inequality for Puerto Rico. If this predicted value is sufficiently different from the observed value, the
hypothesis that the Puerto Rican data are derived from the same
statistical universe as the data for the States is rejected. Whether
the difference is sufficiently great is determined by a *t*-test. The
third stage, then, is to compute the observed *t*-ratio, which is the
difference between the observed and the predicted values for income inequality in Puerto Rico, divided by the standard error of
prediction.

The computed (or observed) t-ratios are $t = 1.50$ for urban Puerto Rico and $t = 2.27$ for total Puerto Rico. For 49 degrees of freedom and a two-tailed test, the critical t-values are 2.0 for a 5 per cent level of significance and 1.7 for a 10 per cent level.

Thus, the relation between income inequality and the education component in Puerto Rico is consistent with the U.S. pattern for the urban male population, but not for the entire male population. This finding is quite reasonable, since the economic environment of urban Puerto Rico is more like that of the mainland than is that of the urban and rural sectors combined.

Mexico

Table 5-3 presents regression results for the log of average monthly earnings on schooling for a sample of 3,901 male workers taken in urban Mexico.[3] A comparison of Mexico (rows 1 and 2 of Table 5-3) with the United States and Canada (Table 5-1) indicates that the inequalities of income and schooling, the adjusted rate of return, and the coefficient of determination are all highest in Mexico.

Striking features of the Mexican data are the high adjusted rate

TABLE 5-3

Results from Regressing the Natural Log of Earnings
on Schooling and Experience for Males in Urban Mexico

Age of Males	Summary Statistics			Regressions				
	SD(ln$E$)	SD(S)	$\frac{AV(\ln E)}{AV(S)}$	$\hat{r}$	b_1	b_2	Var(U)	$\overline{R}^2$
	(1)	(2)	(3)	(4)	(5)	(6)	(7)	(8)
All ages[a]	.89	3.98	6.94	.14	—	—	.46	.42
			6.57	(.003)				
Age 25+[a]	.79	4.26	7.25	.14	—	—	.27	.56
			6.79	(.002)				
All ages[b]	.89	3.98	6.94	.18	.10	−.0013	.22	.73
			6.57	(.002)	(.002)	(.0000)		

Note: E is in pesos per month, S is years of schooling, and T is age minus schooling minus five. Standard errors in parentheses.

Source: Sample provided by Martin Carnoy, including 3,901 individual, ungrouped observations, described in Appendix A-3.

[a] $\ln E_i = (\ln E_0) + (\hat{r}) S_i + U_i$.
[b] $\ln E_i = (\ln E_0) + (\hat{r}) S_i + b_1 T_i + b_2 T_i^2 + U_i$.

---

3. See Appendix A-3 for a discussion of the sample. Since the natural log of earnings is the dependent variable, the use of average monthly earnings (i.e., annual earnings divided by twelve) rather than annual earnings has no effect on the regression slope parameter or the measures of inequality.

of return and explanatory power of schooling. Even in Puerto Rico, where the adjusted rate of return is similar to that in Mexico, the explanatory power of schooling, while great, does not approach the magnitude of that for Mexico. The Mexican workers in the sample were all employed at the time and were asked to report their average monthly earnings. If, as seems plausible, they reported their full-time monthly earnings, then weeks worked were, in effect, held constant in the data. This may explain the high explanatory power of schooling.

The Mexican data contain the variable age (A), which permits an analysis of the effects of schooling (S) and years of labor market experience (T) $(T = A - S - 5)$ on the natural log of earnings.[4] Two interesting conclusions emerge from this analysis (Table 5-3). First, when experience is held constant, the adjusted rate of return from schooling is increased from 14 to 18 per cent.[5] This implies that years of experience and schooling are negatively correlated. Second, the explanatory power of the model is increased from 42 to 73 per cent. That is, in this sample of urban Mexican workers nearly three-fourths of the individual variations in monthly earnings are explained by years of schooling and experience.

Summary

A comparison among the four countries indicates that the inequality of income is positively correlated with the rate of return, the inequality of schooling, and the explanatory power of schooling.

The proportion of the interregional variation in income inequality that can be explained by the education component, the residual variance, and their covariation can be computed using equations (3-21) and (3-22). For earnings data for the U.S. North, U.S. South, and nonfarm Canada, the education component ex-

---

4. If it is assumed that the fraction of earnings invested in experience declines linearly, then the log of earnings is a parabolic function of years of experience. (See Mincer, *Schooling, Experience, and Earnings*, or Chapter 6 of this volume.) Experience is the number of years since leaving school, and is measured as age minus schooling minus five.

5. Recall from Chapter 3 that the slope coefficient of schooling is rk. Therefore, the rate of return is 0.14 when experience is not held constant, if $k = 1$. A $k = 1$ implies that the sum of direct plus opportunity costs of a year of schooling are equal to the earnings the student could have received in that year if he had not attended school. In other words, if the direct costs of the year of schooling equal the earnings the student received that year while attending school, then $k = 1$.

TABLE 5-4

International Explanatory Power of Schooling
(per cent)

Regions	Education Component (1)	Residual (2)	Covariation (3)
U.S. North, U.S. South, Canada (earnings data)	30.2	20.9	48.8
United States, Canada, Puerto Rico (income data)	19.5	28.5	52.2
United States, Canada, Urban Puerto Rico (income data)	25.2	25.2	49.6

Note: See notes to Table 4-5.
Sources: Tables 5-1 and 5-2.

plains 30 per cent and the residual variance explains 21 per cent of the differences in earnings inequality among these three regions (see Table 5-4). For income data in the United States, Canada, and Puerto Rico, the education component explains 20 per cent of the differences in inequality. When the Puerto Rican data are restricted to urban males, the education component and the residual each explain 25 per cent. In a comparison of Table 5-4 with Table 4-5, we note that the education component's direct interregional explanatory power is smaller in the international data than among the fifty-one states (where it is 30.5 per cent).

EARNINGS INEQUALITY AND ECONOMIC GROWTH

Lydall performed the herculean task of collecting data and generating statistics on inequality of earnings and schooling of nonfarm males from several countries at various levels of development.[6] These data are analyzed here to provide additional evidence on the relationship between the distribution of schooling and the distribution of earnings.

Let us recall equations (3-13) and (3-14), which specified that earnings inequality is positively related to the level and inequality of schooling and rates of return from schooling.[7] To test this relationship, Lydall's data are used here for the inequality of earnings

---

6. Harold Lydall, *The Structure of Earnings*, Oxford, 1968, Chapter 5.
7. The equation is:

$$\text{Var}(\ln Y) = \bar{r}^2 \ \text{Var}(S) + \bar{S}^2 \ \text{Var}(r) + \text{Var}(r) \ \text{Var}(S) + \text{Var}(U).$$

and schooling. Data on GNP per capita are used as a proxy for the level of schooling. International data are scarce on the level of the rate of return from schooling, and nonexistent on the variance in rates of return.

Yet, there may be a relation between the level and inequality of rates of return from schooling and secular economic change. During periods of secular economic change, relative prices are in flux; if schooling promotes perceiving and adjusting to changed circumstances, it will raise the level of and inequality in the rates of return and thereby increase income inequality.[8] A discussion of the process through which secular economic change may influence the distribution of rates of return from schooling and the relevant empirical analysis are presented below.

Allocative Efficiency and Rates of Return

The skills created by school and postschool training can be thought of as falling into one of two not easily separable categories—worker efficiency and allocative efficiency.[9] Worker efficiency refers to the ability to perform a particular set of tasks; allocative efficiency refers to the ability to make correct decisions. Learning to use a drill press increases worker efficiency; learning how to decide on the appropriate grade of metal to drill increases allocative efficiency. Again, learning how to apply fertilizer to a field increases one's worker efficiency, while learning how to select a combination of chemicals to apply to a field increases one's al-

---

8. Note that this can be contrasted with the increase in income inequality during business cycle recessions. The decline in employment during recessions is experienced disproportionately by those with low levels of training. In terms of the schooling model of income distribution, the cyclical decline results in an increase in the level and inequality of rates of return from schooling computed from observed annual earnings. For theoretical and empirical analyses of the effect of the business cycle on the distribution of employment and income, see Becker, *Human Capital*, 1974, Part I; and Barry R. Chiswick and Jacob Mincer, "Time-Series Changes in Personal Income Inequality in the United States from 1939, with Projections to 1985," *Journal of Political Economy*, Supplement, May-June 1972.

9. The distinction was made originally by Theodore W. Schultz in *Transforming Traditional Agriculture*, New Haven, Yale University Press, 1964, Chapter 12. It was developed further by Richard Nelson and Edmund Phelps, "Investment in Humans, Technological Diffusion and Economic Growth," *American Economic Review*, May 1966, pp. 69–75; and Finis Welch, "Education in Production," *Journal of Political Economy*, January 1970, pp. 35–59. Welch uses U.S. agricultural data to show that schooling increases allocative efficiency.

locative efficiency. A particular job may, of course, involve varying combinations of allocative and worker efficiency. Allocative skills appear to be of relatively greater importance with higher levels of skill. Indeed, for most professionals, decision-making skills are of primary importance.

The demand for allocative skills is higher the more decisions there are to be made and the higher the payoff is for "better" decisions. In a long-term stagnant economy where relative prices are unchanged, the most efficient procedures would have long been discovered and the knowledge spread to all relevant members of the system. In this situation allocative skills would not be very valuable.[10]

Suppose we now introduce a development that changes relative prices. Those with the greatest allocative skills are the first to learn of this change and the first to implement an appropriate response; as a consequence they receive higher incomes—now allocative skills have achieved more economic value. If this is the only change (and a once-and-for-all change), the premium for this skill will decline as the knowledge spreads to those with lesser allocative skills.[11]

In an environment of continuous economic change, there is the possibility of economic gain by combining factors of production in a different way or by producing a different output. In such a situation premiums for superior allocative efficiency can (and presumably do) persist even in the long run. Allocative efficiency is, therefore, assumed to have a larger payoff the more change there is in the economic environment. Periods of secular economic growth are periods in which the economic environment is in flux and in which gains may be had from recombining factors of production.

Let us return to the simplified internal rate of return formula, $r = d/C$, where d is the annual increment in earnings due to an investment in schooling and C is the dollar cost of the investment. The differential d can, in principle, be decomposed into an allocative efficiency (d_a) and a worker efficiency (d_w) differential, $d = d_a + d_w$. The costs of the investment are the direct costs (C_d) and the opportunity costs, where the latter is the sum of an allocative

---

10. Schultz argues in *Transforming Traditional Agriculture*, p. 8, that the "critical feature of traditional agriculture is the low rate of return to investment in agricultural factors of the type that farmers have been using for generations." For an elaboration of this point, see ibid., Chapter 6.

11. For an analysis of the spread of an innovation, see Zvi Griliches, "Hybrid Corn and the Economics of Innovation," *Science*, July 29, 1960, pp. 275-280.

(C_a) and a worker efficiency (C_w) component. Then, $C = C_d + C_a + C_w$. The rate of return is written as:

$$r = \frac{(d_a + d_w)}{C_d + C_a + C_w}. \tag{5-1}$$

Suppose a change in the economic environment increases the return to allocative efficiency by $100t$ per cent. The new rate of return is

$$r' = \frac{(1 + t) d_a + d_w}{C_d + (1 + t) C_a + C_w}, \tag{5-2}$$

if direct costs are not affected by the change. This implies an increase in the level of the rate of return.[12] If we allow for individual differences in worker and allocative efficiency, the variance in rates of return is likely to increase when the premium for allocative skills increases.[13]

Thus, it is hypothesized that more rapid economic change increases opportunities for a larger premium to allocative skills. Since allocative skills differ among individuals, and since these skills are likely to increase in relative importance for those with higher levels of skill, the expanded opportunities increase both the level and variance in rates of return from schooling—and consequently income inequality.[14]   Hence, since economic growth is associated

---

12. The rate of return increases as long as $r' > r$, $\dfrac{(1 + t) d_a + d_w}{C_d + (1 + t) C_a + C_w} >$ $\dfrac{d_a + d_w}{C_d + C_a + C_w}$, or $\dfrac{d_a}{d_w} > \dfrac{C_a}{C_d + C_w}$. If C_d is nonnegative, $\dfrac{d_a}{d_w} > \dfrac{C_a}{C_w}$, if allocative skills rise in importance as skill level increases. Thus, r' is greater than r as long as allocative skills do not fall in relative importance as skill level increases.

13. This is easy to show if we make several assumptions. Let us assume those without the investment have no allocative efficiency, and the increased premium is a constant proportion $100t$ per cent. The new rate of return is $r' = \dfrac{(1 + t) d_a + d_w}{C}$. The variance in rates of return is $S^2(r) = (1/C)^2$ $[S^2(d_a) + S^2(d_w) + 2 \text{ Cov }(d_a, d_w)]$, and $S^2(r') = (1/C)^2 [(1 + t)^2 S^2(d_a) + S^2(d_w) + 2(1 + t) \text{ Cov }(d_a, d_w)] = (1/C)^2 [S^2(d_a) + S^2(d_w) + 2 \text{ Cov }(d_a, d_w)] + (1/C)^2 [(t^2 + 2t) S^2(d_a) + 2t \text{ Cov }(d_a, d_w)]$. For a positive t, $S^2(r')$ is greater than $S^2(r)$ as long as $(t + 2) S^2(d_a) + 2 \text{ Cov }(d_a, d_w) > 0$. This necessarily holds if individual differences in allocative and worker skills are not negatively correlated.

14. The scanty international data that are available on rates of return support this hypothesis. Although there appears to be no relation between the level of output per capita and the rate of return, in Latin America at least,

with a changing economic environment, growth may be a *cause* of greater inequality in labor market income.

Empirical Analysis[15]

We can now test the hypotheses that earnings inequality is greater the larger the inequality of schooling, the higher the level of schooling, and the more rapid the secular economic change.

Lydall's measure of earnings is money wages and salaries before taxes for nonfarm males.[16] He uses three percentile measures of relative income inequality. The percentile measure of income inequality $P(X)$ is the ratio of the income of the individual in the Xth percentile from the upper end of the distribution $(p(X))$, relative to the median income (i.e., $p(50)$), multiplied by 100.[17]

rates of return are higher in the more rapidly growing countries. (See Martin Carnoy, "Rates of Return to Schooling in Latin America," *Journal of Human Resources*, Summer 1967, pp. 354–374, and T. Paul Schultz, "Returns of Education in Bogota, Colombia," *RAND* Memorandum, Santa Monica, 1968, Table 9.) Using time series data, Schultz found that the partial correlation between income inequality and the *secular* growth rate of output was positive in the United States and the Netherlands, although it was significant only for the latter. ("Secular Trends and Cyclical Behavior of Income Distribution in the United States: 1944-1964," in Lee Soltow, ed., *Six Papers on the Size Distribution of Income and Wealth*, New York, 1969, p. 87.) In his cross-sectional analysis of farm family income in the United States, Gardner used "research and extension expenditures and the growth of output per farm" to serve as an "indicator of the dynamism of a state's agriculture." When schooling inequality, migration, and several other variables were held constant, Gardner's variables for "dynamism" had a positive effect on income inequality. (Bruce R. Gardner, "An Analysis of U.S. Farm Family Income Inequality, 1950-1960," Ph.D. dissertation, University of Chicago, 1968, pp. 62-63 and Tables 6 and 7.)

15. The empirical analysis is based on my "Earnings Inequality and Economic Development," *Quarterly Journal of Economics*, February 1971, pp. 21-39.

16. *The Structure of Earnings*, pp. 60 and 153.

17. A Schematic Representation of the Distribution of Income

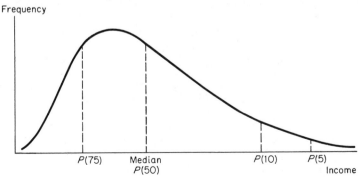

$(P(X) = [p(X)(100)]/[p(50)]$.) $P(5)$ and $P(10)$ are measures of inequality in the upper half of the distribution, their values exceed
100, and larger values imply greater inequality. $P(75)$ is a measure
of inequality in the lower half of the distribution, has values less
than 100, and larger values imply less inequality. $P(5)$ (or $P(10)$)
and $P(75)$ are highly negatively correlated, which implies that regions with greater inequality in the upper half of the earnings distribution tend to have greater inequality in the lower half, and
therefore tend to have greater overall earnings inequality.[18]

Lydall's measure of schooling inequality is the "Lorenz coefficient," $(LC(S))$, a measure of relative rather than absolute dispersion. He computed it for nonfarm males in ten countries for
which he calculated personal earnings inequality.[19] Data on the
level of schooling are not available, so GNP per capita is used as a
proxy. The average per capita GNP is in constant 1967 prices
(dollar equivalents) for the 1950–1960 period, except for Japan,
where the period covered is 1952–1960.[20] The secular rate of
change is measured by the per cent change in per capita GNP in
constant 1967 prices (dollar equivalents) for the same periods.

The cross-sectional data on level and growth rate of output are
available for only nine of the ten countries for which Lydall calculated Lorenz coefficients of schooling, and for two of these there
are no estimates of $P(75)$. Thus, the empirical analysis of the effects of income level (Y'), growth rate of output $(\%\Delta Y)$, and
schooling inequality $(LC(S))$ on $P(5)$ and $P(10)$ is performed for
nine countries, and on $P(75)$, for seven countries.[21] Due to ex-
tremely small samples the results can only be suggestive.

Table 5-5 contains the analysis of earnings inequality for the
upper tail of the distribution, $P(5)$ and $P(10)$. The simple correlations between average income and $P(5)$ and $P(10)$ are negative and

---

18. The correlation coefficients for twenty-two countries are
$R[P(5),P(10)] = 0.98, R[P(5),P(75)] = -0.80, R[P(10),P(75)] = -0.83$.

19. Lydall, *The Structure of Earnings*, pp. 209–211.

20. U.S. Agency for International Development, *Gross National Product,
Growth Rates and Trend Data by Regions and Countries*, Documents No.
RC-W-138, April 25, 1969 (Statistics and Reports Division, Office of Program and Policy Coordination). An index of per capita consumption con-
structed by W. Beckerman and R. Bacon ("International Comparisons of Income Levels: A Suggested New Measure," *Economic Journal*, Vol. 76,
September 1966, pp. 519–536) was tried as a substitute for GNP per capita,
but the results were not significantly different and are not reported.

21. $LC(S)$, the Lorenz coefficient of schooling, is a measure of relative
inequality; higher coefficients imply a greater inequality of schooling.

The seven are Argentina, Canada, France, Japan, Mexico, United Kingdom, and United States. The two additional countries are Brazil and Chile.

TABLE 5-5

Analysis of $P(5)$ and $P(10)$

	P(5)	P(10)	Y'	%ΔY	LC(S)	$\overline{R}^2$
			Correlation Matrix			
P(10)	0.97					
Y'	-0.67	-0.68				
%ΔY	0.03	0.02	-0.26			
LC(S)	0.80	0.73	-0.61	-0.27		
			Regressions			
Dependent			-0.016	87.3	0.339	0.56
variable P(5)			(-0.43)	(0.66)	(2.12)	
Dependent			-0.017	21.1	0.137	0.40
variable P(10)			(-0.75)	(0.26)	(1.36)	

Note: The larger $P(5)$ and $P(10)$, the larger the earnings inequality. There are 9 observations; t-ratios are in parentheses. Critical values for correlations $R_{0.95} = 0.58$; for regression coefficients $t_{0.95} = 2.02$. Symbols are defined as follows:
$P(i) = \dfrac{100\,pi}{p_{50}}$, where pi is earnings at the ith percentile from the upper end of the distribution, and p_{50} is the median, for nonfarm males.

Y'—average per capita GNP in constant 1967 prices (dollar equivalents) for 1950-1960 (Japan, for 1952-1960).

%ΔY—percentage change in GNP per capita in constant 1957 prices (dollar equivalents) from 1950 to 1960 (Japan, 1952 to 1960).

$LC(S)$—Lorenz coefficient of quantity of schooling.

See footnote 21 for a list of countries involved.

Sources: P(i)—Harold Lydall, *The Structure of Earnings* (Oxford, 1968), p. 153, Table 5.5.

Y' and %ΔY—*Gross National Product, Growth Rate and Trend Data by Regions and Countries*, Document No. RC-W-138 (April 25, 1969), Statistics and Reports Division, Office of Program and Policy Coordination, U.S. Agency for International Development.

$LC(S)$—Lydall, *The Structure of Earnings*, p. 211, Table 7.1.

significant. When the rate of output growth and the Lorenz coefficient of schooling are held constant, however, the partial relation remains negative but becomes insignificant. Thus, although countries with lower levels of development are associated with greater earnings inequality, low income does not seem to have a direct effect, but operates through other variables (like the inequality of schooling, for example).

The growth rate of output has positive but insignificant simple and partial correlations with $P(5)$ and $P(10)$. The positive simple correlations of schooling inequality with $P(5)$ and $P(10)$ are significant, and although the significance declines, the partial relation remains positive, and is significant at the 5 per cent level for $P(5)$.

The dependent variable $P(75)$ declines with greater earnings inequality. Thus, the positive simple correlation shown in Table

TABLE 5-6

Analysis of $P(75)$

	$P(75)$	Y'	$\%\Delta Y$	$LC(S)$	$\overline{R}^2$
			Correlation Matrix		
Y'	0.63				
$\%\Delta Y$	-0.68	-0.43			
$LC(S)$	-0.47	-0.48	-0.24		
			Regressions		
Dependent		-0.0008	-24.55	-0.027	0.81
variable $P(75)$		(-0.46)	(-3.81)	(-3.05)	

Note: The smaller $P(75)$, the larger the earnings inequality. There are 7 observations; t-ratios are in parentheses. Critical values for correlations $R_{0.95} = 0.67$; for regression coefficients $t_{0.95} = 2.35$. For definition of symbols, see note to Table 5-5.

Sources: See footnote to Table 5-5.

5-6 between $P(75)$ and average income means that a smaller earnings inequality is associated with a higher level of income. This coefficient is barely significant at a 5 per cent level. The partial relation between Y' and $P(75)$ is not significant. The growth rate of output has a significant, and schooling inequality, an insignificant negative simple correlation with $P(75)$. Schooling inequality becomes highly significant and the growth rate of output increases in significance in the multiple regression.

The multiple regression analysis for $P(75)$ gives the expected signs for the three independent variables, and the schooling inequality and growth rate variables are significant. The results for $P(5)$ and $P(10)$ are weaker, but the signs for schooling inequality and the growth rate of output are consistent with our expectations. The differences between the $P(75)$, the $P(5)$, and $P(10)$ regressions may be due to the different samples or to the different aspects of inequality reflected in the three measures. To separate these effects, the regressions for $P(5)$ and $P(10)$ were run for the seven countries used in the $P(75)$ analysis. Although the results for $P(5)$ and $P(10)$ become more consistent with our expectations, they are not as consistent as the $P(75)$ results.[22] Thus, the differences between the $P(75)$ seven-country and the $P(5)$ and $P(10)$ nine-country analyses are partly due to the different sections of

---

22. For $P(5)$ the seven-country partial slope coefficient for schooling inequality is positive and significant ($t = 2.59$), and insignificantly positive for the growth rate of output ($t = 1.49$) and the level of output ($t = 0.29$). For $P(10)$ the three coefficients are positive, significant for schooling inequality ($t = 2.83$), but insignificant at the 5 per cent level (one-tailed test) for the growth rate of output ($t = 1.96$) and level of output ($t = 0.23$).

the earnings distribution encompassed by these variables. $P(75)$ measures dispersion closer to and below the median, while $P(5)$ and $P(10)$ reflect the extreme upper end of the distribution. The model, therefore, seems a better predictor for the center of the distribution of earnings than for the upper tail.

Conclusions

Although it is based on a very small sample, the international cross-sectional analysis with data on earnings inequality of non-farm males tends to confirm the hypotheses derived from the schooling model of income distribution. The observed negative simple correlation between the earnings inequality of nonfarm males and the level of development does not appear to be directly due to development, since the partial relation is insignificant. If the level of development has an effect on earnings inequality it operates through other variables. A greater inequality of schooling and a higher growth rate of output appear to increase earnings inequality. The model is more successful in explaining earnings inequality around the median than between the median and the upper tail of the distribution.

MASS MIGRATION AND INCOME INEQUALITY IN ISRAEL

The variables examined in this volume are affected by historical events. It has been well established, for example, that historical events shaped the pattern of income distribution among the Jewish population of Israel. The exogenous changes in labor supply due to mass migration resulted in changes in Israeli income inequality, the rate of return from schooling, and the correlation of income with schooling which are consistent with our model.

Trends over Time

At the time of Israel's establishment in 1948, its Jewish population was composed primarily of immigrants from Europe.[23] Their migration was largely motivated by noneconomic considerations.[24] They came in large numbers to an underdeveloped econ-

---

23. See A. Hovne, *The Labor Force in Israel*, Jerusalem, Falk Project for Economic Research in Israel, July 1961, p. 19.

24. R. Bachi, "Immigration into Israel," in B. Thomas, ed., *Economics of International Migration*, London, Macmillan, 1958, pp. 315-318.

omy and often found that their previous training was of little economic value. The result: a low skill differential and, consequently, a low rate of return from schooling and a low correlation between earnings and schooling.[25]

Few immigrants brought capital with them, and previous Jewish settlement had been too recent for the development of a substantial group of property owners. National, public, and cooperative ownership of land and development enterprises tended to dominate the economic scene. The result was a small inequality among Jews in the distribution of nonlabor wealth and property income. The low rate of return from schooling and small inequality of property income led to a small inequality of total income.[26]

The residual variance, in turn, was affected by the small inequality of wealth and low rates of return from human capital. Skill differentials were sufficiently low to permit residual factors (such as ability and luck) to exert a relatively important effect on income distribution and to result in a small explanatory power of schooling.

Thus, it appears that the exogenous increase in the supply of skilled workers depressed the rate of return from schooling and generated a small inequality of income and a low correlation between income and schooling—a pattern which is consistent with our model.

The mass immigration after independence in 1948 once again was not motivated by conventional economic forces.[27] The new immigrants had less schooling than the immigrants who had come in the 1920s and 1930s.[28] They were also at a disadvantage as to other forms of human capital: many came from refugee camps in Europe and poor countries of the Middle East and North Africa, and we may assume that their level of health was lower than that of prestatehood immigrants. Moreover, knowledge of the language and "way of life" of a country and information concerning labor markets are also part of human capital. Hovne finds that "prestate immigrants of the same age, level of education, and continent of

25. Giora Hanoch, "Income Differentials in Israel," *Fifth Report, Falk Project for Economic Research in Israel*, 1961, p. 43.

26. Hanoch (ibid., Chapter 1) shows that in 1957–58, income inequality was relatively small, yet larger than nearly a decade earlier.

27. Bachi, "Immigration into Israel," pp. 319–320.

28. In 1957 the mean and variance of years of schooling for all male Jews of fifteen years and over were 6.6 and 17.9, respectively, and for those designated as "veterans" (in Palestine in 1947), 7.8 and 17.4, respectively.

The five schooling intervals were assigned the following numerical values:

origin were at an advantage,"[29] presumably because they had already acquired these forms of capital.

The increased supply of unskilled workers decreased the average level of schooling and other human capital, and changed relative scarcities.[30] As would be expected, skill differentials increased. Bahral reports that "the relative wage differentials of workers performing different jobs (when comparing high and low wage groups), on the average, widened during the first ten years of the state. This is true for the first years of mass immigration and for the period of the second wave of immigration, 1955–58."[31] He adds that "this relative price of highly paid labor services in Israel should be stressed in view of the downward trend of occupational differentials found in most modern economies and in mandatory Palestine up to the end of the second World War."[32] Hanoch, too, shows that income inequality increased in the first decade after independence.[33]

Since the average rate of return increased and the inequality of schooling remained nearly unchanged (see footnote 29 below), the education component (the product r^2 Var (S)) increased. It seems plausible that the residual variance increased too, due to higher returns on other forms of capital and a possible growth in the inequality of human capital other than schooling. The effects of some variables in the residual (ability and luck, for example) probably prevented it from rising at the same rate as the education component, and thereby resulted in an increase in the correlation between income and schooling. This is consistent with Hanoch's

Schooling Interval	Years
1. Did Not Attend School	0.0
2. Partial Primary Education	3.0
3. Completed Primary Education	7.0
4. Completed Secondary Education	12.0
5. Completed Higher Education	16.0

Source: Computed from *Statistical Abstract of Israel: 1957–58*, Jerusalem, Central Bureau of Statistics, 1958, Section S, Education, Table 28, p. 365.

29. Hovne, *The Labor Force in Israel*, p. 45.

30. Hanoch reports that "from a relative abundance of persons with secondary and higher education, and of experts, there developed a quite serious shortage." See his "Income Differentials in Israel," p. 44.

31. Uri Bahral, *The Effects of Mass Migration on Wages in Israel*, Jerusalem, Falk Project for Economic Research in Israel, 1965, pp. 5–6.

32. Ibid., p. 6.

33. "Income Differentials in Israel," pp. 44–52.

finding a negligible correlation between income and schooling in 1948 and a significant one in 1957.[34]

Thus, the postindependence migration lowered the level of schooling, raised the rate of return, left the variance of schooling unchanged, and consequently increased the education component $(r^2 \operatorname{Var}(S))$. The results, as predicted by our analysis, were an increase in the inequality of income, in the explanatory power of schooling, and possibly also in the residual variance. The Israeli experience demonstrates that the parameters under study were influenced by historical events, and that the direction of the changes in the parameters was consistent with our previous findings.

Comparison with the United States

It is interesting to compare Israel in the late 1950s with the United States of approximately the same period. For urban heads of households in Israel in 1957, Klinov-Malul calculates internal rates of return (based on total money costs to society) of 17.0 per cent for eight years of elementary education, 6.5 per cent for secondary education, and 7.5 per cent for higher education.[35] These are considerably lower than rates of return in the United States.[36]

The variance of schooling in 1957 for male Jews of fifteen years of age and over was 17.9 years-squared and the average was 6.6 years. (See footnote 29 on p. 99). With the same grouping for schooling, the variance for white U.S. males between the ages of twenty-five and sixty-four in 1960 was 12.0 years-squared,[37] or two-thirds the Israeli inequality. Comparisons of U.S. and Israeli rates of return and schooling inequality indicate that the education component, $r^2 \operatorname{Var}(S)$, is smaller in Israel than in the United States,[38] and that the same is true of the level of schooling.

---

34. For 1948, see Hanoch, p. 43. For 1957, see footnote 40 below.

35. Ruth Klinov-Malul, "Profitability of Investment in Education," *Fifth Report, Falk Project for Economic Research in Israel*, Jerusalem, 1961, pp. 138–146.

36. For U.S. internal rates of return, see Table 4-2.

37. *United States Census of Population, 1960, Subject Reports: Educational Attainment*, Washington, D.C. Bureau of the Census, Table 6.

38. If $\operatorname{Var}(S)_{US} = (2/3) \operatorname{Var}(S)_I$, the education component would be smaller in Israel if $r^2_{US} \operatorname{Var}(S)_{US} > r^2_I \operatorname{Var}(S)_I$, $(2/3) r^2_{US} > r^2_I$, or $(0.775) r_{US} > r_I$. Comparisons of Klinov-Malul's internal rates of return with estimates for the United States by Becker, Hansen, and Hanoch (see Table 4-2) indicate that the internal rates are sufficiently low in Israel to result in a smaller education component.

There is considerable evidence that income inequality is smaller in Israel than in the United States.[39] This is consistent with the smaller education component and lower level of schooling. As for the residual variance, the small inequality of personal wealth discussed above would preclude a relatively large variance, and indications are that it is, in fact, smaller in Israel.

Parameters given in Hanoch's paper on Israel permit a calculation of the coefficient of determination between schooling and earnings for urban heads of households in 1957. The unadjusted explanatory power for earnings (not log of earnings) is 16.9 per cent.[40] When earnings in 1959 are regressed on schooling of U.S. adult males (all males as well as white males), the unadjusted explanatory power is 12.2 per cent and 11.0 per cent, respectively.[41] It appears that for earnings the explanatory power of schooling is larger in Israel than in the United States. A greater explanatory power but a smaller income variance than in the United States implies that the residual variance is smaller in Israel.

To sum up, in Israel (1957-58) the inequality in ownership of nonhuman wealth, the rate of return, the level of schooling, and the education component are smaller than in the United States (1959), while the inequality of schooling is larger. The smaller education component and dispersion of nonlabor income result in a smaller dispersion of income in Israel. The explanatory power of schooling is greater in Israel. Altogether, the results of the time series analysis and the comparison with the United States are consistent with the interregional relationships found in Chapter 4 and the model developed in Chapter 3.

GREAT BRITAIN VERSUS THE UNITED STATES

In view of the fact that the inequality of wealth is greater in Great Britain than in the United States, many observers are under

39. See Hanoch, "Income Differentials in Israel," 1961, pp. 39-42; and Irving B. Kravis, *The Structure of Income: Some Quantitative Essays*, Philadelphia, The Wharton School, University of Pennsylvania, 1962, pp. 244-249.

40. Designating earnings by 1, continent of origin and place of immigration by 2, and level of education by 3, Hanoch states that $R^2_{12.3} = 0.064$ and $R^2_{12.3} = 0.220$. (See "Income Differentials in Israel," p. 105, Table 24.)

It can be shown that $R^2_{12.3} = (R^2_{12.3} - R^2_{13})/(1 - R^2_{13})$. (See T. Johnston, *Econometric Methods*, New York, McGraw-Hill, 1963, p. 60.) Then, $R^2_{13} = 0.169$.

41. *U.S. Census of Population, 1960, Subject Reports, Occupation by Earnings and Education*, Washington, D.C., Table 1.

the impression that Britain also has a greater inequality of income, and are surprised to find that income inequality is approximately the same in the two countries.[42] The analysis developed in this study can explain this pattern.

Note, first, that the inequality of earnings is smaller in Britain than in the United States.[43] Secondly, inequality is related to the rate of return from schooling and the level and inequality of schooling. Private rates of return from schooling in Britain have been estimated at 13 per cent for those who stay at school three years beyond the age of fifteen and at 14 per cent for those with three additional years of schooling.[44] These are similar to the calculated rates of return for high school and college in the United States (see Table 4-2). As can be seen from Table 5-7, in Great Britain the level of schooling is lower and schooling is more equally

TABLE 5-7

Distribution of the Labor Force by Years of Schooling
in the United States and the United Kingdom

Years of Schooling	Per Cent Distribution	
	U.S., 1957	U.K., 1951
0 to 7	17.3	2.1
8	16.1	7.6
9	6.1	63.1
10	7.3	12.2
11	5.9	7.8
12	29.5	2.8
13	3.4	1.6
14	3.5	0.4
15	1.7	0.6
16	5.5	0.6
17 or more	3.7	1.3
	100.0	100.0

Source: Edward F. Denison, "Measuring the Contribution of Education (and the Residual) to Economic Growth," in *The Residual Factor and Economic Growth*, Paris, OECD, 1964, p. 43, Table 10.

42. See Kravis, *The Structure of Income*, pp. 249–250; and Lydall and Lansing, "A Comparison of the Distribution of Income and Wealth in the United States and Great Britain," *American Economic Review*, March 1959.

43. Lydall and Lansing, ibid., or Lydall, *The Structure of Earnings*, Table 5.5, p. 153.

44. D. Henderson-Stewart, "Appendix: Estimate of the Rate of Return to Education in Great Britain," *Manchester School*, September 1965, pp. 252–261.

distributed.[45] The similar rate of return and the lower level and inequality of schooling are consistent with the smaller inequality of earnings in Britain.

Thus, income inequality is approximately the same in Great Britain as in the United States because the smaller inequality of earnings in Britain (due to a lower level and inequality of schooling) is combined with a greater inequality of property income.[46] These findings are consistent with my schooling model of income inequality.

---

45. The table is for the United Kingdom (i.e., Great Britain plus Northern Ireland), but a similar education distribution would emerge if Northern Ireland were removed from the data.

46. If Y were total income, E earnings, and W property income, $Y = E + W$, and Var $(Y) =$ Var $(E) +$ Var $(W) + 2$ Cov (E,W). If, for simplicity, the covariance term were assumed to be the same in both countries, a larger inequality of property income combined with a smaller inequality of earnings could result in the same inequality of total income.

For an analysis of the effect of minimum schooling laws in Great Britain on the parameters under study, see my "Minimum Schooling Legislation and the Cross-Sectional Distribution of Income," *Economic Journal*, September 1969, pp. 495-507.

PART C

Income as a
Function of Schooling
and Market Experience

6

The Expanded Human
Capital Model

This chapter presents a model in which an individual's income can be related to his years of schooling, years of labor market experience, and level of employment (weeks worked) during the year. It is a brief exposition of what has come to be called the expanded "human capital earnings function."[1] The mean and variance of the function are computed and used empirically in Chapters 7 and 8 to explain interstate differences in the income distribution of the United States and Canada.

INVESTMENT IN TRAINING

If earnings were due only to investments in training and employment lasted the full year, there would be a simple relationship between earnings and training parameters. Suppose Y_0 is a full year's earnings of an individual with zero training, and he invests (direct and opportunity costs) $100k$ per cent of his potential income in year 1. If he does not undertake additional investments, and there is no depreciation of his stock of capital, his earning in year 2 and in all subsequent periods will be

$$Y_1' = Y_0 + r_1(k_1 Y_0) = Y_0(1 + r_1 k_1), \qquad (6\text{-}1)$$

where r_1 is his average rate of return on the investment and $k_1 Y_0$

1. The expanded human capital earnings function was developed by Jacob Mincer in his *Schooling, Experience, and Earnings*, Part 1, NBER, 1974.

is the dollar value of the investment. If he invests in N periods of training, his earnings after training will be shown by the identity

$$Y'_{Nj} = Y_0 \prod_{j=1}^{N} (1 + r_j k_j), \qquad (6\text{-}2)$$

where r_j is the average rate of return on the investment in the jth period and k_j is the fraction of potential earnings in year j that was invested.[2]

The earnings an individual could receive if he did not invest in training after N years is his gross or potential earnings (Y'_N). Net earnings (Y_N) are gross earnings after investment costs are deducted. That is,

$$Y_N = Y'_N - k_{N+1}(Y'_N) = Y'_N(1 - k_{N+1}),$$

where k_{N+1} is the fraction of potential (gross) earnings invested in year $N + 1$. Net earnings are equal to observed (or reported) earnings in a year only if all training costs are opportunity costs. If some training costs involve direct or out of pocket expenditures, gross earnings exceed observed earnings, which exceed net earnings.

During some years of formal schooling direct costs are substantial. During postschool investment in on-the-job training direct costs are negligible to the worker since the direct costs of the training provided by the firm are deducted from the "trainee's" wages.[3] The net earnings of a worker investing $100k_{N+1}$ per cent of his potential earnings are

$$Y_N = Y_0 \prod_{j=1}^{N} (1 + r_j k_j)(1 - k_{N+1}). \qquad (6\text{-}3)$$

---

2. From the principle of mathematical induction, if a relationship holds for $j = 1$, and if, when it holds for $j = N$ it also holds for $j = N + 1$, then it holds for all values of j. The relation was shown to hold for $j = 1$ in the text.

If $Y'_N = Y_0 \prod_{j=1}^{N} (1 + r_j k_j)$, and an $N + 1$st year of investment is undertaken,

$$Y'_{N+1} = Y'_N + r_{N+1}(k_{N+1} Y'_N) = Y'_N(1 + r_{N+1} k_{N+1}) = Y_0 \prod_{j=1}^{N+1} (1 + r_j k_j).$$

Thus, the expression is valid for all values of j.

3. While firms provide training, they do not finance any general training (training useful in many firms) and finance only part of specific training (training useful only in that specific firm). See Gary Becker, *Human Capital*, 1974, Ch. 2, and Donald Parsons, "Specific Human Capital: An Application to Quit Rates and Layoff Rates," *Journal of Political Economy*, November-December 1972, pp. 1120–1143.

WEEKS WORKED

The model thus far assumes full employment of the worker during the year. Actual "net annual earnings" are lower than "net full-year employment earnings" to the extent that the worker is unemployed or absent from the labor force during part of the year. Employment will be expressed in terms of weeks worked, since this is the form used for employment data in the empirical analysis. If weekly wages were independent of the number of weeks worked, we could write

$$Y_N = Y_0 \left[\prod_{j=1}^{N} (1 + r_j k_j)(1 - k_{N+1}) \right] (WW) \qquad (6\text{-}4)$$

where Y_N is now annual net earnings, Y_0 is the worker's earnings if he had not invested, the terms in square brackets represent the contribution of past and current human capital investments to his current net earnings, and (WW) is the fraction of weeks in the year $N + 1$ in which he works.[4]

Within the human capital framework, there are two reasons for believing that weekly wages and weeks worked are not independent of each other. First, those who have greater investments in training specific to a firm have higher wage rates and lower quit and layoff rates, and consequently work more weeks per year.[5] Second, those who have higher weekly wages because of greater investment in training (regardless of whether it is general or specific) face a higher opportunity cost of time and will work more during the year if the substitution effect outweighs the adverse effect on work effort produced by the increase in wealth due to the investment.[6] These points are part and parcel of the human capital analysis of earnings.

---

4. It is assumed that investments in training are proportional to time spent working.

5. See Becker, *Human Capital*, Part 1, and Parsons, "Specific Human Capital" for the relation between specific training and quit and layoff rates. Workers with lower levels of skill have more frequent spells of unemployment, and a slightly longer duration per spell. See R. Morganstern and N. S. Barrett, "Occupational Discrimination and Changing Labor Force Participation: Their Effects on Unemployment Rates of Blacks and Women," 1971, Mimeo.

6. Investments in human capital increase wealth only to the extent that the internal rate of return (r) on the investment exceeds the opportunity cost of the funds invested (R). For an investment of C dollars with a constant annual return and an infinite life the increase in wealth is $\dfrac{C\,(r - R)}{R}$.

Outside of the human capital framework there are additional reasons for a connection between weeks worked during the year and weekly earnings. First, if the higher weekly wage for the weeks actually worked is due to cyclical or seasonal sensitivity of employment in an industry, there will be a negative correlation between weeks worked and weekly wages, ceteris paribus.[7] Second, those whose weekly wages are higher for reasons other than investment in human capital or seasonal fluctuations (for example, due to ability, luck, or discrimination) will wish to work more weeks if their supply curve is upward rising. That is, if the price effect of the higher wage exceeds the wealth (income) effect, they will supply more labor to the market.

Finally, it has been observed that there is a positive correlation between weeks worked per year and hours worked per week.[8] Since those who work more hours per week have higher weekly wages, a positive correlation between hours per week and weeks per year, holding investment in human capital constant, results in a positive correlation of weekly wages with weeks worked. Note, however, that this is not a statistical artifact—this correlation is related to human capital analysis and labor supply theory. Those human capital and labor supply forces that encourage a greater labor supply in terms of weeks also encourage a greater labor supply in terms of hours.

Let us define γ as the elasticity of annual earnings with respect to the fraction of weeks worked per year. Human capital theory, upward rising labor supply curves, and the positive correlation of hours worked per week with weeks worked per year all predict that those with higher weekly wages work more weeks per year. This implies a γ greater than unity. The backward bending labor supply curve and cyclical or seasonal sensitivity of employment predict that those with higher weekly wages have a larger annual income but work fewer weeks per year. They predict a γ greater than zero but less than unity.[9] Empirically, Mincer found $\gamma = 1.17$, which was significantly greater than unity, for white nonfarm, nonstudent

---

7. The third of Adam Smith's five points which "make up for a small pecuniary gain in some employments, and counterbalance a great one in others" is "the constancy or inconstancy of employment in them." (*Wealth of Nations*, Modern Library Edition, 1937, p. 100.) The effect of seasonality of employment on weekly wages is analyzed in Chapter 2 of this study.

8. Victor Fuchs, *Differentials in Hourly Earnings by Region and City Size, 1959*, NBER, Occasional Paper 101, p. 4.

9. Define Y as observed annual earnings, Y' as full year employment earnings, and W as the number of weeks worked. If those with higher weekly wages work more weeks during the year, $Y'/52 > Y/W$, where $W < 52$. Since

males with earnings from the 1/1,000 sample of the 1960 Census of Population.[10]

Thus, the human capital earnings function is written as:

$$Y_N = Y_0 \left[\prod_{j=1}^{N} (1 + r_j k_j) (1 - k_{N+1}) \right] (WW)^\gamma, \qquad (6\text{-}5)$$

where γ is the elasticity of annual earnings with respect to the fraction of weeks worked. Weeks worked and γ are not simply standardizing variables, but, rather, integral parts of the human capital model and labor supply theory.

EMPIRICAL FORMULATION

The human capital earnings function in equation (6-5) relates annual net earnings (Y_N) to the number of periods of investment (N), the fraction of potential earnings which was invested in the past ($k_j, j = 1, \ldots, N$), the fraction of potential earnings invested in the current year (k_{N+1}), the fraction of weeks worked during the year (WW), and the relation between weekly wages and weeks worked (γ). This functional form, however, is not desirable for several reasons. First, with the exception of N and WW, these variables are not readily measurable. Second, linear models are easier to estimate empirically than nonlinear models. Third, if the variance of both sides of the equation is computed, the variance of income is a function of the variance of a product of terms. However, interest in income inequality is greater for relative than for absolute inequality. Relative inequality is devoid of units and therefore

---

$Y = Y' \, (ww)^\gamma$, where $ww = \dfrac{W}{52}, \dfrac{Y'}{52} > \dfrac{Y' \, (W/52)^\gamma}{W}$ or $(52)^{\gamma-1} > (W)^{\gamma-1}$. This holds if $\gamma > 1$.

If those with higher weekly wages work fewer weeks per year, $Y'/52 < Y/W$ where $W < 52$. Then, $\dfrac{Y'}{52} < \dfrac{Y' \, (W/52)^\gamma}{W}$ or $(W)^{\gamma-1} > (52)^{\gamma-1}$. This holds if $\gamma < 1$. However, if annual earnings are higher for those with more weeks of employment, $Y' > Y$ or $Y' > Y' \, (W/52)^\gamma$. For $W < 52$, this is true only if $\gamma > 0$. Thus, if those with higher weekly wages have higher annual incomes but work fewer weeks, $0 < \gamma < 1$.

10. This value—and further references to Mincer's data—are taken from the 1972 mimeographed version of his *Schooling, Experience, and Earnings*. The data in the 1974 version differ only slightly from the earlier ones and do not alter the substance of my arguments.

facilitates intercountry comparisons. Moreover, computing the variance of a product of terms is more difficult than computing a sum of terms.[11] Thus, the algebraic manipulations of equation (6-5) that follow are designed to convert the equation into a functional form which facilitates the theoretical and empirical analysis of income distribution.[12]

Taking the natural logarithm of both sides of equation (6-5), and using the relation that the natural log of one plus a small number is approximately equal to that small number,[13] we obtain (approximately)

$$\ln Y_N = \ln Y_0 + \sum_{j=1}^{N} r_j k_j + \ln(1 - k_{N+1}) + \gamma(\ln WW). \quad (6\text{-}6)$$

The N years of training can be decomposed into S years of schooling followed by $N - S$ years of postschool training if it is assumed that schooling precedes on-the-job training. The $T = N - S$ years of postschool training can also be approximated as $T = A - S - 5$, where A is age and it is assumed the worker is investing in training in each of the years since the age at which he left school ($S + 5$ years). If we assume that during the years of schooling the opportunity costs and direct costs of schooling are approximately equal to the potential or gross earnings of students,[14] we can write $k_j = 1$ for the schooling years. Let us also assume that the rate of return from schooling is constant for an individual for all levels of schooling.[15] Then we can write

$$\sum_{j=1}^{N} r_j k_j = rS + \sum_{j=S+1}^{N} r_j k_j.$$

---

11. See Leo Goodman, "On the Exact Variance of a Product," *Journal of the American Statistical Association*, December 1960, pp. 708–713.

12. These manipulations of the postschool training variables were developed in Mincer, *Schooling, Experience, and Earnings*, Part 1, and reported in Chiswick and Mincer, "Time Series Changes in Income Inequality," *Journal of Political Economy, Supplement*, May-June 1973.

13. $\ln(1 + r_j k_j) \approx r_j k_j$. Since r_j is likely to be in the neighborhood of 10 to 20 per cent, and k_j is not likely to be greater than unity, $r_j k_j$ is sufficiently small to make the approximation quite close.

14. Becker, *Human Capital*, Chapter 4; and G. Hanoch, "An Economic Analysis of Earnings and Schooling," *Journal of Human Resources*, Summer 1967, pp. 310–329.

15. There is some empirical support for this assumption. Using data for white nonfarm, nonstudent males with earnings, Mincer found no evidence of a higher (or lower) rate of return for higher levels of schooling when weeks worked and experience were held constant. (*Schooling, Experience, and Earnings*, Part 2.)

To evaluate the postschool training expression $\sum_{j=S+1}^{N} r_j k_j$ we must make some assumption concerning the temporal behavior of k_j, the fraction of gross earnings invested. There are several reasons for believing that k_j declines over time.[16] First, if labor market experience raises the productivity of time devoted to employment more than that devoted to the production of additional training, the opportunity cost of time invested in experience rises with additional experience. This decreases the profitability of additional investment. Second, additional experience reduces the length of the remaining working life and consequently the profitability of investment. Finally, if an investment is profitable, it is more profitable (i.e., has the highest net present value) the earlier it is undertaken. The decline with experience of the fraction of potential earnings that is invested is consistent with the observed concavity of the age-earnings profile.

Thus, it is assumed that k declines monotonically over a lifetime. For simplicity's sake, we assume that k_j declines linearly: $k_j = k_0 (1 - T/T^*)$, where T is the number of years of postschool training, T^* is the number of years of positive net investment, and k_0 is the fraction of potential income invested in the initial ($T = 0$) year of postschool training. T^* is a large number. Converting to continuous time,

$$\int_0^T r_j k_j \, dT = (r_j k_0)T - \left(\frac{r_j k_0}{2T^*}\right) T^2 , \qquad (6\text{-}7)$$

and the effect on the log of earnings of past investments in experience is a parabolic function of years of experience (T).

By assuming k_j declines linearly with experience, the term $\ln (1 - k_j)$ can be evaluated as a function of experience (T) by a Taylor expansion. Using a Taylor expansion evaluated around T^* taken to the third term, and ignoring the remainder,

$$\ln (1 - k_{T+1}) = - k_0 \left(1 + \frac{k_0}{2}\right) + \left(\frac{k_0}{T^*}\right) (1 + k_0) T + \left[\frac{- k_0^2}{2 (T^*)^2}\right] T^2 .$$
$$(6\text{-}8)$$

Let us assume that variations across individuals in Y_0, k_0, T^* and γ appear in a residual U_i. Then, using the subscript i to desig-

16. See Yoram Ben-Porath, "The Production of Human Capital and the Life Cycle of Earnings," *Journal of Political Economy*, August 1967, pp. 352–365; and Gary Becker, *Human Capital and Personal Income Distribution*, Ann Arbor, 1967.

nate individuals, combining the several previous steps, and rearranging terms,

$$
\ln (Y_i) = \left[\ln Y_0 - k_0 \left(1 + \frac{k_0}{2} \right) \right] + r_i S_i + \left[r_i^* k_0 + \frac{k_0}{T^*} (1 + k_0) \right] T_i
$$
$$
- \left[\frac{r_i^* k_0 T^* + k_0^2}{2 (T^*)^2} \right] T_i^2 + \gamma \, (\ln WW_i) + U_i, \tag{6-9}
$$

where r_i is the rate of return from schooling and r_i^* is the rate of return from postschool training.

Equation (6-9) expresses the log of income as a linear function of years of schooling, years of experience, years of experience squared, and the log of weeks worked. While data are generally not available for dollar investments in schooling or postschool training, data for investments measured in years exist in abundance. Indeed, much of public policy appears to be framed in terms of years of investment rather than dollar investments.

In this monograph the variable "experience squared" (T^2) is deleted for two reasons. First, in the analysis of income level, the mean levels of experience and experience squared are so highly correlated that multicollinearity becomes a problem. Second, in the analysis of income inequality, retaining experience squared necessitates computing the third and fourth moments of experience, but the additional explanatory power is not likely to be large. However, deleting the term experience squared biases the slope coefficient of experience downward. When experience squared is deleted, the coefficient of experience is designated r_i'. The term r_i' is the slope of the experience log income profile.

The variable experience (T) is replaced by age minus schooling minus five. Public policy can change the distribution of schooling independently of age, but if it does so, the distribution of experience is necessarily altered. There is also more concern with the distribution of earnings by age group than by experience group. Thus, it would be desirable to express earnings as a function of schooling and age (A). Fortunately, this is easy to do if we assume $T = A - S - 5$. The assumption, however, that an individual is continuously acquiring experience in the labor market after leaving school means that this formulation of the model is more relevant to an analysis of the income of males than to that of females, since the latter frequently have long periods of absence from the labor force.[17]

---

17. For an analysis of the effect of labor market experience on the earnings of women, see Jacob Mincer and Solomon Polachek, "Family Investments in Human Capital: Earnings of Women," *Journal of Political Economy*, *Supplement*, March 1974, pp. S76–S109.

With these modifications, equation (6-9) becomes

$$\ln Y_i = X + r_i S_i + r_i' (A_i - S_i - 5) + \gamma (\ln WW_i) + U_i, \quad (6\text{-}10)$$

where X is the intercept and U_i is a residual. The residual, U_i, reflects individual differences in earnings for given levels of schooling, rates of return from schooling, age, and employment. It includes the effects of differences in the dollar amounts of post-school training in each year of experience, the nonpecuniary aspects of jobs, nonlabor income (if this is included in the income concept), luck, and errors of measurement, among other variables. We assume that the residual is a random variable.

For the purpose of human capital analysis, equation (6-10) has several desirable features. First, the available data sources permit us to measure investments in human capital in terms of years of schooling and years of labor market experience rather than dollar investments, and equation (6-10) relates income to years of training. Second, since income is more closely approximated by a log normal than a normal distribution, the structure in equation (6-10) will have residuals which are more homoscedastic than the structure in equation (6-5). Finally, there appears to be more interest in the relative than in the absolute level and inequality of income, and equation (6-10) is better suited to an investigation of relative income. Thus, this equation shall serve as the basic human capital earnings function in my analysis of the income level and inequality of adult males.

In the following two chapters the mean and variance of both sides of the human capital earnings function will be computed. Computing the mean of a product of two variables ($r_i S_i$ and $r_i' T_i$) is easy. This is not true, however, of the variance of a product of two random variables, unless these variables are statistically independent.[18] For the analysis of income inequality, the plausible assumptions will be made that r_i is independent of S_i and r_i' is independent of T_i. There is both theoretical and empirical support for these assumptions.[19]

For a nontechnical analysis, see also Council of Economic Advisers, *Economic Report of the President, 1974*, Washington, D.C. 1974, pp. 154–161.

18. Goodman, "On the Exact Variance of a Product," December 1960.

19. The theoretical support relies on the model dealing with supply and demand for funds to be invested in human capital. Individuals with greater "training ability" have, for a given cost of funds, a higher average and marginal rate of return, and thus tend to invest more. Those with lower levels of wealth, holding "training ability" constant, invest more but have a lower average and marginal rate of return. If greater wealth and greater "ability" are positively correlated, the relation between level of investment and marginal and average rates of return is ambiguous. Empirical support is found in the

RACIAL DIFFERENCES IN THE AGE-INCOME PROFILE

Much of the analysis of racial differences in the level of income in Chapter 7 and of income inequality in Chapter 8 will focus on the parameter r' in equation (6-10), the slope of the cross-sectional age–log-of-income profile, when schooling and weeks worked are held constant. A cross-sectional profile represents the income of persons at different ages at a moment in time (for example, the year 1959). This is shown by the curve BB in Figure 6-1. The slope of the profile is the per cent change in income as we look at older persons.

There is abundant evidence from many different data sets that the slope of the cross-sectional age–log-of-income profile is flatter for nonwhite males than for white males.[20] A flatter cross-sectional profile can occur for one or both of the following reasons. First, it may be that nonwhites have a flatter cohort profile. A cohort profile is obtained by observing the income of a group (cohort) of individuals as they age. Three cohort profiles ($A_1 A_1$, $A_2 A_2$, $A_3 A_3$) for three different age groups are shown in Figure 6-1. A nonwhite cohort could have a flatter age-income profile than a white cohort because of the former's smaller investments in postschool training or their lower rates of return from this training. This may occur if nonwhites invest in less postschool training because of a lower level of wealth or in a poorer quality of schooling, if they are discriminated against in training opportunities, or if nonwhites who acquire postschool training are subject to more wage and occupational discrimination than less well-trained nonwhites. Ceteris paribus, a set of flatter cohort profiles would translate into a flatter cross-sectional profile.

Second, nonwhites may have a flatter cross-sectional profile

---

absence of a significant partial effect for schooling squared when the log of earnings is regressed on schooling, schooling squared, experience, and the log of weeks worked. See Becker, *Human Capital and the Personal Distribution of Income*; Becker and Chiswick, "Education and the Distribution of Earnings," *American Economic Review*, May 1966, pp. 358–369; and Mincer, *Schooling, Experience, and Earnings*, Part 2.

20. See, for example, Jacob Mincer, "On-the-Job Training: Costs, Returns, and Implications," *Journal of Political Economy*, Supplement, October 1962, pp. 50–79; Thomas Johnson, "Returns from Investment in Human Capital," *American Economic Review*, September 1970, pp. 546–560; Finis Welch, "Black-White Differences in the Returns to Schooling," *American Economic Review*, December 1973, pp. 893–907; and Council of Economic Advisers, *Economic Report of the President, 1974*, Washington, D.C., 1974, pp. 150–154.

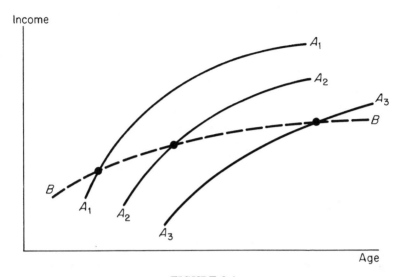

FIGURE 6-1
Hypothetical Cross-Section and Cohort Age-Income
Profiles for Males

than whites because the height of the cohort profiles is rising faster over time for young nonwhites than for young whites. This could occur if there has been a secular decline in discrimination against nonwhites, particularly young nonwhites, in the labor market (in wages or in occupation) or in the quality of schooling. Recent studies suggest that there has been, indeed, a decline in labor market and school quality discrimination.[21]

---

21. The ratio of nonwhite to white expenditures per student in public schools in the South decreased dramatically from 1890 to 1915, but increased thereafter. For example, in Georgia the ratios of nonwhite to white expenditures per student were as follows:

Year	Ratio
About 1890	0.67
1915	0.21
1930	0.22
1945	0.38
1954	0.61

See Richard B. Freeman, "Labor Market Discrimination: Analysis, Findings, and Problems," paper presented at Econometric Society meeting of December 1972, Table 7. Similar evidence is reported in Finis Welch, "Black-White Differences in Returns to Schooling," *American Economic Review*, December 1973, pp. 893–907. In addition, Welch reports in the same article that in the 1960s the ratio of the nonwhite to white rate of return from schooling is higher for younger cohorts. This could be due to reduced discrimination in schooling or in the labor market.

TABLE 6-1

Income of Nonwhite Males as Percentage of Income of White Males,
1949, 1959, and 1969
(per cent)

Type of Income by Age Group	1949	1959	1969
Annual income:			
25–34 years	57	57	65
35–44 years	48	52	56
45–54 years	46	49	53
55–64 years	45	48	51
Weekly income:			
25–34 years	61	61	67
35–44 years	52	57	58
45–54 years	48	52	55
55–64 years	47	51	53

Note: Data for 1949 and 1959 relate to races other than white, data for 1969 relate to blacks only.
Sources: Council of Economic Advisers, *Economic Report of the President, 1974*, Washington, D.C., 1974, Table 39, p. 152.

Table 6-1 presents data on the income of nonwhite males as a percentage of the income of white males by age group for the three years 1949, 1959, and 1969. The ratio of the nonwhite to white cross-sectional age-income profile is obtained by reading down the columns of the table. The data suggest a flatter cross-sectional profile for nonwhites than for whites. Reading across the rows reveals a rise in the ratio of nonwhite to white incomes over time (with age held constant). That is, cohort profiles for nonwhites are rising at a faster rate than for whites.

If we read down the diagonals of Table 6-1 we follow a cohort as it ages. The data suggest that, as a cohort ages, the ratio of nonwhite to white income does not decline, or declines at a much slower rate than the cross-sectional profile. Thus, the flatter nonwhite cross-sectional profile is only partially due to a possibly somewhat flatter cohort profile.

7

The Level of Income

How does the level of average income relate to the distributions of schooling, age (experience), and employment in a region? This question is explored in the following pages, in an analysis that applies the human capital earnings function (equation 6-10) to data for the United States and Canada.[1]

Regional differences in the level of income in the two countries have received considerable attention from economists, even aside from the economic development literature.[2] This analysis differs from the others by taking an explicit human capital approach to the examination of state differences in the income (or earnings) of adult males. Most U.S. regional studies in this subject area are concerned with explaining differences among all (or white) males, or the white-nonwhite income ratio. Here, in addi-

---

1. See Appendix A-2 for a description of the data.

2. For example, see Frank Hanna, *State Income Differentials, 1919–1954,* Duke, 1959; Victor Fuchs, *Differentials in Hourly Earnings by Region and City Size, 1959,* Occasional Paper 101, NBER, 1967; Gerald W. Scully, "The North-South Manufacturing Wage Differential, 1869-1919," *Journal of Regional Science,* Vol. 11, No. 2, 1971, pp. 235-252, and "Inter-State Wage Differentials: A Cross-Section Analysis," *American Economic Review,* 1969, pp. 759-773; A. Hurwitz and C. P. Stallings, "Interregional Differentials in Per Capita Real Income Changes," *Regional Income,* Studies in Income and Wealth, Vol. 21, NBER, 1957; and S. E. Chernick, *Interregional Disparities in Income,* Staff Study No. 14, Economic Council of Canada, August 1966. For an international study, see Anne O. Krueger, "Factor Endowments and Per Capita Income Differences Among Countries," *Economic Journal,* September 1968, pp. 641-659.

tion to these variables, interstate differences in income levels among nonwhites are also explicitly examined.

Using the human capital earnings function to study income levels has various advantages. It suggests which variables are relevant, indicates a form for entering these variables, and provides an economic interpretation of the slope coefficients and, consequently, testable hypotheses about the observed distributions.

The intraregional microequation presented in Chapter 6 is converted into an equation to explain interregional differences in the level of income—the mean log of income or the log of the geometric mean—by computing the mean value of both sides of the microrelation. The characteristics of this model are then explored, followed by the empirical analyses of interregional differences in the income level of white and nonwhite males in the United States and of nonfarm males in Canada. Finally, a summary concludes the chapter.

STATISTICAL IMPLEMENTATION OF THE MODEL

The Level of Income Equation

Let us recall that in Chapter 6 the human capital earnings function was converted to the form

$$\ln Y_i = X + r_i S_i + r_i' (A_i - S_i - 5) + \gamma (\ln WW_i). \qquad (7\text{-}1)$$

This equation relates the years of schooling (S), years of experience ($A_i - S_i - 5$), and log of weeks worked ($\ln WW_i$) of an individual to the natural log of his income, or earnings. Rearranging the experience term,

$$\ln Y_i = (X - 5r_i') + (r_i - r_i') S_i + r_i' A_i + \gamma (\ln WW_i). \qquad (7\text{-}2)$$

If it is assumed that the coefficients of S_i and A_i are random parameters but the coefficient of $\ln WW_i$ is constant across individuals, computing the mean value of equation (7-2),[3]

$$
\begin{aligned}
(\overline{\ln Y}) = {}& X - 5\bar{r}' + (\overline{r - r'}) \, \overline{S} + [R_{r-r',S} SD \, (r - r')] \, SD \, (S) \\
& + \bar{r}' \, \overline{A} + [R_{r_i',A} \, SD \, (r')] \, SD \, (A) \qquad (7\text{-}3) \\
& + \gamma \, (\overline{\ln WW}),
\end{aligned}
$$

---

3. If A_i and B_i are variables with a nonzero correlation ($R_{A,B}$),

$$(\overline{AB}) = (\overline{A}) \, (\overline{B}) + \text{Cov} \, (A,B) = (\overline{A}) \, (\overline{B}) + R_{A,B} \, SD \, (A) \, SD \, (B).$$

where *SD* designates standard deviation and *R* is the correlation coefficient.[4]

Equation 7-3 relates the mean value of the natural log of income in a region to the distributions of schooling, age, and employment in that region. The mean of the log of a variable is the same as the log of its geometric mean.[5] Thus, its use represents an analysis of regional differences in the geometric mean of income. Converting equation 7-3 to the form of a multiple regression and adding a random residual, U_i,

$$(\overline{\ln Y}) = b_0 + b_1 \overline{S} + b_2 SD\ (S) + b_3 \overline{A} + b_4 SD\ (A) + b_5 (\overline{\ln WW}) + U_i.$$

$$(7\text{-}4)$$

The economic interpretations of the coefficients are:

$$b_0 = (X - 5\overline{r}') \qquad\qquad b_3 = \overline{r}'$$
$$b_1 = (\overline{r_i - r_i'}) \qquad\qquad b_4 = R_{r',A} SD\ (r') \qquad (7\text{-}5)$$
$$b_2 = R_{r-r_i',S} SD\ (r - r') \qquad b_5 = \gamma,$$

where r_i and r_i' are the *i*th person's rate of return from schooling (assuming $k = 1$ for the years of schooling) and the slope of his experience log income profile, respectively, and γ is the elasticity of earnings with respect to the fraction of weeks worked. If the regression slope coefficients are constant across the states, or if they are random variables independent of the explanatory variables, the computed slope coefficients are not biased.[6]

Equation (7-4) serves as the basic regression equation in the

---

4. An alternative approach which does not explicitly delete the squared experience term of equation (6-9) was tried but discarded because of multicollinearity. If

$$\ln Y = a_0 + a_1 T + a_2 T^2 + \cdots,$$

and the coefficients are assumed constant,

$$(\overline{\ln Y}) = a_0 + a_1 \overline{T} + a_2 (\overline{T^2}) + \cdots,$$

where $(\overline{T^2}) = (\overline{T})^2 + \text{Var}\ (T)$. The simple correlation between $\overline{T}$ and $(\overline{T^2})$ is 0.9969 for data on males in the continental states. (See Appendix A-2 for source.)

5. $\ln[GM\ (Y)] = \ln \left[\left(\prod_{i=1}^{N} y_i\right)^{1/N}\right] = \dfrac{1}{N} \sum \ln Y = (\overline{\ln Y}).$

6. In the case of one explanatory variable, there is no bias if the slope coefficient is not correlated with either the independent variable or the square of the independent variable. If $Y_i = b_0 + b_i X_i + U_i$ where U_i is a random residual, $Y_i = b_0 + \overline{b} X_i + [(b_i - \overline{b})X_i + U_i]$. The mean value of $b_i - \overline{b}$ is zero. Then, $\text{Cov}\ [X_i, (b_i - \overline{b})X_i + U_i]$ equals zero if b_i is not correlated with X_i or X_i^2. For a proof, see Chapter 3, footnote 16.

analysis of state and provincial differences in the level of income and earnings of males. It does not, however, adjust for the effects of race differences on incomes.

Let Y^* be the income of a white worker of a given level of schooling, age, and employment. If nonwhites receive proportionately lower ($100d$ per cent lower) incomes, we could describe the income of any male of a given schooling-age-employment class by

$$Y_i = Y_i^* \, (1 - d)^{(NW_i)}, \tag{7-6}$$

where NW_i is a dichotomous variable taking the value of 1 for a nonwhite and zero for a white individual. Then,[7] for any class or cell,

$$\ln Y_i = \ln Y^* - (d) \, (NW_i), \tag{7-7}$$

and the cell mean would be

$$(\overline{\ln Y}) = (\overline{\ln Y^*}) - dp, \tag{7-8}$$

where p is the per cent nonwhite (the mean of the variable NW_i).[8] Thus, in the all-male analysis, the variable nonwhite (p) per cent of the male labor force is added to measure the partial effect of the relative presence of nonwhites on the overall level of income.

The Variables

Equation (7-4) is a theoretical equation that relates the level of income to a set of human capital and employment variables. The variables used in the actual statistical implementation of the equation and the predictions of the effects of each of the explanatory variables are discussed in the following pages.

The Dependent Variables

The dependent variables for the United States studied here are the average natural logs of (a) the 1959 income of males, age twenty-five and over, with income, and (b) the 1959 earnings of males, age fourteen and over, with earnings. Neither measure is ideal, since the model pertains to the earnings of males who have completed their schooling and the explanatory variables are computed for males between twenty-five and sixty-four years of age.[9]

---

7. The relation $\ln (1 - d) \approx -d$ if d is small.

8. If d is not constant across states but a variable independent of p, equation (7-8) still holds, but d is now interpreted as the mean value of the per cent difference in income.

9. See Appendix A-2 for definitions and computation of independent and dependent variables.

Average Schooling

The slope coefficient of the level of schooling, b_1, is expected to be positive and significant. The coefficient is hypothesized to be smaller for nonwhites than for whites. This hypothesis is based on the finding of a lower rate of return from schooling and a lower slope of the cross-sectional experience-earnings profile for nonwhites.[10]

Standard Deviation of Schooling

If individual differences in the rate of return from schooling (r_i) and in the slope of the cross-sectional age-log income profile (r_i') exist, the sign of the slope coefficient of the standard deviation of schooling, b_2, depends on the simple correlation of S_i with $(r_i - r_i')$. A priori arguments do not predict a sign for the correlation coefficient, but there is empirical evidence that suggests it is positive.[11]

Average Age

The model predicts a positive slope coefficient, b_3, for the level of age. Holding schooling and weeks worked constant, a higher level of age implies a greater number of years of experience or postschool training. The greater the postschool training financed by the worker, the lower are observed earnings during the early years of experience and the higher observed earnings in subsequent years. Thus, the level of income is expected to rise with age.[12]

Suppose, however, that there are no investments in postschool training ($k_0 = 0$ in equation 6-9)—age would have no effect on in-

---

10. For empirical evidence on the lower nonwhite rate of return from schooling around 1960, see Gary S. Becker, *Human Capital*, 2nd. ed., New York, 1974, and Finis Welch, "Black-White Differences in Returns to Schooling," *American Economic Review*, December 1973, pp. 893–907. For empirical evidence on the lower slope in the cross section of the experience-earnings profile for nonwhites, see Chapter 6 of this volume, p. 116–118.

11. Using microdata for the country as a whole, the slope coefficient of schooling from a regression of log of earnings on schooling is approximately the same when the regression is computed for all age groups or within narrow age groups. When log of earnings is regressed on years of low, median, and high levels of schooling for all age groups—but experience is not held constant—the slope coefficient increases with the level of schooling. These findings suggest a positive correlation between S_i and $(r_i - r_i')$. See Chapter 4, Table 4-1.

12. This is reinforced by the accumulation of nonhuman assets with age when income, rather than earnings, is the dependent variable.

come. Now let us introduce the depreciation or obsolescence of the human capital acquired by schooling and the pure labor component of income: here one expects a negative relation between age and income. Suppose, in addition, the quality of a given year of schooling rising over time or the extent of labor market discrimination against new entrants falling over time: in this case, too, one would expect a negative association between age and income.

A positive slope coefficient for age level is predicted for all males and white males, but a lower coefficient is predicted for nonwhites than for whites. This last point is based on assuming a lower level of investment in postschool training by nonwhites, as well as a secular rise in the quality of schooling and in job opportunities for young nonwhites relative to young whites due to a secular decrease in discrimination.[13]

The Standard Deviation of Age

Holding the level of age constant, the model predicts that a larger variance in age generates a lower level of income, since those who are older have lower slopes to their age-log income profile (i.e., A_i and r_i' are negatively correlated).[14] The effect on the level of income of the negative correlation $R_{r'A}$ depends on the dispersion of r'. The larger the dispersion of r', the lower (i.e., more negative) is the slope coefficient of the inequality of age.[15] Since it appears that nonwhites have a flatter cross-sectional age-income

---

13. See the discussion in Chapter 6 of racial differences in the slope of the age-income profile.

14. Theoretically as well as empirically, age-income profiles are concave; income rises with age, but at a decreasing rate.

15. The effect of a negative correlation of A_i and r_i' can be clarified by an example. Suppose we have two situations, each with two persons who, at age forty, have $\ln Y = 10$.

In situation A, one person is forty-one, and has $\ln Y = 11$ (slope = .10), while the other is thirty-nine, and has $\ln Y = 8$ (slope = .20). Mean $\ln Y$ is 9.5, and there is a negative correlation of age with the slope of the age-log income profile.

In situation B, one person is forty-one, and has $\ln Y = 14$ (slope = .40), while the other is thirty-nine, and has $\ln Y = 8$ (slope = .20). Mean $\ln Y$ is 11.0, and there is a positive correlation between age and the slope of the age-log income profile.

For the same level and dispersion in age, the level of income is lower in the situation in which the correlation of age (A_i) and the slope of the age-log income profile (r_i') is negative.

For a given negative correlation between A_i and r_i', the income level is lower the larger the dispersion in age. Suppose the slope of the age-log in-profile, the absolute dispersion of the slopes of their age-log of income profiles is likely to be smaller and their slope coefficient of the standard deviation of age higher (less negative) than for whites.

Thus, a negative slope coefficient of the standard deviation of age, b_4, is hypothesized for all males and white males, and a less negative one (i.e., with lower absolute value) is hypothesized for nonwhites than for whites.

Furthermore, because of the accumulation of nonlabor income with age, the slope of the age-log income profile does not decline with age as rapidly as the slope of the age-log earnings profile. The slope coefficient of the standard deviation of age will, therefore, be less negative (i.e., smaller absolute value) in the income than in the earnings analysis.

Average Log of Weeks Worked

The model yields the mean log of weeks worked as the employment variable to be used for explaining interregional differences in the level (average log) of income. The regression slope coefficient is $b_5 = \gamma$, where γ is the elasticity of earnings with respect to the fraction of weeks worked. Computed values of γ shall be tested against the hypotheses that the population values are 1.0 and 1.17. A coefficient of unity implies that weekly wages are not correlated with the number of weeks worked,[16] while 1.17 was the value Mincer obtained in a microdata analysis of the 1960 1/1,000 sample.[17]

A third hypothesis is that γ is lower for nonwhites than for whites. This is based on two interrelated points. First, nonwhites may obtain less general training, and presumably also less specific training, than do whites. Therefore, a major factor tending to pro-

---

come profile for ages above forty is .05, but .10 for ages below forty. At age forty, $\ln Y = 10$.

Situation A		Situation B	
Age	ln Y (approx.)	Age	ln Y (approx.)
39	9.0	38	8.0
41	10.5	42	11.0
Mean	9.75	Mean	9.50

16. See the discussion in Chapter 6.

17. See Chapter 6, footnote 10. Although Mincer's estimate of $\gamma = 1.17$ is a sample value and therefore has a standard error, the standard error is small, and will be assumed to equal zero. His data cover nonfarm white males with earnings, not enrolled in school, and fourteen years of age or older.

duce a γ greater than unity may be weaker for nonwhites. Second, nonwhite males experience greater seasonality in employment than white males.[18] Due to the forces of competition, seasonal jobs offer higher weekly wages for fewer weeks of employment per year, and hence tend to generate a γ less than unity.[19]

The coefficient γ is expected to be lower in the income regressions than in the earnings regressions. Income data contain nonlabor income, and, with the weekly wage held constant, higher nonlabor incomes tend to reduce the number of weeks worked. This factor would reduce the magnitude of γ, although the causation is from income to work.[20]

This hypothesis also implies that, given the smaller nonlabor income of nonwhite males, the difference between γ estimated from earnings and that estimated from income should be smaller for nonwhite males than for white males.

Race and Region

In the all-male analysis, a race composition variable, the nonwhite percentage of the male labor force, p, is introduced to capture the (average) effect of racial differences in income within schooling, age, and employment cells. This variable has a negative partial slope coefficient if nonwhites have lower weekly incomes, with schooling and age held constant.

A region dummy variable, *NSD*, where *NSD* = 1 in the seventeen Southern states, is also introduced to test for the persistence of regional differences in the level of income. A race-region linear

---

18. Indices of seasonality exist for employment of white and nonwhite males of twenty and over, but not cross-classified by occupation, schooling, or age. The factors for 1959 are:

	White	Nonwhite		White	Nonwhite
January	98.10	96.61	July	101.10	100.99
February	98.10	96.41	August	101.20	100.91
March	98.60	98.10	September	101.00	102.31
April	99.50	99.29	October	101.00	103.10
May	100.40	101.09	November	100.50	101.71
June	101.20	100.91	December	99.40	98.59

The sum of the absolute deviations from 100 is 12.7 for white males and 22.1 for nonwhite males. The monthly factors were computed from the ratio of "Original Data" to "Seasonally Adjusted Data" for employed white and nonwhite males of twenty and over in 1959. See unpublished Bureau of Labor Statistics employment data (1972), and letter to author from Hyman B. Kaitz, Bureau of Labor Statistics, January 5, 1973.

19. See Chapter 2.

20. The distributions of schooling and age can be thought of as controlling for the weekly wage.

interaction variable ($p \cdot NSD$) is included to test for regional differences in the effect of race composition on the level of income.[21]

Summary

The preceding discussion has shown how the human capital earnings function of Chapter 6 (equation 6-10) can be converted into a relation between the level of income and the distribution of schooling, age, and employment. The dependent variable, the average log of income, is a linear function of the levels of schooling, age, and the log of weeks worked, and of the standard deviations of schooling and age. The slope coefficients have economic meaning.

The dependent variables are the average log of (a) the income of males of twenty-five years and over and (b) the earnings of males of fourteen years and over. The independent variables are for males between the ages of twenty-five and sixty-four. The slope coefficient of average schooling is expected to be positive, but lower for nonwhites than for whites because of the former's lower rate of return from schooling and flatter cross-sectional age-log income profile. The slope of the standard deviation of schooling is expected to be positive on the basis of microdata analysis.

With schooling held constant, higher levels of age imply higher levels of experience, and hence higher incomes. The slope coefficient of average age is expected to be lower for nonwhites than for whites, since nonwhite males have a flatter cross-sectional age-income profile. This may have occurred because nonwhites invest less in postschool training than whites and have experienced a greater secular rise in the quality of schooling and job opportunities than have young whites. The partial slope coefficient of the standard deviation of age is hypothesized to be negative because the slope of the age-log income profile declines with higher levels of experience.

The average log of weeks worked captures the effects on the dependent variable of differences in employment level. The computed regression coefficient (γ) will be tested against alternative hypotheses about the population value. In addition, γ is hypothesized to be lower for nonwhites than whites, and lower in the income analyses than in the earnings analyses.

---

21. If $(\overline{\ln Y}) = a + b_6 p + b_7 NSD + b_8 p \cdot NSD$, then $\dfrac{\partial\,(\overline{\ln Y})}{\partial p} = b_6 +$ $b_8 (NSD)$. If b_6 and b_8 are negative, an increase in the fraction nonwhite has a more depressing effect on the level of income in the South than in the North.

Three additional variables are included in the all-male analysis: a race (nonwhite per cent of the male labor force), region (North-South dummy variable), and race-region interaction term. These variables test for the effects of the relative number of nonwhites and the applicable region on interstate differences in the mean log of income.

To sum up, the hypothesized signs for the human capital and employment variables are the following:

Variable	Symbol	Hypothesized Sign
Average schooling	$\overline{S}$	+
Standard deviation of schooling	$SD(S)$	+
Average age	$\overline{A}$	+
Standard deviation of age	$SD(A)$	−
Average log of weeks worked	$(\overline{\ln WW})$	+

EMPIRICAL APPLICATION

The model developed above to explain interregional differences in the level of income (mean log of income)—equation 7-4—is applied here to interstate data for all males, white males, and nonwhite males in the United States, and to an interprovincial analysis for nonfarm males in Canada. The data sources are discussed in Appendix A-2.

U.S. Males

The regression results for the mean log of income or earnings for all males in the fifty states and the District of Columbia—to be referred to as the fifty-one states—appear in columns (1) and (2) of Table 7-1. The model has a high explanatory power for earnings ($\overline{R}^2 = .71$), but does less well for income ($\overline{R}^2 = .41$). All of the variables have the hypothesized sign, except for the average log of weeks worked in the income analysis.

For earnings, the level of schooling and the standard deviation of age are highly significant, while the level of age and the dispersion of schooling have significant positive effects at a 5 per cent level. In the income analysis, schooling level is the only significant variable. As was hypothesized earlier in this chapter, the effect of the dispersion in age is more negative and that of the level of weeks worked more positive in the earnings than in the income analysis, although the differences are not significant.

TABLE 7-1

Regression Results, Log of Geometric Mean of Income
or Earnings of All Males
(fifty-one states)

Independent Variables	Dependent Variables			
	Level of Income (1)	Level of Earnings (2)	Level of Income[a] (3)	Level of Earnings[a] (4)
$\bar{S}$	0.2504	0.2589	0.2764	0.2562
	(4.33)	(7.19)	(5.40)	(7.38)
$SD(S)$	0.1546	0.1457	0.1503	0.2206
	(1.18)	(1.79)	(1.15)	(2.51)
$\bar{A}$	0.0429	0.0658	0.0135	0.0569
	(0.69)	(1.70)	(0.25)	(1.56)
$SD(A)$	-0.3142	-0.5349	-0.0572	-0.3804
	(-1.35)	(-3.69)	(-0.26)	(-2.61)
$\overline{(\ln WW)}$	-0.6583	0.1824	-0.7291	-0.1126
	(-0.77)	(0.34)	(-0.95)	(-0.22)
p	-0.2651	-0.1747	0.3338	0.0498
	(-0.87)	(-0.92)	(1.11)	(0.25)
NSD	—	—	0.3332	0.0357
			(3.02)	(0.48)
$p \cdot NSD$	—	—	-1.8692	-0.7758
			(-4.10)	(-2.52)
Constant	—	—	0.7466	6.9272
			(0.27)	(3.65)
N	51	51	51	51
R^2	0.4778	0.7441	0.6293	0.7896
$\bar{R}^2$	0.4066	0.7091	0.5587	0.7495

Note: Student t-ratios are in parentheses.
Source: See Appendix A-2.
[a]Regional dummy and race-region interaction terms are added.
The covariances of the slope coefficients are:

	col. (3)	col. (4)
(p, NSD)	0.0116	0.0053
$(p, pNSD)$	-0.0653	-0.0298
$(NSD, pNSD)$	-0.0314	-0.0143

Regional dummy and race-region interaction terms are added
in columns (3) and (4) of Table 7-1. The adjusted coefficients of
determination are increased to .75 and .56 for earnings and income, respectively. In the earnings analysis, it is worth noting that
average age becomes nearly significant at the 5 per cent level and
that the dispersion in schooling becomes highly significant. There
are no noteworthy changes in the slope coefficients for income.

Of the race-region variables in the earnings equation, only the
interaction term is significant. It implies that in the North, differ-

ences in the percentage of nonwhites have no effect on the level of earnings. In the South, however, earnings are lower in states where a larger proportion of the male labor force is nonwhite. Phrased differently, for a given percentage nonwhite, with schooling, age, and employment held constant, earnings are lower in the South than in the North. Thus, a significant regional difference in earnings persists even after controlling for our human capital and employment variables. In the income analysis, the North-South dummy and the interaction term are significant. Assuming $p = .107$ (the average value for the fifty-one states), the model explains one-third of the regional difference in state means for income, and three-fourths for earnings.[22]

For purposes of comparison, the level of income equations, including the race and region terms, are also computed with Alaska and Hawaii deleted from the data (see Table 7-2). These two states have a large proportion of nonwhites, most of whom are nonblack. In spite of the loss of two degrees of freedom, the adjusted coefficient of determination increases five percentage points (to 0.80) for earnings and one percentage point (to 0.57) for income. In the earnings analysis, the levels of schooling, age, and employment and the dispersions in schooling and age have the expected signs and are significant (or nearly significant) at the 5 per cent level. In the income analysis, only the level of schooling is significant.

In the forty-nine–state analysis, the race, region, and race-region interaction variables are significant at the 10 per cent level. In the Northern states the level of earnings and income rises with the proportion of nonwhites, but this is not true in the South. Going from a Northern to a Southern state, assuming $p = .093$ (the mean value), decreases average earnings by 0.11 points. The human capital, employment, and race variables account for approximately 60 per cent of the North-South difference in the mean log of earnings when the analysis is restricted to the forty-nine coterminous states. Average income, however, is increased by a statistically insignificant .04 points. Thus, schooling level and

22. The observed mean values of the dependent variables (in thousand dollar units) are:

	$Av(\ln Y)$	$Av(\ln E)$
North	1.37	1.35
South	1.18	1.08
Difference	0.19	0.27

Source: Appendix A-2.

TABLE 7-2

Regression Results, Log of Geometric Mean of
Income or Earnings of All Males
(forty-nine states)

Independent Variables	Dependent Variables	
	Level of Income[a] (1)	Level of Earnings[a] (2)
$\overline{S}$	0.2529	0.2282
	(4.84)	(7.30)
$SD(S)$	0.0515	0.1442
	(0.35)	(1.65)
$\overline{A}$	-0.0056	0.0582
	(-0.09)	(1.62)
$SD(A)$	-0.0164	-0.3077
	(-0.08)	(-2.39)
$(\overline{\ln WW})$	-0.1866	1.0208
	(-0.19)	(1.75)
p	2.5466	2.7277
	(2.03)	(3.63)
NSD	0.4667	0.2116
	(3.51)	(2.66)
$p \cdot NSD$	-4.0262	-3.4702
	(-3.15)	(-4.53)
Constant	-0.4492	2.2039
	(-0.10)	(0.81)
N	49	49
R^2	0.6452	0.8343
$\overline{R}^2$	0.5742	0.8012

Note: Student t-ratios are in parentheses.
Source: See Appendix A-2.
[a]The covariants of the slope coefficients are:

p, NSD	0.1020	0.0366
$p, pNSD$	-0.0152	-0.5440
$NSD, pNSD$	-0.1210	-0.0433

race differences account for regional differences in the measure of income level.

The slope coefficient of average schooling, to be interpreted as the rate of return from schooling minus the average slope of the age-log income profile, appears to be biased upward.

The slope of the average log of weeks is lower than expected. It is less than unity in all but one of the regressions in Tables 7-1 and 7-2. The slope coefficient is significantly below unity in only one regression (Table 7-1, col. 3). The large standard error relative to the slope coefficient of the mean log of weeks worked appears to be due to the very small interstate variation in this variable for all males.[23]

To summarize: the model can statistically explain over 70 per cent of state differences in the level (log of the geometric mean) of earnings and a somewhat smaller proportion of differences in income. Higher levels of schooling and age and a greater inequality in schooling are associated with higher levels of earnings. A greater inequality of age is associated with a lower level of earnings, presumably because of the decline in the slope of the age-log income profile as age increases. The employment variable has a generally positive slope, but is generally not significant. The low slope coefficient and large standard error appear to be caused by the very small interstate variation in this variable. The variables all have the sign hypothesized by our model.

In the income analysis the relationships are weaker, especially as to level and inequality of age. The slope of the age-log income profile declines less with age than the slope of the age-log earnings profile, which may explain the differential results for the standard deviation of age. This lack of significance of the level of age is surprising.

In the continental North, when the other variables are held constant, a larger proportion of nonwhites than of whites is associated with either no change or a small increase in the level of earnings. This may be due to the concentration of Northern nonwhites in urban industrial areas. In the South, a greater proportion of nonwhites tends to be associated with lower average earnings. This could be due to the greater "ruralness" of Southern states with a larger fraction of nonwhites, or it could reflect a greater racial difference in weekly wages in the South. About 60 per cent of the South–non-South difference in earnings for the coterminous states is due to differences in the schooling, age, and employment variables. There is no significant regional difference for income (when the other variables specified by the model are held constant and the variable per cent nonwhite is given its mean value).

---

23. The interstate means, standard deviations, and coefficients of variation of $\ln WW$ for the forty-nine continental states and for the thirty-nine states for which race-specific data are available are as follows:

		Mean	SD	CV
49 States:	All Males	3.8022	0.0321	0.0084
	White Males	3.8114	0.0301	0.0079
39 States:	All Males	3.7997	0.0346	0.0091
	White Males	3.8113	0.0327	0.0086
	Nonwhite Males	3.6780	0.0807	0.0219

Source: Appendix A-2.

TABLE 7-3

Regression Results, Log of Geometric Mean
of Income or Earnings of White Males

Independent Variables	Dependent Variables			
	Level of Income[a] (1)	Level of Earnings[a] (2)	Level of Income[b] (3)	Level of Earnings[b] (4)
$\overline{S}$	0.2135	0.2506	0.2043	0.2656
	(4.29)	(8.26)	(3.19)	(7.38)
$SD(S)$	0.1694	0.1664	0.1432	0.1167
	(1.73)	(2.78)	(1.07)	(1.56)
$\overline{A}$	0.0762	0.0996	0.0774	0.0863
	(1.22)	(2.62)	(0.94)	(1.86)
$SD(A)$	-0.2840	-0.4657	-0.2726	-0.4928
	(-1.39)	(-3.73)	(-1.06)	(-3.41)
$(\overline{\ln WW})$	-1.1288	0.3561	-1.1913	0.0088
	(-1.17)	(0.60)	(-0.96)	(0.01)
Constant	2.6594	4.4588	2.9180	6.6790
N	49	49	39	39
R^2	0.3023	0.6750	0.2542	0.6916
$\overline{R}^2$	0.2212	0.6372	0.1413	0.6449

Note: Student t-ratios are in parentheses.
Source: See Appendix A-2.
[a] 49 observations.
[b] 39 observations.

U.S. White Males

This section presents the empirical analysis for white males, defined as white males in the thirty-nine continental states for which separate race-specific data exist in the 1960 Census of Population, and all males in the remaining ten continental states.[24] Table 7-3 contains the regression results for the level of earnings and income for the forty-nine and thirty-nine–state samples. The model's explanatory power is higher for earnings than income.[25] All of the variables have the expected sign, except for the insignificant "weeks worked" variable in the income analysis.

---

24. The ten states, and the per cent of males between twenty-five and sixty-four in 1960 who were nonwhite, are Idaho (1.5), Maine (0.7), Montana (3.6), Nevada (7.6), New Hampshire (0.5), North Dakota (2.0), Rhode Island (2.5), Utah (2.0), Vermont (0.2), and Wyoming (2.2).

25. Adjusted R^2 for white males:

	Income	Earnings
49 states:	.22	.63
39 states:	.14	.64

Source: Table 7-3.

For the earnings data, the four schooling and age variables are all significant at a 5 per cent level, except for the standard deviation of schooling in the smaller sample. On the income side, the only significant variables are the level of schooling and, for the forty-nine–state sample, the standard deviation of schooling.

The level of weeks of employment again does not differ from zero. Moreover, it is significantly lower than 1.0 and 1.17 for income, but not for earnings. Indeed, the coefficient is negative in the income data. The lower partial slope coefficient for the income analysis may be demonstrating the adverse effect of nonlabor incomes on the labor supply to the market when the weekly wage is held constant. The small interstate variation in the weeks worked may also be responsible for the large standard error in the slope coefficient.

As in the all-male regression analysis, the slope coefficient of the average level of schooling appears to be biased upward. The slope of the standard deviation of age is lower in absolute value in the income than in the earnings data; this is consistent with the different changes in the slope of the age-log income and age-log earnings profile as age increases.

A comparison of the income and earnings equations reveals a lower absolute value for the slope of the standard deviation of age, and a less positive slope for the level of weeks worked. (Both phenomena are explained above.) The slope coefficient of schooling is also lower in the income equation, but this is not surprising since the slope is interpreted as $\bar{r} - \bar{r}'$. The slope of the age-income profile ($\bar{r}'$ for income) is expected to be steeper than the slope of the age-earnings profile ($\bar{r}'$ for earnings). A lower slope appears in the income analysis than in the earnings analysis, too, for the average age variable. Note, however, that the income data are for males of twenty-five years of age and over while the earnings data are for males of fourteen years of age and older; a unit increase in average age has a smaller (average) effect on income (or earnings) in a population of twenty-five and over than in one of fourteen and over because the income (or earnings) profile is much steeper at young ages.

Comparing the slope coefficients and t-ratios of the income and earnings regressions, we find generally larger standard errors of slope coefficients for income—a major reason for the poorer performance of the income equation. This suggests that the inclusion of nonlabor income may be increasing "purely random" errors in the dependent variable. Such random errors do not bias regression slope coefficients, but they do enlarge the standard error of the slope coefficients and thereby decrease t-ratios. If this explanation of the poorer performance of the income equation for white males is correct, it should perform better in a population with less nonlabor income in this group. A comparison of the income equation for white males with that for nonwhite males below will provide a test for this hypothesis.

U.S. Nonwhite Males

Here the human capital earnings function is used to analyze interstate differences in the log of the geometric mean of income and earnings of nonwhite males from the thirty-nine continental states for which separate race data were made available in the 1960 Census of Population. In the first part of this chapter certain implications regarding racial differences in the regression slope coefficients were developed on the basis of the following set of assumptions: Nonwhites, compared to whites, (a) receive a lower rate of return from schooling, (b) have a flatter cross-sectional experience-earnings profile,[26] and (c) face greater seasonality of employment. Thus, the regression coefficients are expected to be positive but algebraically lower for nonwhites than for whites for the mean levels of schooling, age, and the log

TABLE 7-4

Regression Results, Log of Geometric Mean
of Income or Earnings of Nonwhite Males

Independent Variables	Dependent Variables	
	Level of Income (1)	Level of Earnings (2)
$\overline{S}$	0.1822	0.1968
	(8.41)	(8.60)
$SD(S)$	0.1238	0.1745
	(1.30)	(1.73)
$\overline{A}$	-0.0295	-0.0200
	(-1.13)	(-0.73)
$SD(A)$	-0.2358	-0.1993
	(-1.84)	(-1.47)
$(\overline{\ln WW})$	0.8404	0.6373
	(2.59)	(1.86)
Constant	0.4670	6.1210
N	39	39
R^2	0.8236	0.8062
$\overline{R}^2$	0.7967	0.7769

Note: Student *t*-ratios in parentheses.
Source: See Appendix A-2.

---

26. For a discussion of this point, see Chapter 6, pp. 116–118.

of weeks worked, and the slope of the standard deviation of age is expected to be less negative.

Table 7-4 presents the actual regression results for nonwhite males. The model has a high explanatory power both for income ($\bar{R}^2 = 0.80$) and earnings ($\bar{R}^2 = 0.78$). All of the variables, except the level of age, have the sign predicted by the human capital model (see p. 128). The effect of schooling level is highly significant in both equations, and the rate of return implied by the slope coefficient of schooling is high and appears to be an upward-biased estimate, as in the preceding regressions. The nonwhite coefficient is lower, but not significantly so, than the value for whites. The slope coefficient of the standard deviation of schooling differs from zero (at a 5 per cent level) only for the earnings data.

When it comes to the age factor, the slope coefficient of the level of age is not significantly different from zero in either the earnings or the income equation. The magnitude of the coefficient is lower for nonwhites than for whites. The slope of the standard deviation of age is lower in absolute value for nonwhites than whites too, but, whereas $SD(A)$ proved significant for all males and white males only in the earnings data, it is significant for nonwhites only in the income data. This difference may be a consequence of the slower rise with age of nonlabor incomes for nonwhites.

As to weeks worked, the slope coefficient of the mean log of weeks worked is positive and significant for nonwhites in both regressions. Although the values of the coefficients are less than unity, they are not significantly lower than hypothesized population values of 1.0 or 1.17.[27] The statistical significance of this variable for nonwhite males—but not for all males or all white males—may be due to its much larger interstate variability.[28]

To what extent is the lower income and earnings level of nonwhites compared to whites due to different values in the independent variables? The answer is provided in Table 7-5, on the basis of the thirty-nine states with separate race data. If nonwhites retained the value of their slope coefficients but had the same values whites had for the explanatory variables, the level of income

---

27. If the null hypothesis is $H_0: \gamma = 1.17$, for the income data $t = \dfrac{.8404 - 1.17}{.3245} = 1.02$, and for the earnings data $t = \dfrac{.6373 - 1.17}{.3426} = 1.55$. For a two-tailed test, 10 per cent level of significance and 33 degrees of freedom, the critical value is $t = 1.70$.

28. See footnote 23 on p. 132.

TABLE 7-5

Mean Values of the Log of Geometric Means for Income and Earnings,
Observed versus Predicted, Thirty-nine States
(in thousands of dollars)

	Income	Earnings
Observed values[a]		
Whites	1.368	1.322
Nonwhites	0.754	0.795
Predicted values[b]		
With nonwhites' slope coefficients, whites' mean values of independent variables	1.241	1.286
With whites' slope coefficients, nonwhites' mean values of independent variables	1.014	1.655

Note: Mean values of independent variables are:

	Whites	Nonwhites
$Av(S)$	10.37	8.00
$SD(S)$	3.60	3.82
$Av(A)$	42.91	42.05
$SD(A)$	10.87	10.86
$Av(\ln WW)$	3.81	3.68

[a]See Appendix A-2.
[b]For slope coefficients: see Table 7-3, cols. 3 and 4, and Table 7-4, cols. 1 and 2. For independent variables: see Appendix A-2.

and earnings of nonwhites would increase substantially. The change would narrow the white-nonwhite gap in the average log of income (Av (lnY)) by 80 per cent, and in the average log of earnings (Av (lnE)), by 92 per cent. This is mainly due to the higher levels of schooling and weeks worked among whites.

Suppose, however, that nonwhites retained the value of their independent variables but had the white values for the regression slope coefficients. The racial gap would be reduced by almost 50 per cent in observed income and would change its sign in earnings. The finding for earnings stems from the effects of the lower slopes of the standard deviation of age and the mean log of weeks worked for whites. However, the slope of the mean log of weeks worked is highly unstable for whites. Indeed, the regression equation appears to be generally less reliable for whites than for nonwhites.

Thus, it appears that the lower income and earnings level (log of the geometric mean) of nonwhites compared to whites is largely due to racial differences in the explanatory variables (particularly the lower levels of schooling and weeks worked) rather than to the effect of these variables on income or earnings.

TABLE 7-6

Regression Analysis, Log of Geometric Mean of Income in Canada

Independent Variables	Dependent Variable: $Av(\ln Y)$	
	Ten Provinces	Ten Provinces and Yukon Territory
$Av(S)$	0.2345	0.2189
	(10.40)	(11.46)
$SD(S)$	0.7276	0.7109
	(4.95)	(4.65)
$Av(A)$	0.0653	0.0620
	(1.38)	(1.26)
$SD(A)$	-0.5927	-0.3493
	(-2.47)	(-2.42)
Constant	0.1413	-2.0022
df	5	6
R	0.9882	0.9874
$\overline{R}^2$	0.9576	0.9582
R^2	0.9765	0.9750

Note: t-ratios are in parentheses.
Source: Appendix A-2.

Canada

Information provided by the 1961 Census of Canada permits us to study the effects of schooling and age on the distribution of income in Canada. The analysis covers nonfarm males of twenty-five to sixty-four years of age in the ten provinces and the Yukon Territory—eleven units of observation referred to as eleven provinces.[29] The very small sample size reduces the meaningfulness of tests of significance, unless regression residuals are assumed to be normally distributed.

Table 7-6 illustrates the regression analysis of provincial differences in the log of the geometric mean of income for a ten- and eleven-province sample. The hypothesized slope coefficients for the four explanatory variables that appear in the data have high t-ratios, except for the level of age, and the slope coefficient of schooling appears to be biased upward. Both the insignificant effect of average age and the significant effect of the variance in age may be explained by the fact that age (experience) exerts a strong influence on earnings at young and old ages but a weak effect in between.

The model's explanatory power is very high, 96 per cent after

29. Although data on weeks worked do exist, they are not useful for this study because the intervals are too broad. See Appendix A-2.

adjusting for degrees of freedom. Altogether, the Canadian results are very similar to those obtained in the U.S. analysis of earnings.

SUMMARY

Chapter 7 is an analysis of interregional differences in the level of income (and earnings) in the United States and Canada within the theoretical framework of a human capital model of income generation. The mean value of both sides of the human capital earnings equation of Chapter 6, relating the log of an individual's annual income to his level of schooling, age, and log of weeks worked in the year, is computed, and the model is analyzed theoretically.

The dependent variable is the average value of the natural log of income—the same as the log of the geometric mean of income. The five explanatory variables are the means and standard deviations of years of schooling and of age, and the mean log of weeks worked. The slope coefficients of the explanatory variables have economic interpretations.

The slope coefficient of the level of schooling ($b_1 = \bar{r}_i - \bar{r}'_i$) is the mean value across individuals of the difference between the average rate of return from schooling ($\bar{r}_i$) and the slope of the experience log of income profile ($\bar{r}'_i$). The coefficient of schooling level is hypothesized to have a positive sign, and to be lower for nonwhites than whites in the United States. The racial difference is based on the assumption that nonwhites have proportionately lower rates of return from schooling and flatter cross-sectional experience-earnings profiles. On the basis of a microdata analysis, the standard deviation of schooling is expected to have a positive slope coefficient.

The slope coefficient of the level of age, when schooling level is held constant, is the average across individuals of the slope of the age-log of income profile ($\bar{r}'_i$). A positive slope is hypothesized, since an increase in age implies more labor market experience and less current investment in training, and thus higher observed earnings. A lower coefficient is hypothesized for nonwhites than whites because the former have flatter experience-earnings profiles.

The predicted sign of the effect of the model's fourth explanatory variable, the standard deviation of age, is the same as the sign of the correlation of age with the slope of the age-log of income profile. Since the slope of the profile declines with age, the model hypothesizes a negative regression coefficient for the standard deviation of age. The coefficient is less negative the flatter the age log of income profile. Hence, a less negative slope of the standard deviation of age is predicted for nonwhites than whites.

The model's fifth variable for explaining interstate differences in the level of income is the average log of weeks worked. The slope coefficient of this variable is the elasticity of income with respect to the fraction of weeks worked (γ), and is hypothesized to be positive (those who work more weeks per year have higher annual income), but lower for nonwhites than whites. The hypothesized racial differences are based on two related points—a lower level of investment in job-specific training and a greater relative concentration in seasonally sensitive jobs on the part of nonwhites.

In the empirical analysis, two dependent variables are employed: the average log of (a) the income of males twenty-five years of age and over, and of (b) the earnings of males fourteen years of age and over. The former measure contains nonlabor market income, while the latter includes young males. Since the model was developed to study the earnings of males who have completed their schooling, it is clear that neither measure of the dependent variable is a perfect fit to the theoretical concept of income or the definition of the independent variables. The data are from the 1960 U.S. Census of Population and the 1961 Census of Canada, and the states and provinces are the respective units of observation.

In the U.S. analysis for all males, the human capital and employment model can explain ($\overline{R}^2$) over 70 per cent of interstate differences in the level (log of the geometric mean) of earnings and a somewhat smaller proportion (40 per cent) of differences in income. Higher levels of schooling and age, a greater inequality of schooling, and a smaller inequality of age are associated with higher levels of earnings. These variables have the predicted signs (p. 128). The employment variable, the log of the geometric mean of weeks worked, has a generally positive slope in the earnings analysis, and is significant in the coterminous forty-nine states, but not in the fifty-one states. The employment slope does not differ from unity or 1.17, a value for the elasticity of earnings with respect to weeks worked that was found in microdata for white males. The relationships are weaker for income—the level of schooling is the only significant variable.

About 60 per cent of the South–non-South difference in earnings is explained by differences in the schooling, age, employment, and race composition (per cent nonwhite) variables.

Separate regressions are computed for data restricted to white males. The model has a high explanatory power for earnings ($\overline{R}^2 \approx .64$), but makes a poor showing for income ($\overline{R}^2 = .14$ to .22). All of the variables have the signs hypothesized by the human capital model, except the mean log of weeks worked in the income analysis. The schooling and age variables are significant in the earnings equation, but only schooling level is significant in the income equation. The conclusions regarding white males are similar to those for all males.

In the analysis of data for nonwhite males, the model has a high explanatory power for both earnings ($\overline{R}^2 = .78$) and income ($\overline{R}^2 = .80$). On the assumption that nonwhite males have little nonlabor income, the income data are a better fit to the model's theoretical income concept and the independent variables than are the earnings data. Unlike the results for all males and white males, the adjusted coefficient of determination for the nonwhite income equation is very high, and larger than the explanatory power for earnings. This suggests that the model's relatively poor performance for the income of all males and white males may be due to the inclusion of nonlabor market income.

Levels of schooling and the log of weeks worked have significant positive slopes for nonwhite income and earnings. The racial difference in the significance of the weeks-worked coefficient appears to be due to interstate variations in this variable. The coefficient of variation of the average log of weeks worked is more than twice as large for nonwhite males as for white males or all males. The standard deviation of schooling has a positive partial effect.

As predicted, the absolute value of the slope coefficients of the levels of schooling and age and the standard deviation of age are lower (and less significant) for nonwhites than for whites. Indeed, the two age variables are not significant for nonwhites, and this is consistent with a fairly flat nonwhite age-log of income profile.

Tests are performed to discover whether the lower level of income and earnings of nonwhite males is due to different values of the independent variables (schooling, age, and weeks worked), or to the effects of these variables on income and earnings (i.e., to different values of the regression coefficients). The racial difference in the mean log of income and earnings is found to be largely (80 to 90 per cent) due to racial differences in the explanatory variables, in particular, the lower levels of schooling and weeks worked per year for nonwhites.

Thus, our human capital model of interstate differences in the level of income and earnings of males appears to do quite well ($\overline{R}^2$ = .60 to .80) for the earnings of all males, white males and nonwhite males, as well as for the income of nonwhite males. The model's poor performance in respect to the income of all males and white males may be due to the inclusion of nonlabor income. Empirically, in the case of all males and white males, earnings are an increasing function of the levels of schooling and age and the standard deviation of schooling, and a decreasing function of the standard deviation of age. In the case of nonwhites, the levels of income and earnings are rising functions of the levels of schooling and the log of weeks worked, and, for earnings, also of the standard deviation of schooling. 80 to 90 per cent of the racial difference in the mean logs of income and earnings can be explained by the racial difference in the levels of schooling and weeks worked.

The interprovincial analysis for Canada is limited by the small sample size, but the results are interesting. The four explanatory variables, the levels and standard deviations of schooling and age, have the hypothesized sign, and except for the level of age, they have very high t-ratios. The adjusted coefficient of determination is 96 per cent. The Canadian results are similar to those obtained in the analysis of earnings in the United States.

8

The Dispersion of Income

In this chapter the human capital earnings function—equation 6-10—is applied to generate and test the relation, with the U.S. states and the provinces of Canada as units of observation, between relative income (or earnings) inequality and the distributions of the rate of return from schooling, years of schooling, years of experience, weeks of employment during the year, and race. Using this function instead of ad hoc reasoning has the advantage of specifying the explanatory variables, the manner in which they enter the regression equation, and the economic interpretation of the regression coefficients.

The variance of the natural log of income is generated as the dependent variable. It is a commonly used measure of income inequality, and, devoid of units, facilitates interregional comparisons. There appears to be, moreover, greater social concern with relative than absolute inequality of income. Note that the explanatory power of the regressions, the adjusted coefficient of determination, is at least as high here as via ad hoc specifications.[1]

---

1. Using 1960 census data on family income inequality in the United States, Aigner and Heins obtained $\bar{R}^2$ of .76 to .85, and Al-Samarrie and Miller, of .82 to .84. Conlisk obtained $\bar{R}^2$ = .88, but only after experimenting with his estimating equation and deleting insignificant variables. See A. Al-Samarrie and H. P. Miller, "State Differentials in Income Concentration," *American Economic Review*, March 1967, pp. 59-72; D. J. Aigner and A. J. Heins, "On the Determinants of Income Equality," *American Economic Review*, March 1967, pp. 175-184; and J. Conlisk, "Some Cross-State Evidence

STATISTICAL IMPLEMENTATION OF THE MODEL

The Inequality Equation

Equation (6-10), which expresses the relation between earnings or income and the explanatory variables schooling, age, and weeks worked (employment), was written as:

$$\ln Y_i = X + r_i S_i + r_i' (A_i - S_i - 5) + \gamma \ln (WW_i) + U_i \qquad (8\text{-}1)$$

where U_i is the residual. As indicated in Chapter 6, it is assumed that r_i is independent of S_i and r_i' of $(A_i - S_i)$. The variance of a product of two independent random variables A_i and B_i is[2]

$$\text{Var} (AB) = \bar{A}^2 \, \text{Var} (B) + \bar{B}^2 \, \text{Var} (A) + \text{Var} (A) \cdot \text{Var} (B). \qquad (8\text{-}2)$$

Then, taking the variance of both sides of equation 8-1 results in:

$$\text{Var} (\ln Y) = [(\bar{r} - \bar{r}')^2 + \text{Var} (r) + \text{Var} (r')] \, \text{Var} (S) \qquad (8\text{-}3)$$
$$+ [(\bar{r}')^2 + \text{Var} (r')] \, \text{Var} (A) + \gamma^2 \, \text{Var} (\ln WW)$$
$$+ [2\bar{r}' (\bar{r} - \bar{r}') - 2 \, \text{Var} (r')] \, \text{Cov} (A,S)$$
$$+ [2\gamma (\bar{r} - \bar{r}')] \, \text{Cov} (S,\ln WW) + [2\gamma \bar{r}'] \, \text{Cov} (A,\ln WW)$$
$$+ [\text{Var} (r)] \, \bar{S}^2 + [\text{Var} (r')] \, (\bar{A} - \bar{S} - 5)^2 + \text{Var} (U),$$

if it is assumed that r_i and r_i' are independent of each other.

Equation 8-3 expresses relative income inequality as a function of (a) the distributions of and intercorrelations among schooling, age, and employment (weeks worked), (b) the distributions of the rate of return from schooling (r_i), and (c) the distribution of the slope of the experience-log of income profile (r_i').[3] The data calculated for the states are the means and variances of schooling and age, the variance of the log of weeks worked, the covariance of schooling and age, and the average rate of return from schooling. A discussion of the definition and computation of these variables appears in Appendix A-2.

---

on Income Inequality," *Review of Economics and Statistics*, February 1967, pp. 115–118.

In my study, $\bar{R}^2$ is .88 for the income inequality of adult males, .92 for white males, and .86 for nonwhite males (see Tables 8-1, 8-4, and 8-6).

2. See Leo Goodman, "On the Exact Variance of a Product," *Journal of the American Statistical Association*, December 1960, pp. 708–713.

3. This equation was also used in Chiswick and Mincer, "Time Series Changes in Income Inequality in the United States from 1939, with Projections to 1985," *Journal of Political Economy*, Supplement, May-June 1972, s34–s66.

The regression equation is

$$\text{Var} (\ln Y) = b_0 + b_1 (\bar{r}^2 \, \text{Var} \, (S)) + b_2 \, \text{Var} \, (S) \qquad (8\text{-}4)$$
$$+ b_3 \, \text{Var} \, (A) + b_4 \, \text{Var} \, (\ln WW) + b_5 \, \text{Cov} \, (A,S)$$
$$+ b_6 \, \bar{S}^2 + b_7 \, (\bar{A} - \bar{S} - 5)^2 + V'$$

where the residual V' contains the intrastate residual variance $(\text{Var} \, (U))$ and the covariances of employment with age and schooling.[4] The slope coefficients can be interpreted as:

$$b_1 = 1 \qquad (8\text{-}5)$$
$$b_2 = (\bar{r}')^2 - 2\bar{r}\bar{r}' + \text{Var} \, (r) + \text{Var} \, (r')$$
$$b_3 = (\bar{r}')^2 + \text{Var} \, (r')$$
$$b_4 = \gamma^2$$
$$b_5 = 2\bar{r}' \, (\bar{r} - \bar{r}') - 2 \, \text{Var} \, (r')$$
$$b_6 = \text{Var} \, (r)$$
$$b_7 = \text{Var} \, (r').$$

The Variables

Equation (8-4) is a theoretical equation that relates the inequality of income to a set of human capital and employment variables. How the human capital analysis predicts the effects of each of the explanatory variables used in the actual statistical implementation of the equation is discussed below.

The Dependent Variables

Two dependent variables are under study here for the United States: the variance of the natural log of 1959 income of males, twenty-five and over, with income, and the variance of the natural log of 1959 earnings of males, fourteen and over, with earnings. Neither measure is ideal, since the model is developed for the variance of earnings of males who have completed their schooling, and since the explanatory variables are computed for males between the ages of twenty-five and sixty-four.[5]

Except for the inclusion of nonlabor income, the variance of the log of income is the more desirable dependent variable of the

---

4. Appropriate data are not available for weeks worked in Canada (see Appendix A-2). Because of the small sample size, the model is estimated in a stepwise manner for Canada.

5. See Appendix A-2.

two. Even the inclusion of nonlabor income does not cause serious difficulty in interpreting the results. First, the upper open-end interval of the income variable has $10,000 as the lower bound, and the mean of the interval is estimated by the Pareto equation. The distribution of income among those with large incomes (over $10,000 in 1959) does not affect the measure of inequality used here. Second, owners of nonhuman capital need not "live" in the same state as their capital. (Our model, however, relates income distribution among the residents of a state to human capital and employment in that state, so nonlabor income may be viewed as causing some measurement error in the dependent variable.)

The earnings data have a $10,000 lower bound to the upper open-end interval too, but the data include the earnings of young males, many of whom are also investing in schooling. Thus, using this measure of inequality may result in measurement errors correlated with the explanatory variables and hence generate biased coefficients. For example, with schooling level held constant, states with younger populations will have a lower value for the experience level of adults. Because of the younger population, these states will have a relatively greater proportion of the age fourteen-and-over labor force in the age group between fourteen and twenty-four. The larger the fraction of very young males in the labor force, the larger the inequality of earnings. Hence, the error in measuring the earnings inequality of adults is correlated with an explanatory variable—the level of experience.

The Rate of Return-Schooling Inequality Interaction Variable

No direct calculation of the rate of return from schooling can be made for each of the states for 1959 because of the lack of income (or earnings) data cross-classified by schooling and age. Two different approaches are employed to compute values for the rate of return, and both sets of estimates are used empirically. These are:[6] (a) r_c, the "regression" estimate based on all levels of schooling; and (b) r_m, the "overtaking age" estimate for high school.

The regression estimate for each state and race is the slope coefficient when the natural log of income is regressed on years of schooling, using microdata for the race-specific males in that state. The slope coefficient of schooling is a downward-biased estimate of the rate of return because years of labor market experience is

---

6. The regression estimate of the rate of return is developed and discussed in detail in Chapter 3. The estimation procedure for both rates of return appears in Appendix A-2.

an omitted variable.[7] It is, however, an average rate of return to all levels of schooling.

The overtaking age rate of return (r_m) is computed from the earnings of high school graduates ($\ln Y_{12}$) and grammar school graduates ($\ln Y_8$) at the "overtaking age." The overtaking age is the age at which the upward-rising age-earnings profile of a given level of schooling would cross the horizontal age-earnings profile that would exist if there were no investment in on-the-job training.[8] From knowing the earnings at this age and using the relation $\ln Y_{12} = \ln Y_8 + r_m$ (4), where 4 is the four years of high school, the term r_m can be computed. Because of data limitations, the procedure involves several approximations which generate considerable measurement errors.

A positive partial slope coefficient equal to unity is predicted for the rate of return-schooling inequality interaction term $\bar{r}^2 \operatorname{Var}(S)$. Because of the downward bias inherent in the regression estimate of the rate of return (r_c), the slope coefficient of the rate of return-schooling inequality interaction variable will be greater than unity when this rate of return is used. This bias above unity will be smaller for nonwhites than for whites because the rate of return is biased downward more for whites.[9] When the overtaking age rate of return is used, the regression slope coefficient may be less than unity (but still positive) due to errors of measurement.

Variance in Schooling

No prediction is offered on a priori grounds as to the sign of the coefficient on the variance in schooling when the rate of return-schooling inequality interaction term is held constant. Depending on the magnitudes of the component parameters, b_2 can

---

7. If the expression for weeks worked is deleted from equation 8-1, we have

$$\ln Y_i = X + r S_i + r' (A_i - S_i - 5) + U_i.$$

If experience $(A - S - 5)$ is now deleted, the slope coefficient of S is biased downward because r' is positive and the covariance of S and $(A - S - 5)$ is negative. Cov $(S, A - S - 5) = \operatorname{Cov}(A,S) - \operatorname{Var}(S)$. The secular increase in years of schooling means the covariance of A and S is negative.

8. See Mincer, *Schooling, Experience, and Earnings*, Part 1.

9. The downward bias is due to the negative correlation of schooling with years of investment in experience. Since, for each level of schooling, nonwhites appear to have a flatter cross-sectional experience-income profile (lower r'), the downward bias of r_c will be smaller. See the last section of Chapter 6 for a discussion of racial differences in the slope of the experience-income profile.

be either positive or negative. An examination of microdata parameter estimates, however, suggests that b_2 is negative for all males and for white males.[10]

The slope of the variance in schooling is expected to be less negative for nonwhites. Although nonwhites may have lower rates of return from schooling and have flatter age-earnings profiles (lower $\bar{r}'$), they appear to have a higher coefficient of variation in rates of return from schooling than do whites.[11]

Variance of Age

The variance of age (with level and dispersion of schooling and level of age held constant) is expected to have a significant positive slope coefficient. The larger the dispersion in age, the larger the proportion of young and old workers, and the larger the dispersion in income. Very young workers have lower net earnings than prime age workers of the same level of schooling and employment because they have less previous investment in experience and are making larger current investments. On the other hand, older workers have higher weekly wages than prime age workers due to the accumulated effects of experience, but these are subject to depreciation and obsolescence.

The slope of the variance in age is expected to be lower and less significant for nonwhites than for whites because of the flatter nonwhite cross-sectional experience-earnings profile.

Covariance of Schooling and Age

The covariance of schooling and age is negative due to the secular increase in years of schooling. It varies across states due to migration and different secular trends in schooling. For the same overall levels and inequalities of schooling and age, a stronger

---

10. b_2 is negative if $b_2 = (\bar{r}')^2 - 2 (\bar{r}) (\bar{r}') + \sigma^2 (r) + \sigma^2 (r')$ is negative. For nonfarm white males, Mincer (in *Schooling, Experience, and Earnings,* 1972 mimeographed version) found that $\bar{r} = .11$ and that the coefficient of variation in the rate of return from schooling and postschooling human capital is approximately one-third. If the coefficient of variation of the slope of the age-earnings profile (r') is also one-third, b_2 is negative if

$$(\bar{r}')^2 - 2 (.11) (\bar{r}') + (.11)^2 (.33)^2 + (\bar{r}')^2 (.33)^2 < 0,$$

since $\sigma^2 (r) = [\bar{r} \, C.V. \, (r)]^2$. This holds if the slope of the experience-log of earnings profile $(\bar{r}')$ is equivalent to $.006 < \bar{r}' < .192$. Hence it is hypothesized that b_2 is negative.

11. See my "Racial Differences in the Variation in Rates of Return from Schooling," G. von Furstenberg et al., eds., *Patterns of Racial Discrimination,* Vol. 2, *Employment and Income,* D.C. Heath, 1974.

secular trend implies a more negative (algebraically lower) covariance of schooling and age. Since the square of the standard deviations of schooling and age are being held constant, interstate variations in the covariance really reflect differences in the correlation between schooling and age [Cov $(A,S) = R (A,S) \cdot SD (A) \cdot SD (S)$].

If we assume no depreciation of human capital with age and a uniform quality of schooling over time, an increase in the algebraic value of the correlation of schooling and age (i.e., a lower secular trend) increases the inequality of income if b_5 is positive (see equation 8-5). An examination of microdata parameter estimates suggests the hypothesis that the slope coefficient of the covariance of schooling and age (b_5) is positive.[12]

For the moment let us assume that there are no investments in postschool training ($\bar{r}'$ and $\sigma^2 (r') = 0$). Age-earnings profiles would be horizontal and b_5, the coefficient of the covariance of schooling and age, would be zero. Suppose there were secular increases in the quality of schooling or in job opportunities. Younger workers would have higher earnings for the same number of years of schooling than older workers. For the same overall level and dispersion of schooling and age, income inequality would be greater if younger workers were concentrated in the higher schooling categories. Thus, given secular increases in schooling quality or job opportunities, the greater the algebraic value of the correlation of schooling and age (i.e., the weaker the secular trend), the smaller is the inequality of income.

Depreciation of human capital with age has a similar effect as secular improvements in school quality. For a given correlation of schooling and age, the greater the rate of depreciation of earnings with age, the larger is the inequality of incomes.

If we combine the effects of investment in postschool training, secular increases in the quality of schooling or job opportunities, and depreciation of earning potential with age, the sign of the slope coefficient of the covariance of schooling and age be-

---

12. Using microdata on the earnings of nonfarm white males, Mincer found $\bar{r} = .11$ and a coefficient of variation in rates of return from human capital of one-third (*Schooling, Experience, and Earnings*, 1972 mimeographed version). If the coefficient of variation in r' is also one-third, b_5 is positive if

$$2 \bar{r}' (.11 - \bar{r}') - 2 (\bar{r}')^2 (.33)^2 > 0, \text{ or } \bar{r}' < .10.$$

The average slope of the age-earnings profile is less than the slope coefficient of experience when log earnings is regressed on schooling, experience, and experience squared. Mincer found the slope of experience to be .08. Therefore, b_5 is expected to be positive.

comes unclear, a priori. The slope coefficient is more likely to be positive, the more important postschool training is relative to (a) secular changes in the quality of schooling or job opportunities for new labor force entrants and (b) the decline of earnings with age. The previous discussion of racial differences in these parameters suggests that the algebraic value of the slope coefficient (b_5) of the covariance term will be lower for nonwhites than for whites.

Variance of the Log of Weeks Worked

Our model generates relative income inequality as a function of the relative variance of weeks worked (employment). This is the first cross-sectional study of income inequality in which this variable has been used.[13] Previous cross-sectional and time series studies used either the fraction of the labor force or of the population reported as unemployed on a particular date.[14] The dispersion in weeks worked is an analytically superior variable—it gets to the heart of the employment-income relation. Suppose, for example, that weekly wages are independent of weeks worked and that all workers have the same level of skill, but 30 per cent of the labor force works forty weeks per year while the remaining 70 per cent works a full year. Thus, 30 per cent of the work force is unemployed approximately one-fifth of the year, which generates inequality in weeks worked and in annual income. Suppose we have another community where, again, all workers have equal weekly wages and the weekly wage is independent of the number of weeks worked. In this second community, however, everyone works forty weeks and everyone is unemployed approximately one-fifth of the year. In spite of the greater rate of unemployment in the second community, the inequality of annual income is smaller (in fact, zero in this extreme example because there is no dispersion in weeks worked).

In the United States, the unemployment rate and the variance in the log of weeks worked are highly correlated over the business cycle, but weakly correlated across states at any one moment in

---

13. See also Chiswick and Mincer, "Time Series Changes in Income Inequality."

14. See T. P. Schultz, "Secular Trend and Cyclical Behavior of Income Distribution in the United States: 1944–1965," in Lee Soltow, ed., *Six Papers on the Size Distribution of Wealth and Income*, NBER, 1969; and L. Thurow, "Analyzing the American Income Distribution," *American Economic Review*, May 1970, pp. 261–269. See also the articles cited in footnote 1, p. 143, by Conlisk, Al-Samarrie and Miller, and Aigner and Heins.

time.[15] Therefore, for a cross-sectional study of income inequality the relative variance in weeks worked is also statistically superior to the unemployment rate. For a time series study, however, the unemployment rate is a good proxy for the relative inequality of weeks worked.[16]

The regression slope coefficient of the variance in the log of weeks worked is γ^2, where γ is the elasticity of earnings with respect to the fraction of weeks worked. γ^2 shall be tested for statistical significance against the two hypotheses that the population values are 1.0 and 1.37. A coefficient of unity implies that weekly wages are uncorrelated with the number of weeks worked.[17] Recall that Mincer obtained $\gamma = 1.17$ (hence, $\gamma^2 = 1.37$) in a microdata analysis for nonfarm white males in the 1/1,000 sample of the 1960 Census.[18]

A third hypothesis is that the elasticity of earnings with respect to weeks worked (γ) is lower for nonwhite than for white males. The theoretical arguments supporting this hypothesis were developed above (see pp. 125–126).

Average Schooling

The statistical model assumes that neither level nor inequality of rates of return from schooling vary with the level of schooling. On this assumption, the partial slope coefficient of average schooling should be positive, and with the use of microdata, the relative inequality of income within schooling, age, and employment cells should increase with the level of schooling. Empirically, however, with age held constant, the absolute inequality of labor market income increases, but its relative inequality decreases, at higher levels of schooling.[19] This decline in relative income inequality may be due to the decline, with higher levels of schooling, in the relative

---

15. See M. Hashimoto, "Factors Affecting State Unemployment," Ph.D. dissertation, Columbia University, 1971.

16. One reason for this is that in recessions the number of weeks worked per year decreases more for workers who tend to work fewer weeks per year even under normal business conditions (primarily those with low levels of training). This is consistent with the human capital model of investment in job-specific training. (See Becker, *Human Capital*, Part 1 and Chiswick and Mincer, "Time Series Changes in Income Inequality.")

17. See discussion in Chapters 2 and 6.

18. See Mincer, *Schooling, Experience, and Earnings*, Part 2, 1972 mimeographed version.

19. See T. P. Schultz, "Long-Term Changes in Personal Income Distribution," *American Economic Review*, May 1972.

inequality of hours worked per week, the average level of the rates of return, or the variance in rates of return.[20]

Suppose rates of return from schooling decline with higher levels of schooling when the age and employment variables are held constant. Then a negative slope coefficient of the level of schooling could emerge in our regression analysis. A higher level of schooling implies a larger proportion of the population with some college schooling. If the effect of declining rates of return is operative, the downward bias in the coefficient of average schooling will be greater if the measure of the rate of return is the rate for high school (as is the overtaking age rate of return, r_m), rather than a weighted average rate for all levels of schooling (as is the regression estimate, r_c). Thus, if the coefficient of average schooling is algebraically lower when r_m rather than r_c is held constant, there will be indirect evidence of a decline in the rate of return at higher levels of schooling.[21]

Level of Experience

A rise in the level of experience results in an increase in the relative inequality of income if there are differences in the slope of the experience-income profile and if the other assumptions of the statistical model apply. However, the income data are for observed income, that is, income net of the opportunity cost of postschool training. Differential investments in postschool training tend to increase the inequality of observed income for young members of the labor force. The result may be the appearance of an inverted U-shaped relation between the (squared) level of experience and the relative inequality of income.

A less positive (or more negative) relation between experience level and income inequality will emerge as young males assume more importance in the data because of their low level and large

---

20. The relative inequality of weeks worked per year, but not of hours worked per week, is held constant in the empirical analysis.

21. Becker, Hanoch, Hansen, and Johnson all found lower rates of return for college graduates than for high school graduates. They did not, however, hold employment constant. Using the 1960 Census 1/1,000 sample for white males, Mincer found no significant evidence of a higher (or lower) rate of return at higher levels of schooling, holding experience and weeks worked during the year constant.

See Becker, *Human Capital*, Part 2; Hanoch, "An Economic Analysis of Earnings and Schooling"; W. Lee Hansen, "Total and Private Rates of Return to Investment in Schooling," *Journal of Political Economy*, April 1963, pp. 128-140; Mincer, *Schooling, Experience, and Earnings*, Part 2; and Johnson, "Returns from Investment in Human Capital."

inequality of income. Since the earnings data are for males four-teen years of age and over while the income data are for males twenty-five years of age and over, a year's increase in the mean level of experience is expected to have a smaller positive effect on earnings inequality than on income inequality. This expectation is strengthened by the rise in the level and inequality of nonlabor income with experience.

Race Composition and Region

Let us assume Y_w is the earnings of a white worker of a given level of years of schooling, years of experience, and weeks of employment. The earnings of a nonwhite in the same school-ing-experience-weeks worked cell could be written as $Y_{NW} = Y_w (1 - d)$ where d is the per cent difference in earnings between white and nonwhite workers. The variable d is positive if non-whites receive a lower quality of schooling or a lower level of investment in postschool training, work fewer hours per week, or are subject to direct labor market discrimination.

We can write

$$Y_i = Y_{i,w} (1 - d)^{NW_i} \qquad (8\text{-}6)$$

where $NW_i = 1$ for nonwhites and $NW_i = 0$ for whites. Then,

$$\ln Y_i = \ln Y_{i,w} - (d) (NW_i), \qquad (8\text{-}7)$$

if d is a small number, and if individual differences in d_i are placed in a residual,

$$\sigma^2 (\ln Y_i) = \sigma^2 (\ln Y_{i,w}) + (d^2) (p - p^2) + U \qquad (8\text{-}8)$$

where p is the per cent of the population nonwhite and the co-variance of $\ln Y_{i,w}$ and NW_i is in the residual U.[22] The variables which comprise $\text{Var}(\ln Y_w)$ are shown in equation (8-4). By adding the variable $p - p^2$ to equation (8-4) in the analysis of all males we can test for the effect of race composition on the inequality of income among adult males.

A region dummy variable ($NSD = 1$ for Southern states) is added to test for the existence of regional differences in inequality after controlling for the human capital, employment, and race composition variables.

The empirical analysis is performed not only for all males, but also for white and nonwhite males separately as in the previous

---

22. If p is the per cent nonwhite, it is the mean value of the dichotomous variable NW_i, and $\text{Var}(NW_i) = (\overline{NW^2}) - (\overline{NW})^2 = (\overline{NW}) - (\overline{NW})^2 = p - p^2$.

chapter. That is, the variables in equation (8-4) can be race-specific. When this is done, a variable for the nonwhite percentage of the adult male labor force can be added to the equation. For the analysis of white income inequality, this variable's partial slope coefficient measures the effect of the relative number of nonwhites in the states on the inequality of income *among* whites within schooling, experience, and weeks worked cells. It offers a similar interpretation when added to the equation for nonwhite income inequality.[23]

-----

23. The variable per cent nonwhite in the state is added to the white (nonwhite) income inequality equation on the basis of the white (nonwhite) employee discrimination hypothesis.

If white employees act as if they had a taste for discrimination against nonwhite workers, those whites who work with nonwhites receive a positive compensating wage differential. This creates a component of inequality in the income of white males, holding other variables constant. Up to a point, white income inequality increases the more nonwhites there are in the state. A positive slope coefficient for the variable per cent nonwhite in the white income inequality equation would be consistent with the white employee discrimination hypothesis. (A similar analysis applies to the income inequality of nonwhites.) The statistical testing of these hypotheses is developed in detail in Barry R. Chiswick, "Racial Discrimination in the Labor Market: A Test of Alternative Hypotheses," *Journal of Political Economy*, November-December 1973, pp. 1,330-1,352, reprinted in G. von Furstenberg *et al.*, eds., *Patterns of Racial Discrimination*, Vol. II, *Employment and Income*, New York, D.C. Heath, 1974.

A thumbnail sketch of the model follows.

Let Y_i^* be the weekly wage of a white worker of a given level of skill (i.e., schooling and labor market experience) if he does not work with nonwhites. Let X_i be a dichotomous variable that takes the value of unity if he works with nonwhites and the value of zero if he does not. It is assumed that white and nonwhite workers are neither perfect substitutes nor perfect complements in production, and that some white workers have $X_i = 1$ and others $X_i = 0$. Let d_i be a market discrimination coefficient, the per cent increase in wages paid to the white worker if he works with nonwhites. The weekly wage of the ith white worker is

$$Y_i = Y_i^* (1 + d_i X_i).$$

Taking the natural log of both sides of the above equation and assuming d_i is small,

$$\ln (Y_i) = \ln (Y_i^*) + d_i X_i.$$

Evaluating the variance of both sides of this new equation across white males in the state,

$$\sigma^2 (\ln Y_i) = \sigma^2 (\ln Y_i^*) + \sigma^2 (d_i X_i) + 2 \operatorname{Cov} (\ln Y_i^*, d_i X_i).$$

If d_i and X_i are independent,

$$\sigma^2 (dX) = \bar{d}^2 \sigma^2 (X) + \bar{X}^2 \sigma^2 (d) + \sigma^2 (X) \sigma^2 (d)$$

$$= [\bar{d}^2 + \sigma^2 (d)] \sigma^2 (X) + [\sigma^2 (d)] \bar{X}^2.$$

Summary

The human capital earnings function is converted into a model relating the relative inequality of earnings (or income) to the distributions of schooling, age, and employment.

The rate of return-schooling inequality interaction term is hypothesized to have a slope coefficient equal to unity if the rate of return is measured correctly. Due to data limitations two estimates of the rate of return are employed. For the regression estimate of the rate of return (r_c), the slope coefficient is expected to be biased upward (i.e., above unity), and more so for whites than nonwhites. When the overtaking age rate of return (r_m) is used, the slope coefficient is hypothesized to be positive but less than unity due to errors of measurement.

On the basis of parameter estimates from microdata, a negative partial effect is predicted for the variance in schooling for white males and for all males. A less negative effect is hypothesized for nonwhite males.

The slope coefficient of the inequality of age is predicted to be positive, but lower for nonwhites than for whites as a result of lower investments in postschool training by, and the secular decline in discrimination (in schooling as well as in the labor market) against, young nonwhites.

The partial effect of the covariance of schooling and age is not clear a priori. The stronger the upward secular trends are in schooling (i.e., the more negative the correlations of schooling and age), the smaller is income inequality within the framework of the model. However, secular uptrends in the quality of schooling or job opportunities for new entrants, as well as the depreciation of earning potential with age, tend to impart a negative partial effect between the covariance term and income inequality. The lower level of investment in training by nonwhite males, the greater secular improvement in the quality of schooling and job oppor-

---

Let us designate k as an index of labor market integration so that $k = \overline{X}/p$, where p is the per cent nonwhite, then $\overline{X} = kp$ and $\sigma^2(X) = (kp) - (kp)^2$. After these adjustments, our equation can be rewritten as

$$\sigma^2(\ln Y) = \sigma^2(\ln Y^*) + \{k[\overline{d}^2 + \sigma^2(d)]\}\, p + (-\overline{d}^2 k^2)\, p^2 + U.$$

The coefficient of p is positive and that of p^2 is negative.

Differentiating the last equation with respect to p indicates that income inequality is a rising function of p as long as less than half of the whites in a state work with nonwhites. Thus, the white employee discrimination model hypothesizes that, holding $\sigma^2(\ln Y^*)$ constant, *white* income inequality in a state is a rising function of the nonwhite percentage of the male labor force (p).

tunities for young nonwhites, and the larger relative depreciation of earning potential with age for those engaged in less skilled jobs all point to a lower algebraic value for the slope coefficient of nonwhites.

The predicted racial difference in the partial effect of the covariance of age and schooling is quite important for the statistical analysis. Where racial differences are hypothesized for the coefficients of other variables, values closer to zero are predicted for nonwhites. It might be argued, however, that the lower absolute value of observed slope coefficients for these variables is due to greater sampling variability or larger measurement errors in the nonwhite data. Thus, if the slope of the covariance of schooling and age is found to be negative and algebraically lower for nonwhites, there would be evidence that the lower nonwhite slope coefficients for the other variables are not entirely due to sampling and measurement problems.

Another explanatory variable generated by the statistical model is the variance of the log of weeks worked. Here a positive slope coefficient is hypothesized, which, if greater than unity, implies that males of a given age and schooling who work more weeks per year have higher weekly wages. Using microdata, Mincer found the elasticity of earnings with respect to weeks worked (γ) to be equal to 1.17. Thus, two hypotheses to be tested are whether the slope coefficient (γ^2) is equal to unity, or equal to 1.37.

Those with higher weekly wages work more weeks per year if the labor supply curve rises upward, their wages are higher because of greater investments in specific training, or the hours worked per week and weeks worked per year are positively correlated. On the other hand, those with higher weekly wages work fewer weeks per year if labor supply curves bend backward, or if the higher wage is an equalizing differential compensating for seasonal employment. Thus, a third hypothesis is that the slope coefficient γ^2 is lower for nonwhites than whites because of a smaller amount of investment in training and a greater concentration in seasonal occupations.

Assuming a constant level and inequality of rates of return from schooling across schooling levels, the statistical model predicts a positive slope coefficient of the squared level of schooling. If the level or inequality of rates of return declines with schooling, a negative coefficient could emerge. A lower coefficient of average schooling with the rate of return to high school (r_m) rather than a weighted average rate of return to all levels of schooling (r_c) held constant gives indirect support to the hypothesis that average rates of return decline with higher levels of schooling.

The partial effect of the (squared) level of experience on income inequality may be U-shaped. During initial periods of gathering experience, income inequality exists partly because of differential investments in training; in subsequent periods, partly because of the returns on previous investments. Even if absolute income inequality increases with experience, relative inequality may first decline and subsequently increase. Thus, the sign of the level of experience is not clear a priori. Because of the inclusion of young males in the earnings data, the coefficient of experience is expected to be algebraically lower for earnings than for income inequality.

The effect on overall income inequality (i.e., for all males) of racial differences in the incomes of whites and nonwhites within schooling, experience, and weeks worked cells is incorporated through the variance of the dichotomous variable NW_i, which takes the value of 1 for nonwhites and of zero for whites. The variance of this variable is $p - p^2$, where p is the nonwhite percentage of the adult male labor force. This variable is predicted to have a positive slope coefficient, which would be consistent with the hypothesis that nonwhites have lower incomes than whites within schooling, experience, and weeks worked cells. When separate analyses are performed for inequality among whites and nonwhites, a variable (p)—nonwhite percentage of the male labor force—can be added. This variable shows the effect of a state's racial composition on the income inequality of a particular race within that state.

A region dummy variable, NSD (where $NSD = 1$ for Southern states), is included to test for the existence of regional differences in income inequality when the human capital, employment, and race composition variables are held constant.

To summarize, the predicted signs for the human capital and employment variables are the following:

Variable	Symbol	Hypothesized Sign
Rate of return-schooling inequality interaction variable	$r^2 \, \mathrm{Var}(S)$	+
Variance of schooling	$\mathrm{Var}(S)$	−
Variance of age	$\mathrm{Var}(A)$	+
Variance of log of weeks worked	$\mathrm{Var}(\ln WW)$	+
Covariance of age and schooling	$\mathrm{Cov}(A,S)$	[a]
Average schooling squared	$(\mathrm{Av}(S))^2$	[a]
Average experience squared	$(\mathrm{Av}(EXP))^2$	[a]

[a] Sign is ambiguous.

EMPIRICAL APPLICATION

U.S. Males

The human capital income inequality model developed above is applied here to the income inequality of males twenty-five years of age and over and the earnings inequality of males fourteen years of age and over in 1959.[24] The analysis covers the fifty-one states (the District of Columbia is treated as a state) and the forty-nine coterminous states (with Alaska and Hawaii deleted from the data). Separate analyses are performed for the regression estimate and the overtaking age estimate of the rate of return from schooling.

Analysis with Regression Estimate of Rate of Return

Table 8-1 presents the regression results for income and earnings inequality for the fifty-one- and forty-nine-state data sets, using the regression estimate of the rate of return and the schooling, age, and weeks worked variables. The model's explanatory power is very high; the adjusted coefficient of determination is 88 per cent for income and 77 per cent for earnings. Nearly all of the slope coefficients differ significantly from zero at a 10 per cent level.

The slope coefficient of the rate of return-schooling inequality interaction variable (r_c^2 Var (S)) is highly significant. It is larger than unity in all four regressions, the difference from unity being significant for earnings but not quite significant for income.[25]

---

24. The means and standard deviations of the variances of the log of income and earnings for all males are:

	Mean	Standard Deviation
All States (fifty-one)		
Var(ln Y)	0.7867	0.1184
Var(ln E)	0.7743	0.1076
Non-South (thirty-four states)		
Var(ln Y)	0.7241	0.0795
Var(ln E)	0.7283	0.0902
Non-South (excl. Alaska and Hawaii)		
Var (ln Y)	0.7228	0.0760
Var (ln E)	0.7237	0.0809
South (seventeen states)		
Var(ln Y)	0.9119	0.0758
Var(ln E)	0.8662	0.0770

Source: Appendix A-2.

25. For a 10 per cent level of significance and 40 degrees of freedom, $t = 1.68$. The fifty-one-state sample has 43 degrees of freedom, while the forty-nine-state sample has 41 degrees of freedom.

TABLE 8-1

Regression Results, Income Inequality, All Males, with Regression
Estimate of Rate of Return (r_c)

Independent Variable	Dependent Variable			
	Income Inequality		Earnings Inequality	
	51 States	49 States	51 States	49 States
$r_c^2\,Var(S)$	1.2968	1.1239	1.5947	1.6243
	(7.28)	(5.52)	(7.43)	(6.43)
$Var(S)$	-0.0071	-0.0039	-0.0174	-0.0173
	(-1.88)	(-0.91)	(-3.82)	(-3.26)
$Var(A)$	0.0106	0.0110	0.0090	0.0091
	(4.33)	(4.51)	(3.08)	(3.02)
$Var(\ln WW)$	1.0378	0.9138	0.9208	0.8764
	(5.39)	(3.95)	(3.99)	(3.05)
$Cov(A,S)$	-0.0078	-0.0123	-0.0085	-0.0073
	(-2.22)	(-2.70)	(-2.02)	(-1.30)
$(Av(S))^2$	-0.0027	-0.0027	-0.0030	-0.0028
	(-2.16)	(-2.16)	(-1.99)	(-1.76)
$(Av(Exp))^2$	-0.0005	-0.0004	-0.0010	-0.0010
	(-2.06)	(-1.70)	(-3.38)	(-2.80)
Constant	-0.0816	-0.2067	0.6226	0.5601
N	51	49	51	49
R^2	0.8956	0.8982	0.8188	0.8003
$\overline{R}^2$	0.8785	0.8808	0.7893	0.7662

Note: Student *t*-ratio in parentheses.
Source: Appendix A-2.

Based on microdata parameters, the analysis earlier in the chapter predicted a negative partial slope coefficient of the variance in schooling with the rate of return-schooling inequality interaction variable held constant. The expected negative slope emerges in all four regressions. The coefficient is highly significant for the earnings data but presents a mixed picture for the income data. As to the variance in age, it has the expected positive slope coefficient and is highly significant. The size of the slope coefficient is not significantly larger for the income than the earnings data.

The relative inequality of weeks worked is also a highly significant variable. The slope coefficient (γ^2) does not differ significantly from a hypothesized value of 1.0—the *t*-ratios are all less than unity. If the population value of the elasticity of income with respect to weeks worked (γ) is predicted to be 1.17, we can test the hypothesis that $\gamma^2 = 1.37$. The observed γ^2 differ significantly from this value at a 10 per cent level (two-tailed test), but not at a 5 per cent level.[26]

It was argued in the first part of this chapter dealing with the statistical implementation of the model that a priori analysis does not predict a sign for the partial slope coefficient of the covariance of schooling and age. Empirically, in Table 8-1 the covariance term's slope is negative and generally significant. The negative slope of the covariance of schooling and age means that, with variances of schooling and age held constant, states with greater secular increases in years of schooling (i.e., a more negative correlation of schooling and age) have larger inequalities of earnings and income. This implies that the income effects of the secular improvement in schooling quality and job opportunities for young males and of depreciation of earnings potential with age outweigh those of investment in postschool training.[27] When separate analyses are performed for whites and nonwhites (see pp. 163–173 below), the slope of the covariance term is negative and significant only for nonwhites.

Empirically, in the analyses for all males, the squared levels of schooling and experience have significant negative slope coefficients. The negative slope for schooling level is not consistent with the model developed in the first part of this chapter, but would be if the model allowed for either a declining level or variance in marginal rates of return for higher levels of schooling. The negative slope for the level of experience implies that, with schooling distribution held constant, the relative inequality of income is lower in older age groups. As will be shown below, however, when the analysis is performed for white and nonwhite males separately, schooling level and experience level are generally not significant. This suggests an interaction between the effects of race and the effects of schooling and experience level on income inequality.

We can now add the race composition variable $p - p^2$ (where p is the percentage of nonwhite labor force males) and the South-non-South dummy variable ($NSD = 1$ in the South) to the regression equation. When these variables are included the adjusted co-

---

26. To test the null hypothesis $\gamma^2 = 1.37$, the t-ratios are:

Equation	Fifty-one States	Forty-nine States
Income	1.73	1.95
Earnings	1.95	1.72

The critical t-ratios for a two-tailed test, 40 degrees of freedom, are $t = 1.68$ at a 10 per cent level of significance and $t = 2.02$ at a 5 per cent level.

27. This is based on Chapter 7.

TABLE 8-2

Effect of Including Race and Region Variables
on the Unadjusted (R^2) and Adjusted ($\overline{R}^2$) Coefficients
of Determination for All Males

	Race and Region Not Included		Race and Region Included	
	R^2	$\overline{R}^2$	R^2	$\overline{R}^2$
	A: Using r_c			
Income inequality				
51 states	0.8956	0.8785	0.8970	0.8744
49 states	0.8982	0.8808	0.8994	0.8761
Earnings inequality				
51 states	0.8188	0.7893	0.8192	0.7795
49 states	0.8003	0.7662	0.8003	0.7541
	B: Using r_m			
Income inequality				
51 states	0.8142	0.7839	0.8350	0.7987
49 states	0.8543	0.8294	0.8614	0.8294
Earnings inequality				
51 states	0.7473	0.7061	0.7643	0.7127
49 states	0.7522	0.7098	0.7576	0.7016

Sources: Columns (1) and (2) from Tables 8-1 and 8-3. Columns (3) and (4), regressions not reported, see Appendix A-2.

efficient of determination ($\overline{R}^2$) is lower (see Table 8-2, rows 1 to 4). This means that the F-ratio for the inclusion of these two variables is less than unity; adding these variables to the regression equation does not significantly increase the model's explanatory power. The added variables have insignificant slope coefficients, and the slopes and t-ratios of the other variables are barely changed. Thus, in the analysis of income or earnings inequality for all males, after controlling for the regression estimate of the rate of return and the distributions of schooling, experience, and weeks worked, there are no systematic regional or race composition effects. Hence, the observed South-non-South difference in income and earnings inequality must be explained by the model's human capital and employment variables.

Analysis with Overtaking Age Rate of Return

We might ask, however, what would happen if the alternative measure of the rate of return—the overtaking age estimate (r_m)— were used in the empirical analysis. The regression results using r_m rather than r_c appear in Table 8-3. The model's explanatory power

TABLE 8-3

Regression Results, Income Inequality, All Males, with
Overtaking Age Estimate of Rate of Return

Independent Variable	Dependent Variable			
	Income Inequality		Earnings Inequality	
	51 States	49 States	51 States	49 States
$r_m^2 \text{Var}(S)$	0.2218	0.1872	0.3780	0.3649
	(3.26)	(2.98)	(5.24)	(5.04)
$\text{Var}(S)$	−0.0001	0.0026	−0.0114	−0.0109
	(−0.03)	(0.54)	(−2.22)	(−1.98)
$\text{Var}(A)$	0.0114	0.0114	0.0093	0.0090
	(3.47)	(3.90)	(2.68)	(2.67)
$\text{Var}(\ln WW)$	1.0136	0.8664	0.7507	0.7514
	(3.78)	(3.10)	(2.64)	(2.33)
$\text{Cov}(A,S)$	−0.0040	−0.0166	−0.0041	−0.0132
	(−0.86)	(−3.09)	(−0.83)	(−2.13)
$(\text{Av}(S))^2$	−0.0049	−0.0047	−0.0054	−0.0055
	(−3.06)	(−3.23)	(−3.17)	(−3.27)
$(\text{Av}(Exp))^2$	−0.0007	−0.0007	−0.0013	−0.0015
	(−2.03)	(−2.10)	(−3.60)	(−2.33)
Constant	0.2623	0.1299	1.1661	1.2321
N	51	49	51	49
R^2	0.8142	0.8543	0.7473	0.7522
$\overline{R}^2$	0.7839	0.8294	0.7061	0.7098

Note: Student t-ratio in parentheses.
Source: See Appendix A-2.

is approximately 10 per cent lower when we substitute r_m for r_c—at approximately 80 per cent for income and 71 per cent for earnings.

The estimated slope coefficients of the rate of return-schooling inequality interaction variable are significantly greater than zero, but significantly lower than unity. It is not clear whether the apparent downward bias in the slope is due to measurement errors or to a characteristic of the parameter r_m. This uncertainty will be resolved in the future when data become available permitting a direct calculation of the overtaking age rate of return by state. The slope coefficients and t-ratios of the other variables are quite similar to the results obtained using r_c (compare Tables 8-1 and 8-3).[28]

---

28. One difference is that the level of schooling has a more negative slope and a larger t-ratio when the overtaking age rate of return is used. This is consistent with the hypothesis that the level or variance of rates of return from schooling is larger for high school than for higher levels of education.

Summary

Our analysis of the income and earnings inequality of males, using the variables suggested by the model developed in the beginning of the chapter, shows that the human capital and employment variables have a very high explanatory power $(\bar{R}^2)$—88 per cent for income inequality and 77 per cent for earnings inequality. The rate of return-schooling inequality interaction variable, the variances of age, and the log of weeks worked all have the predicted positive slope coefficients and are always statistically significant. The negative partial slope coefficient for the variance of schooling, predicted on the basis of microdata analyses, is obtained here, and is generally significant for earnings but not for income. The covariance of schooling and age, as well as the squared levels of experience and schooling, have negative and usually significant slope coefficients.

The addition of variables for the race composition of the state and region generally results in no significant increase in the model's explanatory power, in only insignificant slope coefficients for race and region, and in minor changes in the slope coefficients and *t*-ratios for the human capital and employment variables. Thus, the human capital and employment variables explain the larger inequality of income observed in the South than in the North.

U.S. White Males

The foregoing analysis for all males is performed here separately for white males in the coterminous states. White males are defined as whites in the thirty-nine states for which a white-nonwhite breakdown of the data was provided in the 1960 Census of Population and for all males in the ten states for which no separate data exist.[29] The analysis, for the sets of forty-nine and thirty-nine states, employs the regression estimate of the rate of return computed from data for white males.

The regressions presented in columns 1 and 2 of Table 8-4 for income inequality indicate a high explanatory power, $\bar{R}^2 = .92$ for the forty-nine states, and $\bar{R}^2 = .93$ for the thirty-nine states. The significant variables in the regressions are the rate of return-schooling inequality interaction term and the variance of age and log of weeks worked. These variables have the expected positive slope.

---

29. These ten states, all non-Southern, contain a small proportion of nonwhites. They are Idaho, Maine, Montana, Nevada, New Hampshire, North Dakota, Rhode Island, Utah, Vermont, and Wyoming.

TABLE 8-4

Regression Results, Income Inequality, White Males

Independent Variable	Dependent Variable			
	Income Inequality		Earnings Inequality	
	49 States	39 States	49 States	39 States
r_c^2 Var(S)	1.9735	1.7600	1.7702	1.4914
	(11.46)	(9.97)	(7.10)	(6.68)
Var(S)	-0.0030	-0.0025	-0.0143	-0.0087
	(-0.91)	(-0.74)	(-2.97)	(-1.99)
Var(A)	0.0102	0.0131	0.0109	0.0146
	(5.48)	(6.58)	(4.03)	(5.77)
Var(ln WW)	0.8585	0.7749	0.9335	0.6178
	(4.14)	(3.36)	(3.11)	(2.12)
Cov(A,S)	-0.0054	0.0014	-0.0055	-0.0059
	(-1.45)	(0.31)	(-1.00)	(-1.00)
$(Av(S))^2$	0.0006	-0.0008	-0.0009	-0.0024
	(0.72)	(-0.81)	(-0.71)	(-1.97)
$(Av(Exp))^2$	-0.0000	-0.0002	-0.0008	-0.0008
	(-0.03)	(-0.86)	(-2.52)	(-2.66)
Constant	-0.8854	-0.8128	-0.0276	-0.1776
	(-4.83)	(-4.25)	(-0.10)	(-0.73)
N	49.0	39.0	49.0	39.0
R^2	0.9297	0.9411	0.7846	0.8676
$\bar{R}^2$	0.9177	0.9278	0.7478	0.8377

Note: Student t-ratio in parentheses.
Source: See Appendix A-2.

The coefficient of the interaction term is significantly greater than unity, which was not the case in the all-male analysis. This is not surprising, however, since the regression estimate of the rate of return is biased downward more for white males than for all males. The slope of the relative inequality of employment is not significantly less than unity, but it is significantly less than 1.37.[30]

Three variables change in the switch from all males to white males from generally significant negative (all males) to insignificant (white males). These are the square of the levels of schooling and experience, and the covariance of age and schooling. Recall that in the all-male analysis these variables retained their generally significant negative slopes even when the race composition variable was added. This suggests that the effect of race differences in the all-male analysis is more complex than would be indicated by an

---

30. For a comparison with a hypothesized population value of $\gamma^2 = 1.37$, the t-ratios are 2.5 and 2.6, respectively, in the analyses for the forty-nine and thirty-nine states.

interstate difference in intercepts depending on the proportion of nonwhites. Indeed, it suggests an interaction of the effect of race composition with the effect of schooling and age levels and the covariance of schooling and age on the inequality of income.

The model's explanatory power is lower for earnings inequality—$\overline{R}^2$ = .75 for forty-nine states, $\overline{R}^2$ = .84 for thirty-nine states (columns (3) and (4) in Table 8-4)—than income inequality, but it is still substantial. Once again, the rate of return-schooling interaction term and the inequalities of age and employment have significant positive slopes. The covariance of age with schooling is not significant. While the squared level of experience has a significant negative slope, the squared level of schooling is not significant at a 5 per cent level.[31]

When earnings inequality for whites is the dependent variable, the coefficient of the rate of return-schooling interaction term is significantly greater than unity. The coefficient of relative inequality of weeks worked is not significantly less than unity, and significantly less than 1.37 only in the thirty-nine-state analysis.[32]

Table 8-5 presents the analysis of white income inequality where race composition and region have been added to the human capital and employment variables.[33] A dummy variable Z is created where $Z = 1$ in the ten states (all non-Southern) where separate race data do not exist. A region dummy variable ($NSD = 1$ in the South) is also added.

A comparison of the regressions with and without the race-

31. In the earnings inequality analysis, the slope coefficient of experience squared is expected to be less positive or more negative than in the income inequality analysis. The earnings data are for males fourteen and over with earnings, but the income data are for males twenty-five and older, and the explanatory variables are for males between twenty-five and sixty-four years of age. With schooling held constant, states with a younger population (i.e., lower level of experience for those between twenty-five and sixty-four) are likely to have a larger proportion of their population between the ages of fourteen and twenty-four. The level of experience may have a negative effect because the other explanatory variables do not adjust for the larger dispersions in hours per week, weeks worked per year, years of experience, and dollar investments in training of white males fourteen years and over than in the over-twenty-five group. That is, the variable "mean experience" may be capturing the effects of youths, tending to raise income inequality.

32. For a comparison with a hypothesized population value of γ^2 = 1.37, the t-ratios are 1.46 and 2.5 for the forty-nine-state and thirty-nine-state analyses, respectively.

33. The race variable is the percentage of nonwhite males between twenty-five and sixty-four years of age.

TABLE 8-5

Regression Results, Income Inequality, White Males,
with Race and Region Variables

Independent Variable	Dependent Variable			
	Income Inequality 49 States		Income Inequality 39 States[a]	
	(1)	(2)[b]	(3)	(4)[c]
$r_c^2 \, Var(S)$	1.8747	1.8562	1.6827	1.7275
	(10.61)	(9.81)	(9.30)	(9.17)
$Var(S)$	-0.0066	-0.0071	-0.0057	-0.0051
	(-1.74)	(-1.83)	(-1.42)	(-1.26)
$Var(A)$	0.0095	0.0099	0.0126	0.0125
	(5.22)	(5.45)	(6.34)	(6.22)
$Var(\ln WW)$	0.8627	0.9677	0.8132	0.8636
	(4.28)	(4.70)	(3.57)	(3.67)
$Cov(A,S)$	-0.0005	-0.0004	0.0005	0.0002
	(-1.62)	(-1.32)	(0.10)	(0.04)
$(Av(S))^2$	0.0002	-0.0004	-0.0011	-0.0011
	(0.20)	(-0.38)	(-1.15)	(-1.18)
$(Av(Exp))^2$	-0.0000	-0.0001	-0.0003	-0.0003
	(-0.19)	(-0.60)	(-1.05)	(-1.01)
p	0.1330	0.1848	0.1061	0.1426
	(1.79)	(2.23)	(1.49)	(1.73)
Z	—	-0.0209	—	—
		(-1.50)		
NSD	—	-0.0242	—	-0.0173
		(-1.22)		(-0.89)
Constant	-0.6788	-0.5687	-0.6554	-0.6590
N	49.0	49.0	39.0	39.0
R^2	0.9351	0.9410	0.9722	0.9729
$\overline{R}^2$	0.9221	0.9255	0.9305	0.9300

Note: *t*-ratio in parentheses.
Source: See Appendix A-2.
[a] Analysis is performed for states with $Z = 0$.
[b] Contains regional dummy variable NSD as well as Z.
[c] Contains regional dummy variable NSD.

region variables indicates that the added variables do not change the slope coefficients or the *t*-ratios of the human capital and employment variables. The adjusted coefficient of determination is 93 per cent. The variable for per cent nonwhite always has a positive slope coefficient. Under a type I error of 5 per cent, p is significant in the forty-nine-state analysis, and in the thirty-nine-state analysis when NSD is held constant.[34]

---

34. See footnote 23 of this chapter for an economic interpretation of the effect of the variable "per cent nonwhite."

The regional dummy variable (*NSD*) and the control dummy variable for separate race data (*Z*) are not separately significant under a two-tailed test, 10 per cent type I error.[35] Taken together, however, they are significant at a 5 per cent level.[36]

To sum up, the model relating human capital and employment parameters to the inequality of income explains statistically ($\overline{R}^2$) 92 per cent of interstate variations in income inequality and 75 to 84 per cent of interstate variations in earnings inequality for white males. The rate of return-schooling inequality interaction variable and the variances of age and log of weeks worked are the most important and significant variables. In addition, they carry the expected positive signs. The covariance of schooling and age and the levels of schooling and experience are generally not significant. The variance in schooling has the hypothesized negative slope, but is significant only in the forty-nine-state regressions.

A significant South–non-South difference in inequality among whites exists for the states before, but not after, controlling for the human capital and employment variables.

Regression analyses for white males—as well as nonwhite males and all males—were also performed for the states within the non-South and within the South. Although the number of degrees of freedom becomes quite small, especially in the South, the qualita-

---

35. The variance of the log of income for white males:

	Non-South (32 states)	South (17 states)
Mean	0.7206	0.8815
Standard Deviation	0.0762	0.0972

The student's *t*-ratio for the difference in mean variances between the South and non-South is $t = 5.7$. Thus, there are significant regional differences in inequality among whites before but not after controlling for the human capital, employment, and race variables. (See Appendix A-2.)

36. If R^2 (with *Z* and *NSD* not included) = .9351, then $\sigma^2(U)$ (with *Z* and *NSD* not included) = $(.0649)\sigma^2(\ln Y)$, and if R^2 (with *Z* and *NSD* included) = .9410, then $\sigma^2(U)$ (with *Z* and *NSD* included) = $(.0590)\sigma^2(\ln Y)$. The incremental explanatory power of *Z* and *NSD* is $R^2 = 1 - [\sigma^2(U)$ (with *Z* and *NSD* included)$]/[\sigma^2(U)$ (with *Z* and *NSD* not included)$] = 1 - (.0590)/(.0649) = 1 - .909 = .091$. Then $R = .301$, which is significant at the 5 per cent but not at the 2.5 per cent level. $R^2 = .091$ means that *Z* and *NSD* explain 9 per cent of the variation in the dependent variable otherwise unexplained after the human capital, employment, and race (*P*) variables are held constant. (See Table 8-5.)

tive findings are essentially the same as for the country as a whole.[37]

U.S. Nonwhite Males

Most interstate studies of nonwhite incomes have focused on the proportion of nonwhites above some poverty line or on the ratio of nonwhite to white incomes. There appears to be little previous research on regional differences in the inequality of the distribution of personal nonwhite income.[38] This section analyzes interstate differences in nonwhite income and earnings inequality for the coterminous thirty-nine states. The analysis is performed in the same manner as the thirty-nine-state analysis of white income and earnings inequality. The regression estimate of the rate of return is computed for nonwhite males in each state.

It would be useful at this point to review some expected differences in the effects of the explanatory variables on white and non-white income inequality developed at the beginning of this chapter. Accordingly, compared to whites, nonwhites appear to invest less in postschool training, may receive a lower rate of return from this training, and may have experienced a greater improvement in the quality of schooling and job opportunities in the decade or two prior to 1960 due to a decline in discrimination. These forces are consistent with the observed flatter experience-earnings profiles estimated from cross-sectional data for nonwhites than for whites. Then, the inequality of age will have a smaller and less significant effect on income inequality for nonwhite males.

Less investment in specific training by nonwhites implies a lower correlation of weekly wages with weeks worked. In addition, nonwhites appear to be subject to greater seasonality of employment, which implies a negative correlation of weekly wages with weeks worked. The elasticity of annual earnings with respect to the fraction of weeks worked (γ) is, therefore, expected to be

---

37. The regression results for the interstate analysis of white male and nonwhite male income inequality within the non-South and within the South are presented in Appendix B of my "Racial Discrimination in the Labor Market: A Test of Alternative Hypotheses," *Journal of Political Economy*, November-December 1973, pp. 1,330-1,352.

38. One study of regional differences in the inequality of income among nonwhites is Sharon M. Oster, "Are Black Incomes More Unequally Distributed?" in *The American Economist*, Fall 1970, pp. 6-20.

lower for nonwhites than for whites, and may even be lower than unity.[39]

The slope coefficient of the rate of return-schooling inequality interaction term will be less upward-biased for nonwhites than for whites. The slope coefficient, hypothesized to be equal to 1, was found to be greater than 1 for all males and white males, presumably because the regression estimate of the rate of return (r_c) is downward-biased. The downward bias is greater, the greater the correlation of schooling with experience and with returns from investments in experience. The flatter nonwhite age-earnings profile implies a smaller downward bias in r_c. Hence, less of an upward bias in the rate of return-schooling interaction term is expected for nonwhites.

The algebraic value of the covariance of schooling and age is expected to be lower for nonwhites than for whites if nonwhites invest in less postschool training and are more heavily concentrated in jobs where productivity declines with age. Also, if the quality of schooling and job opportunities for young nonwhites has been rising faster over time than for young whites, the slope of the covariance term will be lower for nonwhites.

Race and region variables are also introduced. The latter tests for regional differences in income inequality when the human capital, employment, and race variables are held constant. The race variable tests the effect of the proportion of nonwhites in the labor force on the income inequality among nonwhites when the other variables are held constant.[40]

Columns (1) and (2) in Table 8-6 present the regression results. The model has a high explanatory power; approximately 85 per cent of interstate differences in the inequality of income and earnings for nonwhites is attributable to the model's variables.[41]

---

39. A unitary elasticity implies a zero correlation between weekly wages and weeks worked. A positive (negative) correlation means an elasticity greater (less) than unity.

40. A positive slope coefficient for this variable is consistent with the hypothesis that nonwhite workers act as if they had a taste for discrimination against white workers. See footnote 23 above.

41. For the thirty-nine states, the adjusted coefficients of determination ($\overline{R}^2$) are:

	White	Nonwhite
Var(ln$Y$)	.93	.86
Var(ln$E$)	.84	.84

Source: Tables 8-4 and 8-6.

TABLE 8-6

Regression Results, Income Inequality, Nonwhite Males

Independent Variable	Dependent Variable			
	Income Inequality (1)	Earnings Inequality (2)	Income Inequality[a] (3)	Income Inequality[b] (4)
$r_c^2 \text{Var}(S)$	0.9431	0.9125	1.1169	1.0884
	(3.02)	(2.71)	(3.32)	(3.00)
$\text{Var}(S)$	-0.0013	-0.0036	-0.0011	-0.0010
	(-0.34)	(-0.88)	(-0.30)	(-0.25)
$\text{Var}(A)$	0.0033	0.0024	0.0023	0.0024
	(2.13)	(1.41)	(1.31)	(1.31)
$\text{Var}(\ln WW)$	0.5952	0.6704	0.5081	0.5188
	(5.75)	(5.99)	(4.15)	(3.92)
$\text{Cov}(A,S)$	-0.0124	-0.0109	-0.0111	-0.0107
	(-3.08)	(-2.50)	(-2.70)	(-2.40)
$(\text{Av}(S))^2$	0.0004	0.0004	0.0005	0.0005
	(0.55)	(0.53)	(0.72)	(0.70)
$(\text{Av}(Exp))^2$	-0.0000	0.0000	0.0000	0.0000
	(-0.28)	(0.30)	(0.28)	(0.17)
p	—	—	-0.1160	-0.1243
			(-1.30)	(-1.28)
NSD	—	—	—	0.0059
				(0.24)
Constant	-0.0599	-0.0165	0.0329	0.0314
N	39.0	39.0	39.0	39.0
R^2	0.8843	0.8711	0.9436	0.9437
$\bar{R}^2$	0.8582	0.8420	0.8612	0.8567

Note: t-ratio in parentheses.
Source: See Appendix A-2.
[a]Includes the variable per cent nonwhite (p).
[b]Includes the variables per cent nonwhite (p) and the North-South dummy variable (NSD).

The rate of return-schooling inequality interaction term has a significant positive slope. The slope coefficient is not significantly lower than unity, but is significantly lower than the white slope.[42]

The variance in age has an insignificant effect for earnings inequality but is significant for income inequality. It will be seen below, however, that there, too, the coefficient becomes insignificant ($t = 1.31$) when the racial composition and region variables

---

42. The student t-ratio is $t = (b_w - b_n)/[\text{Var}(b_w) + \text{Var}(b_n) - 2\text{Cov}(b_w,b_n)]^{1/2}$. The correlation of b_w on b_n is positive but less than unity. For the income analysis and the two extremes of $R(b_w,b_n) = 0$ and $R(b_w,b_n) = 1$, $t = 2.23$ and $t = 5.28$, respectively. There are 62 degrees of freedom. (Source: Tables 8-4 and 8-6.)

are added. The slope coefficient of the variance in age is significantly lower for nonwhite males than for white males.[43] The levels of schooling and experience have no effect on state differences in income or earnings inequality.

As to log of weeks worked, the partial effect of the variance is positive and significantly less than unity. The magnitude of γ is smaller than that for whites (compare Table 8-4 with 8-6), but the difference does not appear to be significant.[44] The implied elasticity of earnings with respect to weeks worked for nonwhites is .77 for income and .82 for earnings. The results imply a tradeoff between weekly wages and weeks worked per year.

The covariance of age and schooling, producing an insignificant coefficient for white males, here has a highly significant negative effect for both the earnings and income analyses. The coefficient for nonwhites is lower than the coefficient for whites, especially in the income equation.[45] This suggests that it was not solely greater sampling or measurement error in the nonwhite than in the white data that led to the less significant or nonsignificant coefficients observed in the other explanatory variables in the nonwhite analysis.

Columns (3) and (4) of Table 8-6 contain the regression analysis for nonwhites when race and region variables are added to the income inequality analysis.[46] The variance in age becomes insignificant, and, although the significance of the covariance of

---

43. Since the slope coefficients of the variance in age for whites and nonwhites are likely to be positively correlated, the assumption of $\mathrm{Cov}(b_w, b_n) = 0$ gives a downward bias to the t-ratio. However, when this assumption is made for the income inequality of white and nonwhite males (thirty-nine states) the t-ratio for the difference in slope coefficients of the variance in age is $t = 3.92$. (Source: Tables 8-4 and 8-6.)

44. If it is assumed that the correlation between the white and nonwhite slope coefficient is zero, the t-ratio for the difference in slope coefficients is $t = 0.71$. If the correlation is assumed equal to unity, $t = 1.41$. With 62 degrees of freedom, under a one-tailed test (because of the hypothesis of a lower coefficient for nonwhites), the latter t-ratio is significant at a 10 per cent level. (Source: Tables 8-4 and 8-6.)

45. Since the covariance of the slope coefficients b_w and b_n is likely to be positively but not perfectly correlated across the states, the t-ratio is downward biased if it is assumed $R(b_w, b_n) = 0$. For the income inequality analysis of white and nonwhite males (thirty-nine states), $t = 2.29$ when it is assumed $\mathrm{Cov}(b_n, b_w) = 0$. For earnings inequality, $t = 0.71$ when $R(b_w, b_n) = 0$ and $t = 3.33$ when $R(b_w, b_n) = 1$. (Source: Tables 8-4 and 8-6.)

46. No separate nonwhite data were presented in the census for the ten states for which the dummy variable Z was given a value of 1 in the white analysis.

age and schooling declines, it remains negative and significant. The slope of the relative inequality of employment variable remains greater than zero, but less than unity.

The race and region variables are not significant either separately or as a set. There seems to be no correlation between the relative number of nonwhites in a state and the income inequality among nonwhites, and no regional difference in nonwhite income inequality after controlling for interstate differences in human capital and employment variables.

The mean level of the nonwhites' inequality of income in the thirty-nine states with separate race data is 0.69, compared with 0.80 for whites. The difference is statistically significant. We could ask what the nonwhite inequality would be if nonwhites had the same mean value of the explanatory variables as whites, or if they had the same values for the slope coefficients. Following are the results of such projections for the mean value of income inequality in the thirty-nine states:[47]

(a) Nonwhite means, nonwhite coefficients (observed): 0.6909
(b) White means, nonwhite coefficients (predicted):   0.6949
(c) Nonwhite means, white coefficients (predicted):   0.7742
(d) White means, white coefficients (observed):   0.8005

For nonwhites the effect of racial differences in the mean values of the explanatory variables is small. Three-fourths of the racial difference in income inequality is due to differences in the slope coefficients of the regression analysis.

Weeks worked during the year show significantly greater inequality for nonwhites than for whites. Since nonwhites have a smaller inequality of annual income, it follows that they necessarily have a smaller inequality of weekly wages. This smaller inequality in weekly wages appears to be largely a consequence of flatter cross-sectional experience-earnings profiles and of the lower rate of return from schooling.

To summarize, the human capital and employment model is successful in explaining nonwhite income and earnings inequality— 85 per cent of interstate differences in nonwhite inequality is explained by the explanatory variables. The rate of return-schooling inequality interaction term, the covariance of schooling and age, and the inequality of weeks worked are all significant variables. The inequality of age has a weak positive effect due to the fairly

---

47. See Table 8-7 for (b) and (c); (a) and (d) are the observed average income inequalities.

TABLE 8-7

Predicted Values of Nonwhite Income
Inequality under Alternative Assumptions

	Predicted Income Inequality A[a]		Predicted Income Inequality B[b]	
	White Coefficient	Nonwhite Means	Nonwhite Coefficient	White Means
r_c^2 Var(S)	1.7600	0.0693	0.9431	0.1475
Var(S)	-0.0025	14.6772	-0.0013	13.0627
Var(A)	0.0131	117.9030	0.0033	118.2932
Var(lnWW)	0.7749	0.2440	0.5952	0.1192
Cov(A,S)	0.0014	-13.7768	-0.0124	-10.3256
(AvS)^2	-0.0008	65.9635	0.0004	107.9427
(Av(Exp))^2	-0.0002	849.1903	-0.0000	759.1740
Constant	-0.8128	1.0000	-0.0599	1.0000
Predicted Value		0.7742		0.6947

Sources: Tables 8-4 and 8-6, and Appendix A-2.
[a] White coefficients (from Table 8-4, col. 2) and nonwhite means.
[b] Nonwhite coefficients (from Table 8-6, col. 3) and white means.

flat age-income profile. The differences in the slope coefficients of the explanatory variables in the white and nonwhite analyses are in the expected directions. Three-fourths of the racial difference in income inequality is explained by different slope coefficients. In spite of larger inequality in weeks worked during the year, intrastate inequality is smaller for nonwhites than for whites. This is due to the flatter nonwhite experience-earnings profile and lower rate of return from schooling.

Canada

Utilizing the 1961 Census of Canada, we can see how the distributions of schooling and age affect the income inequality of Canada's nonfarm male population between the ages of twenty-five and sixty-four.[48] Our analysis is performed for the ten provinces and the Yukon Territory—referred to as the eleven provinces. Although the small number of degrees of freedom reduces the meaningfulness of tests of significance, the analysis is

---

48. Appropriate data are not available for the calculation of the variance in the log of weeks worked. See Appendix A-2 for a discussion of the Canadian data.

TABLE 8-8

Regression Results, Income Inequality, Canada

| Independent Variable | Dependent Variable: Var(ln Y) | | | | | |
| | 10 Provinces | | | 11 Provinces | | |
	(1)	(2)	(3)	(4)	(5)	(6)
r_c^2 Var(S)	4.2189	4.1401	2.5866	4.1970	4.1505	2.7452
	(4.43)	(4.94)	(0.81)	(4.63)	(5.25)	(1.77)
Var(S)	—	—	-0.0303	—	—	-0.0290
			(-0.69)			(-0.89)
Var(A)	—	-0.0057	0.0039	—	-0.0013	0.0021
		(-0.57)	(0.12)		(-0.40)	(0.23)
Cov(A,S)	—	-0.0238	-0.0238	—	-0.0216	-0.0237
		(-2.07)	(-1.42)		(-2.18)	(-1.65)
(Av(S))^2	—	—	-0.0053	—	—	-0.0050
			(-0.62)			(-0.96)
(Av(Exp))^2	—	—	-0.0008	—	—	-0.0008
			(-0.61)			(-0.71)
Constant	0.2636	0.7390	1.2554	0.2679	0.2947	1.3683
df	8	6	3	9	7	4
R	0.8426	0.9121	0.9221	0.8394	0.9088	0.9222
$\bar{R}^2$	0.6737	0.7479	0.5511	0.6718	0.7513	0.6260
R^2	0.7100	0.8319	0.8503	0.7046	0.8259	0.8505

Note: *t*-ratios in parentheses.
Source: Appendix A-2.

still of considerable interest. The findings for Canada are similar to those obtained for the United States.

Of the three models presented in Table 8-8, the abbreviated version (which includes only the rate of return-schooling inequality interaction term, the variance of age, and the covariance of age and schooling) has the highest explanatory power—75 per cent—after adjusting for degrees of freedom. This high explanatory power was obtained without including the dispersion in employment (weeks worked) during the year, a highly significant variable in the U.S. analysis that, were it available, would presumably be important in Canada as well.

In the abbreviated version of the model (columns (2) and (5)), the expected positive effect of the rate of return-schooling inequality interaction variable emerges.[49] The covariance of age and schooling has a negative effect. However, the inequality of age has no effect.

---

49. The lack of significance of this variable in the full regression (columns (3) and (6)) is due to the large increase in its standard error, presumably due to multicollinearity and the small sample size (see Table 8-9).

TABLE 8-9

Correlation Matrix for Canada

(11 observations)

	Var(ln Y)	r^2 Var(S)	Var(S)	Var(A)	Cov(A,S)	$(\overline{S})^2$
r^2 Var(S)	0.8225					
Var(S)	-0.1883	-0.3883				
Var(A)	-0.0434	0.1929	-0.3682			
Cov(A,S)	-0.3207	-0.0392	-0.3831	-0.0322		
$(\overline{S})^2$	-0.5965	-0.6617	0.1555	0.1291	-0.2601	
$(\overline{A}\text{-}\overline{S}\text{-}5)^2$	0.4043	0.6604	-0.6170	0.5070	0.3298	-0.7055

Source: Appendix A-2.

SUMMARY

The final chapter of my study is devoted to interregional differences in the relative inequality of income. The model is tested empirically for the states of the United States and the provinces of Canada on the theoretical framework of a human capital model of income generation. The human capital earnings equation presented in Chapter 6 relates the natural logarithm of annual income of an individual to his level of schooling (S), rate of return from schooling (r), age (A), and log of weeks worked in the year (lnWW). In the first part of Chapter 8 the variance of both sides of the equation is computed, and hypotheses are developed concerning the relationship between the explanatory variables and the dependent variable.

The variance of the log of income or earnings—a commonly used measure of inequality—is the dependent variable. The independent variables are: a rate of return-schooling inequality inter-action term (r^2 Var (S)), the inequality of schooling (Var (S)), the inequality of age (Var (A)), the covariance of schooling and age (Cov(A,S)), the relative inequality of weeks worked (Var (lnWW)), and the squared levels of schooling ($\overline{S}^2$) and years of labor market experience [$\overline{EXP}^2 = (\overline{A} - \overline{S} - 5)^2$].

The arguments behind the hypothesized signs of the regression slope coefficients are reviewed. The rate of return-schooling variance interaction term, the variance of age, and the relative variance of weeks worked are expected to have positive effects on income inequality, but of a lower magnitude for nonwhite males than for white males. Several factors influence the coefficient of the covariance of schooling and age; although no hypothesis is offered as to the sign, the algebraic value is predicted to be lower for nonwhites than for whites.[50]

Two measures of the dependent variable are employed for the United States: the variance of the log of income of males twenty-five years of age and over, and earnings of males fourteen years of age and over. Neither measure is a perfect fit to the theoretical concept of income—the labor market income (earnings) of males who have completed their schooling. The low bound to the upper open-end interval ($10,000 in 1959) reduces the effect of large nonlabor incomes on relative income inequality. The independent variables are defined for males between twenty-five and sixty-four years of age.

In the analysis for all males, the human capital and employment variables have a high explanatory power (R^2): 88 per cent for income inequality and 77 per cent for earnings inequality. The rate of return-schooling variance interaction term and the inequalities of age and log of weeks worked have the predicted positive effects, and are significant. The covariance of age and schooling and the squared levels of schooling and experience have negative slope coefficients. Variables designed to reflect the racial composition of males (per cent nonwhite) in a state and region (South or non-South) are not significant, and have no effect on the slope coefficients of the human capital and employment variables. Thus, interstate differences in the independent variables explain the observed larger income inequality in the South.

Applied to an analysis of the income and earnings inequality of white males, the model shows a high explanatory power ($\overline{R}^2$)— 92 per cent for income inequality and approximately 80 per cent for earnings inequality. The rate of return-schooling variance interaction variable and the inequalities of age and log of weeks worked have significant positive effects. The covariance of schooling and age and the squared levels of schooling and experience, which show significant negative effects for all males, are generally not significant for white males. The elasticity of earnings with respect to the fraction of weeks worked does not differ from unity.

When a race composition and a South–non-South dummy variable are added to the analysis of white income inequality, the former has a positive and significant effect, while the latter has no effect. The explanatory variables account for the larger inequality of white income in the South.

---

50. This is the only variable where the model hypothesizes that the non-white slope may be further from zero than the white slope.

A separate analysis is performed for interstate differences in income and earnings inequality of nonwhite males. Once again, the model has a high explanatory power, 85 per cent. For nonwhites, the rate of return-schooling inequality interaction variable and the inequality of weeks worked have positive and highly significant effects, while the variance of age has a positive but generally insignificant effect. The hypothesized lower nonwhite slopes are found as expected, and the white-nonwhite differences are significant, except for the employment variable. The estimated elasticity of income (or earnings) with respect to weeks worked is significantly less than unity, 0.77 for income and 0.82 for earnings. This implies a tradeoff between weekly wages and weeks worked per year.

The slope coefficient of the covariance of age and schooling is negative and significantly lower than the coefficient found in the analysis for whites. This racial difference has an important implication: whereas the lower nonwhite slopes for several variables predicted by the human capital model are also consistent with greater measurement or sampling error in the nonwhite data, this interpretation is not tenable for the slope of the covariance of age and schooling. This provides additional support for the efficacy of the human capital analysis of white and nonwhite incomes.

The slope coefficients of the squared levels of schooling and experience are not significant in the analysis for nonwhites.[51] This suggests that the significant negative slopes obtained in the all-male analysis are due to the interaction of race with the model's variables, and that merely controlling for the proportion of nonwhites within a state is not sufficient for holding constant the effects of racial differences in the variables under study. Race composition of a state and region of the state is found to have no effects on nonwhite income inequality.

---

51. Except for the negative slope in respect to experience level, these slopes were insignificant also in the analysis for white males. The negative slope for experience in the earnings analysis (earnings for males fourteen years of age and over) is interpreted as being a consequence of large investments in human capital for those males with some earnings in the age group fourteen to twenty-four—many of whom are students. The relative inequality of earnings in this group is large and the level of earnings is lower than for males between twenty-five and sixty-four. The independent variables, however, are defined for males in the twenty-five to sixty-four group. Of these the most likely to capture the youth effect on income inequality is the level of experience, which will be lower in states with a younger population. Thus, the significant negative slope for whites—but not for nonwhites—for the squared level of experience in the earnings regression is consistent with a steeper experience-income profile for whites.

The observed income inequality within the states is smaller for nonwhites than for whites. It is not due to differences in the distributions of the explanatory variables. Three-fourths of the racial difference stems from the smaller values of the regression slope coefficients. Since the inequality in weeks worked is larger for nonwhites, it follows that nonwhites have a smaller intrastate inequality of weekly wages. This smaller inequality in weekly wages is primarily caused by a flatter experience-earnings profile and lower rate of return from schooling.

The findings of the interprovincial analysis of income inequality for nonfarm males in Canada are similar to those for nonwhites in the United States. The model's best explanatory power is 75 per cent. The rate of return-schooling inequality interaction term has a positive effect, the inequality of age has no effect, and the covariance of schooling and age has a negative effect.

The theoretical analysis in the first part of this chapter suggests that the algebraic value of the effect on income inequality of the covariance of schooling and age would be lower, the smaller the amount of, and rate of return from, investments in postschool training and the greater the secular increase in schooling level and the depreciation of earning potential with age. These forces also tend to reduce the effect of the inequality of age on income inequality, and may well cause the age effects on income inequality for nonwhite U.S. males and Canadian males.

Thus, based on the findings of this chapter, the human capital approach appears to be highly successful in explaining regional and racial differences in the inequality of income among males.

Appendix A: Data Sets

Appendix A has three parts. The first, A-1, provides a description of the data used in the analysis for the United States and Canada in Part B of the study, including a presentation of the data for the various states and provinces. Appendix A-2 describes the data used in Part C for the United States and Canada, and explains the procedures for computing the regression estimate and the overtaking age estimate of the rate of return from schooling. Finally, Appendix A-3 discusses the sample data for Mexican wage earners.

APPENDIX A-1: DATA FOR PART B: UNITED STATES AND CANADA

This appendix presents (a) regression results for all states of the United States, for whites in seventeen states, and for the provinces of Canada; (b) figures on earnings inequality, overtaking age rate of return, and schooling's "explanatory" power for the fifty-one states in the United States; and (c) means, standard deviations, and coefficients of variation for the states and provinces.

The following symbols are used:

Variable	Symbol	Description
1. Standard deviation of log of income or earnings	SD $(\ln Y)$ or SD $(\ln E)$	
2. Standard deviation of schooling	SD (S)	
3. Regression estimate of rate of return from schooling (or adjusted rate of return)	$\hat{r}$	Slope coefficient from regression of $\ln Y_i$ on S_i within each region (see Chapter 3, or Appendix A-2).
4. Zero schooling level of income	$\ln Y_0$	Intercept from regression of $\ln Y_i$ on S_i within each region.
5. Residual income variance	Var (U)	Residual variance from regression of $\ln Y_i$ on S_i within each region.
6. Intrastate explanatory power	$\bar{R}^2$	Adjusted coefficient of determination from regression of $\ln Y_i$ on S_i within each region.
7. Overtaking age rate of return	r_m	See Appendix A-2.

8. Regression equation: $\ln Y_i = (\ln Y_0) + (\hat{r}) S_i + U_i$.

TABLE A-1

Results from Regressing the Natural Log of Income in 1959
on Schooling for Males of Twenty-five and over in the United States

State[a]	SD(ln$Y$) (1)	SD(S) (2)	ln$Y_{0,1}$ (3)	$\hat{r}_1$ (4)	Var(U)$_1$ (5)	$\bar{R}_1^2$ (6)
Alabama	1.00	4.21	−.22	.13	0.72	.28
			(.24)	(.02)		
Alaska	0.93	3.77	.37	.11	0.70	.19
			(.31)	(.03)		
Arizona	0.91	4.12	.29	.10	0.66	.26
			(.26)	(.02)		
Arkansas	0.99	4.03	−.38	.13	0.73	.14
			(.25)	(.03)		
California	0.84	3.76	.58	.09	0.61	.15
			(.29)	(.02)		
Colorado	0.82	3.67	.41	.09	0.57	.16
			(.29)	(.02)		
Connecticut	0.79	3.80	.64	.09	0.52	.26
			(.26)	(.02)		
Delaware	0.89	3.98	.24	.12	0.59	.16
			(.26)	(.02)		
D.C.	0.91	4.29	.41	.09	0.70	.16
			(.27)	(.02)		
Florida	0.91	4.00	.18	.10	0.68	.18
			(.27)	(.02)		
Georgia	0.97	4.36	−.13	.12	0.66	.30
			(.22)	(.02)		
Hawaii	0.79	4.82	.77	.07	0.51	.17
			(.19)	(.02)		
Idaho	0.83	3.30	.23	.10	0.59	.15
			(.32)	(.03)		
Illinois	0.85	3.60	.51	.09	0.61	.14
			(.29)	(.03)		
Indiana	0.84	3.39	.37	.10	0.60	.15
			(.30)	(.03)		
Iowa	0.91	3.21	.03	.11	0.71	.14
			(.35)	(.03)		
Kansas	0.89	3.38	.13	.11	0.66	.16
			(.33)	(.03)		
Kentucky	0.99	3.90	−.14	.12	0.76	.23
			(.26)	(.03)		
Louisiana	0.98	4.64	.08	.11	0.68	.28
			(.21)	(.02)		

(continued)

TABLE A-1 (continued)

State[a]	SD(ln Y) (1)	SD(S) (2)	$\ln Y_{0,1}$ (3)	$\hat{r}_1$ (4)	Var$(U)_1$ (5)	$\overline{R}_1^2$ (6)
Maine	0.83	3.31	.16 (.30)	.10 (.03)	0.60	.14
Maryland	0.86	4.01	.43 (.25)	.10 (.02)	0.58	.21
Massachusetts	0.80	3.74	.47 (.26)	.09 (.02)	0.53	.17
Michigan	0.85	3.52	.50 (.29)	.09 (.03)	0.62	.14
Minnesota	0.91	3.43	.05 (.32)	.12 (.03)	0.67	.18
Mississippi	0.99	4.13	-.61 (.22)	.14 (.02)	0.67	.32
Missouri	0.95	3.62	.05 (.30)	.11 (.03)	0.75	.18
Montana	0.83	3.37	.31 (.31)	.09 (.03)	0.60	.13
Nebraska	0.87	3.26	.03 (.33)	.11 (.03)	0.64	.16
Nevada	0.82	3.37	.58 (.32)	.09 (.03)	0.60	.11
New Hampshire	0.80	3.41	.39 (.29)	.09 (.03)	0.55	.13
New Jersey	0.80	3.81	.63 (.25)	.09 (.02)	0.53	.17
New Mexico	0.91	4.29	.22 (.24)	.11 (.02)	0.61	.26
New York	0.84	3.90	.54 (.26)	.09 (.02)	0.59	.16
North Carolina	0.96	4.22	-.10 (.23)	.11 (.02)	0.69	.25
North Dakota	0.90	3.39	.08 (.31)	.11 (.03)	0.69	.15
Ohio	0.84	3.52	.44 (.29)	.10 (.03)	0.59	.15

(continued)

TABLE A-1 (concluded)

State[a]	SD(lnY) (1)	SD(S) (2)	$\ln Y_{0,1}$ (3)	$\hat{r}_1$ (4)	$\text{Var}(U)_1$ (5)	$\overline{R}_1^2$ (6)
Oklahoma	0.96	3.91	-.11 (.28)	.12 (.03)	0.71	.24
Oregon	0.85	3.38	.35 (.32)	.09 (.03)	0.63	.13
Pennsylvania	0.82	3.62	.41 (.27)	.09 (.02)	0.56	.16
Rhode Island	0.79	3.67	.45 (.25)	.09 (.02)	0.53	.15
South Carolina	0.96	4.43	-.12 (.21)	.12 (.02)	0.67	.28
South Dakota	0.93	3.22	-.12 (.34)	.11 (.03)	0.73	.15
Tennessee	1.00	4.07	-.20 (.25)	.13 (.03)	0.74	.26
Texas	0.96	4.32	.11 (.25)	.11 (.02)	0.70	.24
Utah	0.78	3.33	.48 (.32)	.09 (.03)	0.54	.12
Vermont	0.86	3.35	.11 (.31)	.10 (.03)	0.63	.14
Virginia	0.94	4.37	.12 (.24)	.11 (.02)	0.67	.24
Washington	0.84	3.43	.33 (.31)	.10 (.03)	0.59	.16
West Virginia	0.95	3.79	.10 (.27)	.11 (.03)	0.75	.17
Wisconsin	0.85	3.45	.34 (.30)	.10 (.03)	0.62	.15
Wyoming	0.82	3.38	.45 (.31)	.09 (.03)	0.58	.13

Source: *U.S. Census of Population: 1960, Vol. 1, Characteristics of the Population*, Parts 2-52, Washington, D.C., Table 138.

[a]Southern states are italic. The data are in 9 income and 8 schooling intervals.

TABLE A-2

Results from Regressing the Natural Log of Income in 1959
on Schooling for White Males of Twenty-five and over in Seventeen States

State[a]	SD(ln$Y$) (1)	SD(S) (2)	ln$Y_{0,1}$ (3)	$\dot{r}_1$ (4)	Var(U)$_1$ (5)	$\bar{R}_1^2$ (6)
Alabama	0.97	3.91	-.15	.13	0.70	.26
			(.27)	(.03)		
Alaska	0.80	3.00	.94	.07	0.61	.06
			(.38)	(.03)		
Arkansas	0.97	3.85	-.29	.12	0.72	.23
			(.27)	(.03)		
Delaware	0.85	3.81	.35	.11	0.55	.23
			(.27)	(.02)		
D.C.	1.02	4.17	.46	.10	0.89	.14
			(.36)	(.03)		
Florida	0.89	3.71	.28	.09	0.68	.14
			(.30)	(.03)		
Georgia	0.94	4.06	-.00	.12	0.66	.25
			(.26)	(.02)		
Hawaii	0.83	3.72	.51	.10	0.57	.18
			(.31)	(.02)		
Louisiana	0.91	4.42	.32	.10	0.65	.22
			(.23)	(.02)		
Maryland	0.83	3.95	.56	.09	0.55	.19
			(.26)	(.02)		
Mississippi	0.99	3.81	-.40	.13	0.74	.25
			(.30)	(.03)		
New York	0.84	3.94	.57	.09	0.59	.16
			(.26)	(.02)		
North Carolina	0.92	4.10	.05	.11	0.66	.22
			(.24)	(.02)		
South Carolina	0.88	4.13	.17	.10	0.62	.21
			(.24)	(.02)		
Tennessee	0.99	4.03	-.17	.13	0.74	.25
			(.26)	(.03)		
Texas	0.94	4.30	.20	.11	0.68	.23
			(.25)	(.02)		
Virginia	0.93	4.25	.19	.11	0.65	.25
			(.25)	(.02)		

Source: U.S. Census of Population: 1960, Vol. 1, Characteristics of the Population, Parts 2-52, Washington, D.C., Table 138.

[a]Southern states are italic. The data are in 9 income and 8 schooling intervals.

TABLE A-3

Results from Regressing the Natural Log of Income in 1960 on Schooling
for Nonfarm Males, Twenty-five to Sixty-four, in the
Provinces of Canada

Province	SD(ln$Y$) (1)	SD(S) (2)	AV(ln$Y$) (3)	AV(S) (4)	ln$Y_{0,1}$ (5)	$\hat{r}_1$ (6)
Newfoundland	0.87	3.27	0.84	6.80	.17	.10
					(.11)	(.01)
Price Edward Island	0.83	2.98	0.95	8.20	.05	.11
					(.15)	(.02)
Nova Scotia	0.80	3.00	1.07	8.39	.21	.10
					(.13)	(.01)
New Brunswick	0.79	3.16	1.03	7.70	.25	.10
					(.11)	(.01)
Quebec	0.77	3.49	1.25	7.81	.60	.08
					(.10)	(.01)
Ontario	0.72	3.40	1.40	9.13	.69	.08
					(.11)	(.01)
Manitoba	0.74	3.26	1.31	8.94	.53	.09
					(.11)	(.01)
Saskatchewan	0.90	3.34	1.18	8.68	.32	.10
					(.14)	(.01)
Alberta	0.78	3.33	1.36	9.23	.58	.08
					(.12)	(.01)
British Columbia	0.72	3.23	1.41	9.39	.77	.07
					(.12)	(.01)
Yukon	0.80	3.46	1.48	8.73	.75	.08
					(.16)	(.02)

Note: Regression equation, columns (5) to (8):

$$\ln Y_i = (\ln Y_{0,1}) + (\hat{r}_1)\, S_i + U_{1,i}.$$

Regression equation, columns (9) to (14):

$$\ln Y_i = (\ln Y_{0,3}) + (\hat{r}_{\not{p}})\, \not{P}_i + (\hat{r}_{\not{s}})\, \not{S}_i + (\hat{r}_H)\, H_i + U_{3,i}.$$

Source: Census of Canada: 1961, Ottawa, Statistics Canada, Table A.11,
unpublished.

S = years of schooling
$\not{P}$ = years of primary schooling
$\not{S}$ = years of secondary schooling
H = years of higher education

TABLE A-3 (concluded)

$\text{Var}(U)_1$ (7)	$\overline{R}^2_1$ (8)	$\ln Y_{0,3}$ (9)	$\hat{r}_Y$ (10)	$\hat{r}_\$$ (11)	$\hat{r}_H$ (12)	$\text{Var}(U)_3$ (13)	$\overline{R}^2_3$ (14)
0.66	.13	.30	.07	.16	.08	0.67	.13
		(.20)	(.04)	(.07)	(.08)		
0.58	.15	.13	.09	.16	.05	0.59	.15
		(.41)	(.07)	(.07)	(.07)		
0.55	.15	.20	.10	.12	.07	0.55	.14
		(.32)	(.05)	(.06)	(.05)		
0.53	.16	.13	.12	.10	.06	0.53	.16
		(.23)	(.04)	(.06)	(.05)		
0.51	.14	.51	.10	.07	.08	0.52	.13
		(.21)	(.03)	(.04)	(.04)		
0.45	.13	.57	.10	.06	.08	0.46	.13
		(.32)	(.05)	(.04)	(.03)		
0.47	.15	.25	.13	.05	.09	0.47	.14
		(.26)	(.04)	(.05)	(.04)		
0.71	.13	.02	.15	.05	.10	0.71	.13
		(.31)	(.05)	(.06)	(.05)		
0.53	.13	.33	.13	.05	.10	0.53	.12
		(.31)	(.05)	(.05)	(.04)		
0.48	.09	.57	.10	.03	.09	0.48	.08
		(.32)	(.05)	(.04)	(.04)		
0.56	.13	.03	.22	-.06	.06	0.52	.18
		(.26)	(.04)	(.06)	(.06)		

TABLE A-4

Earnings Inequality, Estimated Overtaking Age Rate of Return,
and Three Estimates of Schooling's Explanatory Power for the Fifty-one States

State	SD(ln$E$)	r_m	$\dfrac{r_m^2\,\mathrm{Var}(S)}{\mathrm{Var}(\ln Y)}$	$\dfrac{r_m^2\,\mathrm{Var}(S)}{\mathrm{Var}(\ln E)}$	$\dfrac{\hat{r}^2\,\mathrm{Var}(S)}{\mathrm{Var}(\ln E)}$
Alabama	.96	.19	.640	.691	.324
Alaska	.98	.17	.464	.415	.178
Arizona	.92	.14	.390	.381	.200
Arkansas	.96	.23	.839	.898	.300
California	.85	.13	.344	.337	.159
Colorado	.84	.15	.427	.406	.154
Connecticut	.79	.11	.275	.278	.189
Delaware	.87	.14	.370	.387	.301
D.C.	.89	.12	.331	.345	.188
Florida	.86	.17	.585	.658	.217
Georgia	.94	.18	.619	.656	.308
Hawaii	.80	.12	.492	.484	.179
Idaho	.88	.15	.351	.311	.140
Illinois	.82	.13	.280	.303	.157
Indiana	.83	.15	.347	.352	.165
Iowa	.91	.16	.331	.331	.151
Kansas	.89	.16	.360	.357	.173
Kentucky	.96	.19	.531	.567	.239
Louisiana	.93	.17	.610	.679	.302
Maine	.81	.15	.377	.397	.167
Maryland	.85	.12	.298	.306	.224
Massachusetts	.79	.13	.364	.374	.182
Michigan	.85	.12	.251	.249	.138
Minnesota	.91	.17	.425	.426	.205
Mississippi	1.01	.26	1.160	1.120	.330

Note:
Earnings Inequality: Standard deviation of the natural log of earnings in 1959 for males, age fourteen and over, in the civilian labor force; *U.S. Census of Population: 1960, Vol. 1, Characteristics of the Population*, Parts 2-52, Washington, D.C., Table 124.

Overtaking Age Rate of Return: Estimates of rates of return to four years of high school for the earnings of males based on Mincer's overtaking age technique. The computational procedure is discussed in Appendix A-2.

Var(ln Y), $\hat{r}$ and Var(S): Data from Table A-1.

TABLE A-4 (concluded)

State	SD(lnE)	r_m	$\dfrac{r_m^2 \operatorname{Var}(S)}{\operatorname{Var}(\ln Y)}$	$\dfrac{r_m^2 \operatorname{Var}(S)}{\operatorname{Var}(\ln E)}$	$\dfrac{\hat{r}^2 \operatorname{Var}(S)}{\operatorname{Var}(\ln E)}$
Missouri	.90	.17	.391	.438	.197
Montana	.87	.14	.332	.300	.121
Nebraska	.89	.17	.406	.386	.162
Nevada	.83	.12	.256	.251	.134
New Hampshire	.79	.12	.279	.290	.153
New Jersey	.78	.11	.285	.303	.196
New Mexico	.91	.15	.493	.499	.272
New York	.80	.12	.321	.356	.193
North Carolina	.94	.16	.482	.509	.246
North Dakota	.91	.16	.341	.330	.166
Ohio	.82	.13	.306	.324	.186
Oklahoma	.93	.18	.549	.587	.255
Oregon	.84	.14	.292	.302	.132
Pennsylvania	.80	.12	.300	.316	.167
Rhode Island	.76	.12	.332	.363	.191
South Carolina	.95	.17	.580	.591	.312
South Dakota	.93	.17	.330	.331	.145
Tennessee	.97	.20	.669	.711	.298
Texas	.94	.17	.558	.577	.253
Utah	.86	.13	.303	.251	.122
Vermont	.87	.15	.337	.326	.147
Virginia	.94	.14	.436	.435	.261
Washington	.85	.14	.318	.314	.165
West Virginia	.92	.17	.455	.489	.207
Wisconsin	.85	.13	.287	.284	.163
Wyoming	.86	.14	.333	.305	.140

TABLE A-5

Means, Standard Deviations, and Coefficients of Variation
of the Parameters for the Fifty-one States and Eleven Provinces

Parameter[a]	States			Provinces		
	Mean (1)	SD (2)	CV (3)	Mean (4)	SD (5)	CV (6)
$SD(S)$	3.77	0.41	0.12	3.27	0.17	0.05
$Var(S)$	14.38	3.17	0.22	10.69	1.08	0.10
$\hat{r}$	0.10	0.01	0.14	0.09	0.01	0.14
$\hat{r}^2$	0.01	0.00	0.28	0.01	0.00	0.27
$SD(\ln Y)$	0.88	0.07	0.08	0.79	0.06	0.07
$Var(\ln Y)$	0.79	0.12	0.15	0.63	0.09	0.15
$\hat{r}^2 Var(S)$	0.16	0.07	0.42	0.09	0.02	0.21
$Var(U)$	0.64	0.07	0.11	0.55	0.08	0.14
$\ln Y_0$	0.22	0.29	1.30	0.45	0.26	0.57
R^2	0.18	0.05	0.29	0.13	0.02	0.14
$AV(S)$	10.28	0.79	0.08	8.45	0.78	0.09
$AV(\ln Y)$	1.27	0.23	0.18	1.21	0.21	0.17
$SD(\ln E)$	0.88	0.06	0.07			
r_m	0.15	0.03	0.20			

Source: Same as Tables A-1, A-3, and A-4.
[a]For definition of variables, see p. 179.

APPENDIX A-2: DATA FOR PART C: UNITED STATES AND CANADA

The Variables

Variable	Symbol	Source	
		U.S.[a]	Canada[b]
1. Natural log of income– mean and variance	$Av(\ln Y)$ $Var(\ln Y)$	Table 138	b
2. Natural log of earnings– mean and variance	$Av(\ln E)$ $Var(\ln E)$	Table 124	
3. Rate of return from schooling–regression estimate	r_c	Table 138 Tables 103 and 138, and the 1/1,000	b
4. Rate of return from schooling–overtaking age estimate	r_m	sample, 1960 Census of Population	

		Source	
Variable	Symbol	U.S.[a]	Canada[b]
5. Years of schooling–mean, standard deviation and variance	Av(S) SD(S) Var(S)	Table 103	b
6. Years of age–mean, standard deviation and variance	Av(A) SD(A) Var(A)	Table 103	b
7. Covariance of years of schooling and age	Cov(A,S)	Table 103	b
8. Average years of experience (mean age minus mean schooling minus five)	Av(Exp)	Table 103	
9. Natural log of weeks worked–mean, standard deviation and variance	Av(lnWW) SD(lnWW) Var(lnWW)	Table 118	
10. Per cent nonwhite (for the male labor force)	p	Tables 97 and 138	
11. Dummy variable, $Z = 1$, in ten states without separate race data	Z	Table 138	
12. Dummy variable, $NSD = 1$, in the sixteen Southern states (Census definition) and the District of Columbia	NSD		

[a]References are for tables in *United States Census of Population: 1960, Volume 1, Characteristics of the Population*, Parts 2-52, Washington, D.C., Bureau of the Census. The data are from a 25 per cent sample of the population.

[b]*Census of Canada: 1961* (Ottawa: Statistics Canada), Table A.11 for the provinces, unpublished, obtained from Statistics Canada. The data are from a 20 per cent sample of private nonfarm households.

Intervals

Variable	United States	Canada
1. Income	9	13
2. Earnings	9	—
3. Schooling	15	6
4. Age	8	4
5. Weeks worked	6	—

United States

The fifty states and the District of Columbia are used as the units of observation. Variables for white males are defined as the value of the variable for (a) whites in the forty-one states (including the District of Columbia) for which separate white-nonwhite data are available and (b) all males in the ten remaining states.[1] Nonwhites do not constitute more than 7.6 per cent of males between the ages of twenty-five and sixty-four in any of these ten states. The analysis for white males in the subsample of thirty-nine states covers the coterminous states (i.e., excluding Alaska and Hawaii) with separate white-nonwhite data. The analysis of nonwhites is restricted to the thirty-nine coterminous states with separate race data.

The income data used to compute the mean and variance of the natural logarithm of income for all males, white males, and nonwhite males separately for each state cover the 1959 income (wage, salary, self-employment, and property income) of adult males of twenty-five and over who had an income in 1959, as reported in the 1960 Census of Population. Data on labor market income of adult males by state were not reported in the 1960 Census of Population. The mean and variance of the log of earnings is computed for 1959 earnings of males, age fourteen and over, who were in the labor force in 1960. The mean and variance of the natural log of income and earnings for each race-state were computed by using interval midpoints and the Pareto estimate for the upper open-end interval ($10,000 and over). The low value for the open-end interval reduces the impact on the income data of large non-labor incomes.

The means, standard deviations, and variances of years of schooling and years of age, as well as the covariance of age and schooling, were computed for males between the ages of twenty-five and sixty-four. The mean and variance of the natural log of weeks worked in 1959 were computed for males in the same age group who worked in 1959. The age, schooling, and weeks worked variables were computed separately for all males, white males, and nonwhite males.

The variable "per cent nonwhite" is the percentage of males with income, age twenty-five and over, in 1959 who were nonwhite in the forty-one states with separate white-nonwhite data, and the percentage of all males between twenty-five and sixty-four who were nonwhite in the remaining ten states.

---

1. These ten states are Idaho, Maine, Montana, Nevada, New Hampshire, North Dakota, Rhode Island, Utah, Vermont, and Wyoming.

Two measures of the rate of return from schooling are employed in the analysis of income inequality: the regression estimate (r_c) and the overtaking age estimate (r_m).[2] A cross-classification of income (in 1959) by schooling is available for males twenty-five and over with income.[3] The regression estimate of the rate of return is the slope coefficient from a linear regression of the log of income on years of schooling, using grouped microdata within a state. It was computed for each state for all males, and for white and nonwhite males where separate race data were available.

The regression estimate is deficient as a measure of the rate of return because the income data include nonlabor market income, the population includes aged males, and labor market experience is contained in the residual. The last is the most serious problem of the three. Due to the secular increase in schooling, those with low levels of schooling tend to be older and are receiving their return on earlier investments in postschool training. A regression of the log of earnings on years of schooling in which all age groups are pooled therefore results in a downward-biased estimate of the slope coefficient, and hence of the regression estimate of the rate of return. The downward bias would not be eliminated by restricting the regressions to specific age groups. For a given age, a higher level of schooling implies fewer years of experience.

Thus, the omission of experience as an explicit explanatory variable in the regression equation biases the slope coefficient of schooling downward. The absence of a cross-classification for the states of income by schooling and age prevented the computation of an unbiased estimate. The regression estimate, however, reflects the average rate of return for all levels of schooling.

Mincer developed an alternative shortcut technique for calculating unbiased rates of return from a given level of schooling which he calls the "overtaking age rate of return." The overtaking age is the age at which the observed age-earnings profile cuts the horizontal earnings profile that would exist if there were no investment in postschool training.

The estimating procedure requires cross-classified data on in-

---

2. The regression estimate of the rate of return was first used in G. S. Becker and B. R. Chiswick, "Education and the Distribution of Earnings," *American Economic Review*, May 1966, pp. 358–369. Its properties are developed in greater detail in Chapter 3 of this book.

The overtaking age rate of return and the estimating procedure used here were both developed by Jacob Mincer in *Schooling, Experience, and Earnings*, NBER, 1974, Part 1. The calculations were performed by Sarah Paroush.

3. A cross-classification of earnings by schooling for the states does not exist.

come, schooling, and labor market experience (or age). There are no published classifications of income by schooling and age for the states, but a detailed age and income distribution for each schooling group does exist for males in each state. Using the over-taking age technique on these data, estimates of rates of return (r_m) by state were calculated for high school males.

The data permitted the calculation of the average age and the average log of income for elementary school and high school graduates in each state. It was assumed that the mean age-income point so obtained was on the age-log of income profile for that schooling level in the particular state. Using the one-in-a-thousand sample for males in the country as a whole, an age-log of income profile was generated for each level of schooling. The overtaking age for high school and for elementary school graduates was found in the aggregate data. It was assumed that each state's age-log in-come profile had the same shape, but not necessarily the same in-tercept or height, as in the aggregate data. This assumption, and the point for average age and average log of income, permitted the estimation of the log of income at the national overtaking age (or level of experience) for the two schooling levels in each state. The estimate of the overtaking age rate of return (r_m) was then calcu-lated for each state from the overtaking age log of income for high school $(\ln Y_{HS})$, and for elementary school $(\ln Y_E)$, and from the relation $\ln Y_{HS} = \ln Y_E + r_m S$, where S is four years.

This shortcut for estimating the overtaking age rate of return has two disadvantages. First, given the indirect estimating pro-cedure, there are probably significant errors of measurement. Second, for our purpose an estimate of the average rate of return for all schooling levels is required, whereas the overtaking age rate of return used here is for high school education alone. The over-taking age estimate was computed only for all males in the fifty-one states.

The regression and overtaking estimates are highly and signifi-cantly correlated. For males in the fifty-one states the correlation is .73. The estimates of the overtaking age rate of return, however, are consistently larger; the average r_m for the states is equal to .151, while the average r_c is equal to .102.

Canada

The data for Canada come from unpublished tables of the 1961 Census for a 20 per cent sample of private nonfarm house-holds. The data, for each of the ten provinces and the Yukon Territory, represent a cross-classification of income by schooling and by age. The parameters of the distributions of income, schooling, and age and the regression estimate of the rate of return from schooling were computed in the same manner as for the United States. A distribution of weeks worked for nonfarm adult males exists for the provinces, but the intervals are very wide, especially at the upper end of the distribution.[4] There are four intervals: 1 to 13, 14 to 26, 27 to 39, and 40 to 52 weeks. All but 25 per cent of the observations were in the upper interval. The result was little interprovincial variation in the computed mean and variance in the log of weeks worked. By contrast, the intervals for the United States are: 1 to 13, 14 to 26, 27 to 39, 40 to 48, 48 to 49, and 50 to 52.

APPENDIX A-3: MEXICAN WAGE EARNERS SAMPLE

The Mexican data are from a sample of 3,901 male wage earners in the cities of Monterey, Puebla, and the Federal District (Mexico) taken in the summer of 1963 by Martin Carnoy.[5] Carnoy used a stratified sample in which the number of people interviewed within each urban occupational sector was based on the proportion of wage earners in that sector given by the Mexican Census of Population of 1960. However, within an "urban occupational sector" the sample was nonrandom. The sampler depended on the cooperation of management and a relatively small number of contacts that put him in touch with firms. The workers sampled probably contain a disproportionate number from American-affiliated and local "modern" firms. Stratification reduced, but did not eliminate, the nonrandom character of the sample.

The income variable is average monthly (i.e., annual divided by twelve) earnings. The workers were specifically asked to exclude property income but to include earnings from sources other than their primary employment. The education data consist in the number of years of schooling completed. About two-thirds of all those interviewed with sixteen years and more of schooling are in five firms, and these firms do not all fall into any particular sector. The concentration of those with higher education in a few firms may reflect the nonrandomness of the sample.

---

4. *Census of Canada: 1961*, Vol. 3, Part 3, Table 10.

5. M. Carnoy, "The Cost and Return to Schooling in Mexico: A Case Study," Ph.D. dissertation, University of Chicago, 1964, pp. 30 and 120–133. Children, the youngest being a ten-year-old, formed a small proportion of the sample. They were interviewed on the job (selling newspapers, running errands, et cetera) in different parts of the cities.

Appendix B: Comparative Empirical Results

This appendix provides the reader with two comparative results designed to help in evaluating the sensitivity of the text results to the specific definitions of variables and the coverage of the populations studied.

APPENDIX B-1: EFFECT OF INCLUDING NONWHITES ON INTRASTATE AND INTERSTATE PARAMETERS

The regression results for white adult males for the states in which nonwhites are at least 8 per cent of the relevant population appear in Table A-2. Comparing the parameters for the seventeen states, with nonwhites included (Table A-1) or excluded (Table A-2), reveals that the exclusion of nonwhites generally results in small reductions in the rate of return, the variances of income, education, and the residual, and the adjusted coefficient of determination. The intercept, the estimated income of those with zero education, and average levels of income and schooling are increased. Not surprisingly, the changes are smaller, the smaller the proportion of nonwhites in a state. Since the proportion of nonwhites is greater at lower levels of education, and since for any given level of education nonwhites tend to have lower incomes than whites, their exclusion reduces the estimated slope of the regression line and raises the intercept.

TABLE B-1

Matrix of Correlation Coefficients for the Fifty-one States, with Seventeen
Excluding Nonwhites

	Var(lnY) (1)	$\hat{r}_1$ (2)	lnY$_{0,1}$ (3)	$\bar{R}^2$ (4)	Var(S) (5)	Var(U) (6)	$\hat{r}^2$ (7)	$\hat{r}^2$ Var(S) (8)	Av(Y) (9)
$\hat{r}_1$	.83								
lnY$_{0,1}$	-.77	-.93							
$\bar{R}^2$	.66	.78	-.63						
Var(S)	.49	.32	-.17	.77					
Var(U)	.92	.65	-.65	.32	.24				
$\hat{r}^2$	.84	1.00	-.93	.78	.31	.65			
$\hat{r}^2$ Var(S)	.85	.87	-.75	.95	.71	.58	.88		
Av(Y)	-.34	-.52	.67	-.31	-.02	-.27	-.51	-.36	
Av(S)	-.16	-.37	.42	-.42	-.21	.01	-.35	-.35	.81

Note: The critical values for the correlation coefficient (R), under alternative type I errors (α), are $R(\alpha = .05) = .23$, $R(.025) = .27$, $R(.01) = .32$. The critical values are based on 50 degrees of freedom. See note to Table 4-3.

Source: Tables A-1 and A-2.

Correlation coefficients are presented in Table 4-3, with non-whites included in all states, and in Table B-1, where they are excluded from seventeen. A comparison reveals that the qualitative relationships are the same. The inequalities of income, schooling, and residual income, as well as the education component, the adjusted rate of return, and the adjusted coefficient of determination, are all positively correlated with one another. The states with a high proportion of nonwhites tend to have higher than average values for these parameters when only whites are analyzed. Thus, the inclusion of nonwhites tends to exaggerate the interstate differences for white males.

The adjustment of the data for nonwhites slightly reduces the average explanatory power of schooling within states, from 18.4 per cent to 17.4 per cent. The interstate explanatory power is reduced by almost one-third (see Table 4-5). When nonwhites are included, schooling, the residual, and their covariation explain approximately one-third each of the differences in income inequality. When nonwhites are excluded from seventeen states, education explains 22.3 per cent, the residual, 43.2 per cent, and their covariation, 34.5 per cent of interstate differences in the variance of the natural log of income. Although the intrastate and interstate explanatory powers are reduced, schooling is still an important explanatory variable at both levels.

APPENDIX B-2: EFFECT OF INCLUDING THE AGED AND PROPERTY INCOME ON THE U.S. PARAMETERS

Due to data limitations, the state analyses are performed for males twenty-five years of age and older, with the log of income as the dependent variable. To determine whether the results based on these data are due primarily to the effects of nonlabor income and the inclusion of the aged, calculations were made for the South and non-South using the same coverage as for the states.

As indicated in Table B-2, using total income rather than earnings and including aged males increases the variances of income, education, and the residual, the rate of return, and the coefficient

TABLE B-2

Results from Regressing the Natural Log of Earnings and Income in 1959 on Schooling for Males in the United States

	Non-South Earnings (25 to 64)	South Earnings (25 to 64)	Non-South Income (25+)	South Income (25+)
$SD(\ln Y)$	.65	.76	.86	.98
$SD(S)$	3.41	4.03	3.74	4.35
$Av(\ln Y)$	1.63	1.32	1.44	1.09
$Av(S)$	10.67	9.42	10.13	8.95
$\ln Y_{0,1}$	.94	.47	.49	.05
	(.23)	(.20)	(.14)	(.20)
$\hat{r}_1$	.06	.09	.09	.12
	(.02)	(.02)	(.01)	(.02)
$Var(U)_1$	.38	.45	.62	.71
$\overline{R}_1^2$	.10	.22	.16	.26
$\ln Y_{0,3}$	1.09	.66	.49	.04
	(.50)	(.23)	(.23)	(.30)
r_E	.05	.07	.09	.12
	(.09)	(.08)	(.03)	(.05)
r_S	.06	.09	.11	.13
	(.06)	(.07)	(.03)	(.07)
r_H	.08	.09	.08	.09
	(.06)	(.06)	(.04)	(.08)
$Var(U)_3$	.39	.46	.62	.73
$\overline{R}_3^2$	.07	.16	.16	.24

Note: For definition of variables, see notes to Table 4-1.

Sources: U.S. Census of Population: 1960, Subject Reports, Occupation by Earnings and Education, Tables 2 and 3, and *U.S. Census of Population: 1960, Subject Reports, Educational Attainment*, Table 6, Washington, D.C.

of determination. The rise in the estimated rate of return may be related to the positive correlation between schooling and non-human capital.[1] The aged have lower average schooling than adult males and, for each level of schooling, a lower level of income. This, too, tends to bias the regression estimate of the rate of return upward.

The ranking for the two regions of the parameters studied are not altered by the new definitions. The inclusion of property income and aged males in the state data will alter the magnitude of the parameters, but it seems unlikely that the qualitative relationships would change significantly.

---

1. Let $P_i = E_{T,i}/E_{S,i}$, where E_S is the earnings after S years of schooling and E_T is total personal income. The natural log of P may be expressed as a linear function of schooling, $\ln P_i = m + nS_i + v_i$.

Then, using equation (3-12),

$$\ln E_{T,i} = \ln E_{S,i} + \ln P_i = (\ln E_0 + m) + (\bar{r}^* + n) S_i + (U_i + v_i).$$

With income rather than earnings as the dependent variable, the slope coefficient would be biased upward or downward depending on whether n is positive or negative. n is positive if the proportion of total income from sources other than earnings rises with level of schooling.

Bibliography

Aigner, D. J. and Heins, A. J. "On the Determinants of Income Equality." *American Economic Review*, March 1967.

Al Samarrie, A. and Miller, H. P. "State Differentials in Income Concentration." *American Economic Review*, March 1967.

Bachi, R. "Immigration into Israel." Thomas, B., ed. *Economics of International Migration*. London: Macmillan, 1958.

Bahral, U. *The Effect of Mass Migration on Wages in Israel*. Jerusalem: Falk Project for Economic Research in Israel, 1965.

Becker, G. S. *Human Capital*. New York: NBER, 1974.

_____. "Human Capital and the Personal Distribution of Income." Ann Arbor: University of Michigan, 1967.

Becker, G. S. and Chiswick, B. R. "Education and the Distribution of Earnings." *American Economic Review*, May 1966.

Beckerman, W. and Bacon, R. "International Comparisons of Income Levels: A Suggested New Measure." *Economic Journal*, September 1966.

Ben-Porath, Y. "The Production of Human Capital and the Life Cycle of Earnings." *Journal of Political Economy*, August 1967.

Bowman, M. J. "A Graphical Analysis of Personal Income Distribution in the United States." *American Economic Review*, September 1945.

Carnoy, M. "The Cost and Return to Schooling in Mexico: A Case Study." Ph.D. dissertation, University of Chicago, 1964.

_____. "Rates of Return from Schooling in Latin America." *Journal of Human Resources*, Summer 1967.

_____. "Sample of Mexican Wage Earners, 1963," unpublished data set.

Census of Canada: 1961. Population Sample, Incomes of Individuals and *Schooling by Age Groups;* and unpublished data on income, schooling, and age for the provinces. Ottawa: Dominion Bureau of Statistics, 1964.

Chernick, S. E. *Interregional Disparities in Income.* Ottawa: Economic Council of Canada, 1966.

Chiswick, B. R. "An Interregional Analysis of Schooling and the Skewness of Income." W. L. Hansen, ed. *Education, Income and Human Capital.* New York: NBER, 1970.

_____. "Earnings Inequality and Economic Development." *Quarterly Journal of Economics,* February 1971.

_____. "Minimum Schooling Legislation and the Cross-Sectional Distribution of Income." *Economic Journal,* September 1969.

_____. "Racial Differences in the Variation in Rates of Return from Schooling." G. von Furstenberg *et. al.,* eds. *Patterns of Racial Discrimination,* Vol. II: *Employment and Income.* New York: Heath, 1974.

_____. "Racial Discrimination in the Labor Market: A Test of Alternative Hypotheses." *Journal of Political Economy,* November 1973.

Chiswick, B. R. and Mincer, J. "Time Series Changes in Personal Income Inequality in the United States from 1939, with Projections to 1985." *Journal of Political Economy, Supplement,* May 1972.

Conlisk, J. "Some Cross-Sectional Evidence on Income Inequality." *Review of Economics and Statistics,* February 1967.

Courchene, T. "Interprovincial Migration and Economic Adjustment." *Canadian Journal of Economics,* November 1970.

Denison, E. "Measuring the Contribution of Education (and the Residual) to Economic Growth." *The Residual Factor in Economic Growth.* Paris: OECD, 1964.

"Distribution of Income." *Economic Report of the President, 1974.* Washington, D.C.: Council of Economic Advisers, 1974.

Fein, R. "Educational Patterns in Southern Migration." *Southern Economic Journal, Supplement,* July 1965.

Fisher, R. A. and Yates, F. *Statistical Tables.* London: Oliver and Boyd, 1938.

Freeman, R. B. "Labor Market Discrimination: Analysis, Findings and Problems." Paper presented at Econometric Society Meeting, Toronto, December 1972.

Fuchs, V. *Differentials in Hourly Earnings by Region and City Size, 1959.* New York: NBER, 1967.

Gardner, B. R. "An Analysis of U.S. Farm Family Income Inequality, 1950-1960." Ph.D. dissertation, University of Chicago, 1968.

Goodman, L. "On the Exact Variance of Products." *Journal of the American Statistical Association,* December 1960.

Griliches, Z. "Hybrid Corn and the Economics of Innovation." *Science,* July 29, 1960.

Griliches, Z. and Mason, W. "Education, Income and Ability." *Journal of Political Economy, Supplement,* May 1972.

Gross National Product, Growth Rates and Trend Data by Regions and Countries. Washington, D.C.: U.S. Agency for International Development, 1969.

Grossman, M. *The Demand for Health: A Theoretical and Empirical Investigation.* New York: NBER, 1972.

Hanna, F. *State Income Differentials 1919-1954.* Durham: Duke University Press, 1959.

Hanoch, G. "An Economic Analysis of Earnings and Schooling." *Journal of Human Resources,* Summer 1967.

_____. "Income Differentials in Israel." *Falk Project for Economic Research in Israel, Fifth Report.* Jerusalem: 1961.

_____. "Personal Earnings and Investment in Schooling." Ph.D. dissertation, University of Chicago, 1965.

Hansen, W. L. "Total and Private Rates of Return to Investment in Schooling." *Journal of Political Economy,* April 1963.

Hashimoto, M. "Factors Affecting State Unemployment." Ph.D. dissertation, Columbia University, 1971.

Henderson-Stewart, D. "Appendix: Estimate of the Rate of Return to Education in Great Britain." *Manchester School Bulletin,* September 1965.

Hovne, A. *The Labor Force in Israel.* Jerusalem: Falk Project for Economic Research in Israel, 1961.

Hurwitz, A. and Stallings, C. P. "Interregional Differentials in Per Capita Real Income Changes." *Regional Income.* New York: NBER, 1957.

Johnson, N. O. "The Pareto Law." *Review of Economics and Statistics,* February 1937.

Johnson, T. "Returns from Investment in Human Capital." *American Economic Review,* September 1970.

Johnston, J. *Econometric Methods.* New York: McGraw-Hill, 1963.

Kaitz, Hyman. Bureau of Labor Statistics, letter of January 5, 1973 to author.

Klinov-Malul, R. "Profitability of Investment in Education." *Falk Project for Economic Research in Israel, Fifth Report*. Jerusalem: 1961.

Kravis, I. B. *The Structure of Income: Some Quantitative Essays*. Philadelphia: University of Pennsylvania, 1962.

Krueger, A. O. "Factor Endowments and Per Capita Income Differences Among Countries." *Economic Journal*, September 1968.

Leibowitz, A. "Women's Allocation of Time to Market and Nonmarket Activities." Ph.D. dissertation, Columbia University, 1972.

Lydall, H. *The Structure of Earnings*. Oxford: Clarendon Press, 1968.

Lydall, H. and Lansing, J. B. "A Comparison of the Distribution of Income and Wealth in the United States and Great Britain." *American Economic Review*, March 1959.

Malinvaud, E. *Statistical Methods of Econometrics*. Chicago: Rand McNally, 1966.

Michael, R. *The Effect of Education on Efficiency in Consumption*. New York: NBER, 1972.

Miller, H. P. *Income of the American People*. New York: John Wiley, 1955.

Mincer, J. "A Study of Personal Income Distribution." Ph.D. dissertation, Columbia University, 1957.

———. *Schooling, Experience, and Earnings*. New York: NBER, 1974.

———. "Schooling, Experience, and Earnings." New York: Mimeo., 1972.

———. "On-the-Job Training: Costs, Returns and Some Implications." *Journal of Political Economy, Supplement*, October 1962.

———. "The Distribution of Labor Incomes: A Survey." *Journal of Economic Literature*, March 1970.

Morganstern, R. and Barrett, N. S. "Occupational Discrimination and Changing Labor Force Participation: Their Effects on Unemployment Rates of Blacks and Women." New York: Mimeo., 1971.

Mushkin, S. "Health as an Investment." *Journal of Political Economy, Supplement*, October 1962.

Nelson, R. and Phelps, E. "Investment in Humans, Technological Diffusion and Economic Growth." *American Economic Review*, May 1966.

O'Neill, J. "The Effect of Income and Education on Inter-Regional Migration." Ph.D. dissertation, Columbia University, 1970.

Oster, S. M. "Are Black Incomes More Unequally Distributed?" *American Economist*, Fall 1970.

Parsons, D. "Specific Human Capital: An Application to Quit Rates and Layoff Rates." *Journal of Political Economy*, November 1972.

Podoluk, J. *Education and Earnings*. Ottawa: Dominion Bureau of Statistics, 1965.

Rahm, C. M. "Investment in Training and the Occupational Structure of Earnings." Ph.D. dissertation, Columbia University, 1971.

Schultz, T. P. "Returns to Education in Bogota, Colombia." Santa Monica: Rand Corporation, 1968.

_____. "Secular Trends and Cyclical Behavior of Income Distribution in the United States: 1944 to 1964." Lee Soltow, ed. *Six Papers on the Size Distribution of Income and Wealth*. New York: NBER, 1969.

_____. "The Distribution of Income: Case Study of the Netherlands." Ph.D. dissertation, Massachusetts Institute of Technology, 1965.

Schultz, T. W. *Transforming Traditional Agriculture*. New Haven: Yale University Press, 1964.

Scully, G. W. "Interstate Wage Differentials: A Cross-Sectional Analysis." *American Economic Review*, December 1969.

_____. "The North-South Manufacturing Wage Differential, 1869–1919." *Journal of Regional Science*, August 1971.

Smith, A. *The Wealth of Nations*. New York: Modern Library, 1937.

Statistical Abstract of Israel: 1957–58. Jerusalem: Central Bureau of Statistics, 1958.

Thurow, L. "The Determinants of the American Distribution of Income." *American Economic Review*, May 1970.

U.S. Census of Population: 1960, Characteristics of the Population, Vol. I, Parts 1 to 53. Washington, D.C.: Bureau of the Census, 1963.

U.S. Census of Population: 1960, Subject Reports: Educational Attainment. Washington, D.C.: Bureau of the Census, 1963.

U.S. Census of Population: 1960, Subject Reports: Occupation by Earnings and Education. Washington, D.C.: Bureau of the Census, 1963.

Ullman, C. "The Rise of Professional Occupations in the American Labor Force." Ph.D. dissertation, Columbia University, 1972.

Walker, H. M. and Lev, J. *Statistical Inference*. New York: Holt, Rhinehart and Winston, 1953.

Welch, F. "Black-White Differences in Returns to Schooling."
    American Economic Review, December, 1973.
_____. "Education in Production." *Journal of Political Economy*,
    January 1970.
Wilkenson, B. "Some Economic Aspects of Education in Canada."
    Ph.D. dissertation, Massachusetts Institute of Technology, 1964.

Index